Social and Economic Control of Alcohol

The 21st Amendment in the 21st Century

PUBLIC ADMINISTRATION AND PUBLIC POLICY

A Comprehensive Publication Program

EDITOR-IN-CHIEF

EVAN M. BERMAN
Huey McElveen Distinguished Professor
Louisiana State University
Public Administration Institute
Baton Rouge, Louisiana

Executive Editor

JACK RABIN
Professor of Public Administration and Public Policy
The Pennsylvania State University—Harrisburg
School of Public Affairs
Middletown, Pennsylvania

Available Electronically

Principles and Practices of Public Administration, edited by
Jack Rabin, Robert F. Munzenrider, and Sherrie M. Bartell

PublicADMINISTRATION*netBASE*

Social and Economic Control of Alcohol

The 21st Amendment in the 21st Century

Edited by

Carole L. Jurkiewicz
Louisiana State University
Baton Rouge, Louisiana, U.S.A.

Murphy J. Painter
Louisiana Department of Revenue
Baton Rouge, Louisiana, U.S.A.

CRC Press
Taylor & Francis Group
Boca Raton   London   New York

CRC Press is an imprint of the
Taylor & Francis Group, an **informa** business

CRC Press
Taylor & Francis Group
6000 Broken Sound Parkway NW, Suite 300
Boca Raton, FL 33487-2742

© 2008 by Taylor & Francis Group, LLC
CRC Press is an imprint of Taylor & Francis Group, an Informa business

No claim to original U.S. Government works
Printed in the United States of America on acid-free paper
10 9 8 7 6 5 4 3 2 1

International Standard Book Number-13: 978-1-4200-5463-7 (Hardcover)

Library of Congress Cataloging-in-Publication Data

Jurkiewicz, Carole L., 1958-
    Social and economic control of alcohol : the 21st amendment in the 21st century / Carole L. Jurkiewicz.
        p. cm. -- (Public administration and public policy)
    Includes bibliographical references and index.
    ISBN 978-1-4200-5463-7 (alk. paper)
    1. Temperance--United States. 2. Drinking of alcoholic beverages--United States. 3. Liquor laws--United States. I. Title.

HV5085.J87 2008
362.292'609973--dc22   2007018725

Visit the Taylor & Francis Web site at
http://www.taylorandfrancis.com

and the CRC Press Web site at
http://www.crcpress.com

Dedication

CLJ: For Spencer and Crosby

MJP: To all my friends and family who have stayed the course by my side, and especially to former Governor Murphy J. Foster Jr. who gave me the opportunity to be commissioner of the Office of Alcohol & Tobacco Control for the State of Louisiana.

Contents

Foreword

When Prohibition (the Eighteenth Amendment) was repealed by State ratification of the Twenty-first Amendment in December 1933, I was a teenager, but already familiar with beverage alcohol. My initial contact was through religion; for centuries alcohol in beverage form had been part of the customs of many organized religions, customs that were and are part of the traditions of my Jewish faith. During Prohibition, I had consumed alcohol in a family environment and also participated in the sale of alcohol. Our family owned the Buchman Wine Company in lower Manhattan Borough, New York City, and the sale of sacramental wine was permitted. Our largest customer was the Archdiocese of New York, Roman Catholic Church.

At that latter stage of my youth, it was not difficult to recognize that the sacramental and medicinal sales of beverage alcohol during Prohibition were not the only exceptions to principles of control over the access to beverage alcohol. The speakeasy was not a myth, nor were the racketeer and bootlegger. There was great disrespect for the rule of law. Compounding control over the defects in Prohibition was the enormous weight imposed upon the people and the nation's institutions by the unemployment and human misery inflicted during the Great Depression. It was no surprise that there was rejoicing by many when repeal was enacted, because it was seen by them to be a signal of hope and opportunity for the future. It certainly presented opportunities for me.

It was an exciting time for someone who grew up in the industry. For several years following repeal, I was busy completing university education, while working as a plant manager, then comptroller of a multi-state wine producer and importer of foreign wines. By 1939, I had begun a law partnership with my late brother, Henry. That firm and its progeny have served clients in the beverage and hospitality industries since then, and continue under our family name today.

I witnessed the federal government's initial control of the alcoholic beverage industry encounter difficulties. That federal system, based upon codes established under the National Industrial Recovery Act of June 16, 1933 and the Federal Alcohol Control Administration set up by presidential executive order, became unraveled as a consequence of the U.S. Supreme Court decision in *Schechter Poultry*

Corp. vs. United States, 295 U.S. 495 (May 27, 1935). A good part of the efforts of Congress during the Summer of 1935, which I was able to monitor in Washington D.C., was directed at hearings and debates over what became the Federal Alcohol Administration Act of August 29, 1935 (27 U.S.C. 201, et seq.).

The state governments, however, seemed to fare better in the execution of their initial control over alcohol. Perhaps this was because of the vigorous public debates that took place in connection with the process of ratification of the Twenty-first Amendment, or with the contribution of information infused into the crafting of regulatory systems that was extended by a singular forward-looking individual bearing a family name familiar to many, even today.

Well before repeal of Prohibition, John D. Rockefeller, Jr., who utilized the Rockefeller family fortune to establish scores of philanthropic enterprises, foresaw and supported its coming, as the widespread disregard for the law was, in his view, an evil even greater than intemperance. A lifelong personal teetotaler and supporter of total abstinence, he commissioned a study to help prepare careful plans of control, so that the evils against which Prohibition initially was invoked could not easily return. His intentions were expressed in the foreword he penned for the publication of that study: *Toward Liquor Control* (Raymond B. Fosdick and Albert L. Scott, Harper & Brothers, 1933).

The results of that study are the subject of contrast, evaluation, and enhancement in the works presented in the pages that follow here. Unlike Mr. Rockefeller, I cannot acknowledge any role in commissioning this undertaking almost seventy-five years later. I am, however, pleased and honored to have been asked to preface the introduction to you, and to present a few thoughts of my own about events since repeal....

America, except for its Native Peoples, was and is a nation of immigrants. Each culture has brought with it to these shores its own customs and religions, many of which incorporate the use of beverage alcohol. Prohibition was doomed from inception. The lawlessness during Prohibition was fueled by the criminal exploitation of the desire of the masses, not the glamorous image of the speakeasy. As long as Americans cherish personal and religious freedoms, Prohibition will not return.

Liquor control power has diminished as a function of government over the years, except for revenue generation. Priorities for the uses of resources have shifted away from fostering temperance. In contrast, consider, for example, that the first "commissioner" in New Jersey was personally designated by law to serve for no less than seven years and provided personal compensation of $13,000 (P.L. 1933, c. 436). In short, he essentially was free of political pressure and paid, in 2006 value, $201,600 a year. The New Jersey Governor's current maximum salary is $175,000.

Long after World War II, the nation was largely rural, with areas of urban concentration. Brewers and even distillers were regional in nature. Wholesale distributors were numerous and local. The local tavern or restaurant was an institution of social gathering, even more so, when it presented the first public access to broadcast television. Largely, these businesses were owned by individuals who lived in the community. A confluence of two emerging trends illustrates a fundamental change that took place. Over several decades, Eisenhower's interstate highway network fueled suburban flight and weakened the nation's rail mass transit system. The automobile became a necessity. Broadcast television initially also was regional in nature, until a new program format was introduced to permit the entire nation to view an event at the same time. It was football on Monday nights; soon to be followed universally by both national network programming and commercial advertising of all kinds.

Before all this, the liquor control system was balanced by principles of local option: dry or wet communities, different hours of sale and types of licenses and, until the late 1980's, legal drinking age. Out of the family and local ethnic and political communities grew social expectations regarding responsible consumption or temperance, together with liquor control and law enforcement responses consistent with those communities' values. What has emerged over the decades is a larger more homogeneous national community, whose values and norms largely now are the product of other sources outside the traditional family.

Multiple generations of Americans have been educated about alcohol by way of advertising and entertainment communicated by an ever increasing number of new technologies. Cable television, the Internet, even telephones are interactive. Messages, images, and ideas are presented with speed and brevity. While apparently well intended, the information communicated often creates mixed or conflicting signals. Consider the advertising campaign for now ingrained proposition of the designated driver. While it is directed at highway safety, by implication it also inversely communicates another message. In essence, often it is acceptable for the intended passengers to over-consume, because there is an abstainer driving. Consider the signal sent by beverage alcohol brands sponsoring drivers and cars in the sport of motor racing. Addressing the impact of advertising and marketing upon intemperate consumption is the challenge for the future and requires both a narrowly tailored level of restraint upon commercial free speech and an authority empowered to articulate acceptable standards. The fortitude and leadership of the "liquor czars" of the earlier post-Prohibition period have been disabled over the passage of time. Some new champion of the principles of moderation and temperance is needed, if liquor control is to be reinvigorated.

Please turn now to the newer insights of the contributors who seek to move the process forward.

Abraham M. Buchman[*]
Mentoring Partner
Buchman Law Firm, LLP

---

[*] "Abe" Buchman passed away July 8, 2007. This preface is but a small part of his legacy. Again, our thanks and condolences to his family.

The Authors

Marc Belanger received his master's degree in health communication from Emerson College. His career spans both the nonprofit and public health sectors as program and marketing manager for civil rights, substance abuse prevention, cancer control, and smoking cessation organizations. He can be reached at MarcusBelanger@gmail.com.

Susan C. Cagann's practice focuses on providing innovative solutions and sound risk assessment to business leaders in the wine, food, and retail industry. She is special counsel in Farella Braun + Martel's Business Transactions practice. Prior to private practice, Cagann served in both executive and legal capacities for Kendall-Jackson Wine Estates and Jackson Family Farms, a management services company for Jackson's luxury wine portfolio. Her many roles included counsel on and management of the full range of legal matters facing this wine industry powerhouse, including environmental regulations compliance, including water rights and quality issues; federal and state regulations on the production, marketing, and distribution of wine; and Proposition 65 compliance. Cagann was also a senior attorney at Safeway Inc., where she managed legal compliance in sales and marketing; advertising; consumer protection and privacy; e-commerce; weights and measures; unfair trade practices; transportation; and environmental regulations.

A frequent author and speaker, Cagann has lectured on a variety of legal topics in national venues, such as the National Conference of State Liquor Administrators, National Alcohol Beverage Control Association Legal Symposium, and the Food Marketing Institute Legal Conference.

Cagann is admitted to practice in California and Illinois.

Raymond W. Cox III is a professor in the Department of Public Administration and Urban Studies at the University of Akron. He is the author of some forty-five academic and professional publications, including two books. His recent work has been focused on issues of discretion in decision-making and police ethics. In addition to his teaching experience, Dr. Cox has more than sixteen years of government service, including four as chief of staff to the lieutenant governor of New Mexico and five at the National Science Foundation.

Kelley A. Cronin is an assistant professor of political science/criminal justice at Notre Dame College in Cleveland, Ohio. Her research interests include management reforms in public administration and how customer-service ideas are permeating administrative approaches and practices in public safety management.

Mark R. Daniels is professor and chair of political science at Slippery Rock University of Pennsylvania. He is the author of *Terminating Public Programs: An American Political Paradox* and has edited books and journal symposia on a variety of public policy issues, including Medicaid reform, sustainable community programs, and policy termination.

Stephen Diamond has a J.D. and a Ph.D. in American history. He has written on the history of taxation in the United States and the jurisprudence of Justice Holmes. His teaching and research now focus on U.S. and comparative alcoholic beverage and food law.

Carole L. Jurkiewicz, is the Woman's Hospital Distinguished Professor of Healthcare Management in the Public Administration Institute of the E.J. Ourso College of Business at Louisiana State University. Her work in the area of alcohol control focuses upon analyzing the effects of regulatory and enforcement policies on alcohol consumption, and their ensuing social consequences. She has published widely in the areas of organizational and individual performance, ethics, power, and leadership, bringing to her academic career many years experience as a key executive in private and nonprofit organizations. She has served as a consultant to many governmental, nonprofit, and proprietary organizations.

Since graduating from the Boston University School of Law in 1967, **Evan T. Lawson** has devoted his professional life to the art and science of trial work, amassing extensive experience in all aspects of dispute resolution and appellate practice. In 1969 he was appointed legal counsel to the Massachusetts Alcoholic Beverages Control Commission, where he served for three years developing a specialty in state and federal regulation. In 1973 he founded Lawson & Weitzen, LLP, which is now a 34-attorney firm in Boston.

Lawson's practice concentrates on civil litigation with an emphasis on alcoholic beverages licensing and regulation, and supplier-wholesaler disputes. He has been the principal attorney in over 100 appellate cases, including leading Massachusetts decisions concerning the alcoholic beverages industry. In 1996 he successfully represented a Rhode Island liquor retailer before the United States Supreme Court in *44 Liquormart v. State of Rhode Island*, which established a First Amendment right to advertise prices, and overturned a previous Supreme Court ruling that the 21st Amendment gave an "added presumption of validity" to state regulation of alcoholic beverages.

Lawson frequently serves as a panelist for legal education seminars on licensing, administrative law and media law. He has also published articles on constitutional law and alcoholic beverages regulation. Lawson was named by his peers in *Boston Magazine* as one of Massachusetts' "Super Lawyers" for trial work, and for the past ten years has been named to the Woodward/White directory for the "Best Lawyers in America" for First Amendment Law.

Jeffrey W. Linkenbach is a member of the research faculty at Montana State University where he directs The National MOST OF Us Institute for Social Norms (www.mostofus.org). Linkenbach is a well respected social entrepreneur, lecturer and author who has developed national award winning programs related to alcohol-related prevention. Linkenbach is a licensed addictions counselor, who has over 25 years experience in designing innovative approaches to solving complex problems, by translating social science into social action. The Montana Model of Social Norms Marketing has become the standard for effective social norms interventions across North America and beyond.

Murphy J. Painter is commissioner of alcohol and tobacco control for the State of Louisiana, a post he has held for the past decade. He holds a master's degree in public administration and is a graduate of the FBI National Academy. He is past president and executive director of the National Conference of State Liquor Administrators, and has received numerous awards for his work including the American Society of Public Administrator's Ethics in Practice Award and distinguished recognition from the U.S. Attorney's Office. He has written on the topic of alcohol control for both professional and scholarly publications, and speaks on these issues to organizations across the U.S.

Terrel L. Rhodes is vice president for quality, curriculum, and assessment at the Association of American Colleges and Universities in Washington, D.C. As such, he works with campuses across the country on reform of undergraduate education and student learning. He served previously as vice provost at Portland State

University. He recently completed a term as ethics section chair for the American Society for Public Administration.

He is the author of three books, several articles, and book chapters. He received his B.A. at Indiana University in Bloomington, and his M.A. and Ph.D. in political science at the University of North Carolina at Chapel Hill. He has held previous faculty appointments at St. John's University in Minnesota, the University of North Carolina at Charlotte, and Portland State University.

Doug Schwalm has a Ph.D. in Economics from the University of California Berkeley, and is currently an assistant professor of Economics at Illinois State University. His research and teaching interests include topics in health, labor economics, and applied econometrics.

Elissa R. Weitzman is an assistant professor of pediatrics and adolescent medicine at Harvard Medical School and Children's Hospital, Boston, and a social and behavioral scientist at the Harvard School of Public Health. Her training includes a bachelor's in psychology (Brandeis University), a master's in health policy and a doctorate in health and social behavior and psychiatric epidemiology (Harvard School of Public Health). She is a former fellow of medical ethics at Harvard Medical School, and was the Norman E. Zinberg fellow of public health in psychiatry in the division of addictions at Harvard Medical School. She leads multiple national studies of the epidemiology of alcohol, tobacco, and other substance use among college youth including evaluation studies of the long term effects of environmental prevention models targeting alcohol availability and accessibility on risks for heavy and harmful drinking, tobacco, and other drug use. She is also pioneering the field of public health informatics, evaluating the use of newly mature informatics technologies for supporting behavioral surveillance and health promotion goals. Her published work includes studies of: environmental determinants of heavy and harmful drinking in college; evaluation studies of environmentally oriented drinking prevention programs; epidemiologic analyses of alcohol abuse, depression, and smoking/drinking comorbidities among youth; behavioral and mental health risks among young adult children of alcoholics; assessments of alcohol abuse and patterns of treatment need/use among college youth, and health services studies of perceived risk for chronic health problems and health protecting behaviors.

Colleen M. West is a Florida-licensed clinical psychologist at the Miami Department of Veterans Affairs Medical Center with adjunct faculty appointments in the University of Miami School of Arts and Sciences (Department of Psychology) and the School of Medicine (Department of Medicine, Division of Gerontology and Geriatric Medicine). She received her doctoral degree from the University of Arizona and received extensive post-doctoral training in gero-psychology and behavioral medicine. For over twenty years she has provided end-of-life care within a full range of psychology services (including assessment, intervention and consultation) for medically fragile patients and their families.

Jonathan P. West, a professor in the Department of Political Science and director of the Master of Public Administration Program, has published close to 100 articles and chapters and eight books. His most recent books include *Human Resource Management in Public Service: Problems, Paradoxes, and Processes* (M.E. Sharpe, 2006), *American Politics and the Environment* (Longman, 2002), *The Professional Edge: Competencies for the Public Service* (M.E. Sharpe, 2004), and *American Public Service: Radical Civil Service Reform and the Merit System* (Taylor & Francis, in press). He is the managing editor of a journal titled *Public Integrity* published by M.E. Sharpe and co-sponsored by the American Society for Public Administration, the Council of State Governments, the Council on Government Ethics Laws, the Ethics Resource Center, and the International City/County Management Association.

Chapter 1

Why We Control Alcohol the Way We Do

Carole L. Jurkiewicz, Ph.D.
Murphy J. Painter, M.P.A.

Contents

> Alcohol gives pleasure as well as pain, and any government which fails to acknowledge that fact is unlikely to take the people with it.

(WHO, 1994)

From the 1870s to 1933 the control of intoxicating liquors, as they were then called, was a hot-button issue well beyond the extent to which it is debated today. Powerful single interest pressure groups such as the Anti-Saloon League, and later the Association Against the Prohibition Amendment, wielded great influence both socially and politically. Alcoholic beverages dominated political debate; and their regulation tended to swing in wide oscillations from deregulation to prohibition. In time, Americans tired of the incensed debate and moved toward a more rational approach in declaring that true temperance came from a balance between control

1

and accessibility, facilitated by effective regulation which reflected, and also helped shape, public opinion.

According to Fosdick and Scott (1933), "The attempt to control by law the use of intoxicating beverages is many centuries old. In America, legal restrictions surrounded the sale of liquor from the earliest colonial days. Temperance movements have come and gone; organized efforts for moderation, backed by moral suasion, have had their day; but in all the struggle with one of the most difficult human problems law has remained our chief weapon in trying to curb the social consequences of excess."

History of Alcohol Control in the U.S.

Alcohol has figured prominently in societies reaching into antiquity, from the Phoenicians to Egyptians during the period of King Tutankhamun (around 1340 B.C.) to pre-Islamic Arabic-speaking countries (Heath, 2000). The spread of alcohol into new societies was largely a function of religious sacramental use, gardeners' passions for new varietal plants including those found to be instrumental in alcohol production, and as a means to establish colonialism throughout the world (Jankowiak and Bradburd, 1996). In some societies, the effects on the community remained minimal, and alcohol policies did not develop. Europe has had a widely disparate approach to alcohol regulation and the debate continues today (Institute of Alcohol Studies, 2005). Research has demonstrated, however, that weaker alcohol regulation in European countries is highly correlated with higher consumption rates and concomitant social and health problems (http://www.medscape.com/viewarticle/556169). In other countries, such as the U.S., the increase in alcohol consumption was viewed as a precursor to the proliferation of crime, violence, health woes, and various economic concerns — essentially creating resource burdens on society.

Alcohol regulation arose in historical times as societies became more cultured, and was first instituted in ancient Greece, Mesopotamia, Egypt, and Rome (Ghalioungui, 1979). Greek statesmen of the 6th century B.C. introduced supervised festivities as an alternative to the theretofore popular Dionysian revelries that promoted drunkenness. In 594, the death penalty was prescribed for drunken magistrates, and all wine was ordered to be diluted with water before being sold. For over 2000 years, strategies such as these were devised by monarchs, governments, and the clergy across the European continent to prevent alcohol-related problems that eventually arrived in America along with the colonists. Not teetotalers by any measure, the Puritans sailed to Massachusetts with 42 tons of beer, 10,000 gallons of wine, and 14 tons of water on board. Additional drinking water could be acquired by catching rainwater, but beer was considered more sanitary than most available water sources other than rainwater (Lee, 1963). The colonists made modest attempts at controlling overindulgence, acting in response to the demands of their fledgling society. For example, taverns in the early 1700s were required to maintain staff on duty to serve alcoholic beverages to visitors and travelers should they happen by (Miller and Johnson, 1963), a law that was later modified in response to claims of loud and disruptive behavior emanating from such establishments (Cherrington, 1920). From the first law enacted in the colonies in 1629 to disallow excessive drunkenness among ministers to today's interchange of federal and state sanctions, America's response to vocalized public concern over abuse of alcohol has often been to outlaw the action, followed by modifications to the law due to unforeseen adverse economic impact (Tropman, 1986).

What is meant by alcohol control in the 21st century? It has been defined to include all strategies and measures used by administrations to influence the availability of alcohol (e.g., Bruun, Edwards, and Lumio, 1975), and less often as informal social control mechanisms that exert control over when and where alcohol can be accessed (e.g., Yalisove, 2004). Control of alcohol encompasses fiscal, economic, public health and safety, and political interests (Osterberg and Karlsson, 2002; Makela, Room, and Single, 1981) and addresses the process from production and distribution to consumption.

Reflecting upon the pattern of alcohol regulation in the U.S. before prohibition, what emerges is a cyclic transfer of locus of control from the individual to the government and back again. As evidence, the following annotated time line is offered:

1633   Massachusetts enacted a law to limit sales of alcohol in taverns to two drinks per person, amended to exempt strangers.

1638   Law enacted to prohibit drinking of health tonics; abandoned shortly after passage.

1650-1750s   No new laws; social custom effectively exerted pressure upon those for whom excessive drinking resulted in unseemly behavior.

Early 1700s   New regulatory controls focused on licenses, excise taxes, and fines for sales to drunks or Indians in reputed effort to reduce overindulgence (Krout, 1967).

1735   Consumption of beer encouraged while first prohibitory statute against alcohol-related ribaldry passed.

1766   Taverns became customary meeting places for revolutionary groups allowing alcohol consumption and loud conversation.

The three events listed below were in response to the growing popularity of taverns as social and political venues, and led to an increase in excise taxes as a means to discourage consumption:

1773   John Adams declares taverns staging areas for disorderly conduct and loose morals; John Wesley follows this proclamation with a call for prohibition on distilling.

1752 First health argument in favor of temperance introduced by Nathaniel Ames.

1785 Dr. Benjamin Rush, a signer of the Declaration of Independence and member of the Continental Congress and one of the leading minds for forming the new government, published an influential book declaring that drinking led to diseases of body and mind.

These events in turn led to:

1791 Frontier farmers in western Pennsylvania organized the Whiskey Rebellion against high excise taxes, requiring 15,000 militia to quell the uprising and resulting in political pressure that led to the lowering of excise tax rates.

1802 Federal tax on distilling and importing spirits repealed.

1813–1817 New federal taxes on distilling enacted, repealed in 1862 as the temperance movement gained momentum with various social and religious groups, feminists, abolitionists, and utopians joining in a collective voice to castigate the government for collecting revenue from the profits of evil.

1818–1862 In response to the growing sentiment of profiting from evil pursuits, alcohol was tax free.

1835 American Temperance Society formed, first of many such organizations.

1847 Various states pass total abstinence measures, each vetoed by the governor, repealed by the state legislature, or invalidated by the state supreme court.

1850 Outcry by temperance groups in response to federal government approval of requests to sell liquor. Chicago attempts temperance statute, resulting in riots and storming of the business district, and repeal of the law.

1849–1851 Father Thoebal Matthew received pledges of total abstinence from 600,000 citizens, and was rewarded with a formal dinner at the White House followed by a Senate reception at which Congressman Gerrit Smith gave the first official government speech in support of total abstinence.

Mid 1850s In response to anti-alcohol sentiment, patent medicine formulas became 40-plus proof and saw a dramatic increase in sales.

1860s To fund the Civil War, the tax per gallon of alcohol rose from 20 cents to $2, resulting in a dramatic reduction of sales and ultimate loss of revenue, increased fraud, and stockpiling.

1863 First industry lobby, the U.S. Brewers Association, formed and launched a vigorous legislative campaign succeeding in reducing taxes on beer from 1 dollar to 60 cents.

1869 Government responds to reduced sales by lowering taxes on liquor from 2 dollars to 50 cents and saw an immediate rise in revenue from $13.5 million in 1868 to $45 million in 1869 and $55 million the following year; government introduces mandatory stamps to prevent counterfeiting and tampering.

1902   Temperance movement continues to grow and anti-alcohol education required in all schools except for those in Arizona.

1913   Becoming more activist, prohibition movement fields candidates for public office (all lose), and publications claim alcohol responsible for divorce, poverty, insanity, child desertion, and crime, and religious organizations proclaim that if prohibition passes the kingdom of God would come to the U.S. Further, it was opined that sobriety would result in expanded productivity, increased bank deposits, improved debt collection, and stimulated retail trade (Timberlake, 1963). Producers of non-alcoholic beverages such as Welch's Grape Juice, sensing a market opportunity, capitalized on this sentiment in their advertising and experienced a resulting sales jump.

Nine states were under prohibition by statute; in 31 additional states local option laws were implemented. Through law and various regulatory efforts, over 50 percent of the U.S. was under prohibition. The demands of the Anti-Saloon League were formally presented to Congress by the Committee of One Thousand.

1917   The resolution to prohibit the manufacture, sale, transportation, or importation of alcoholic beverages in the U.S. was approved by Congress and sent to the states for ratification (Cherrington, 1920). National Prohibition Act, otherwise known as the Volstead Act, was enacted on October 28, and was to become effective on January 17, 1920.

1919   Three months before Volstead Act was to go into effect, liquor worth half a million dollars (in 1919 value) was stolen from government warehouses.

1920   Within six months of implementation, federal courts were overwhelmed with pending liquor violation trials, 600 in Chicago alone (Sinclair, 1962). Within 3 years, 30 prohibition agents had been killed, and the number of saloons in New York City alone increased from 15,000 to 32,000 (Lerner, 2007).

1921–1930   After 95,933 illicit distilleries were seized, the numbers increased annually to 282,122 in 1930; 34,175 people were arrested in 1921, rising yearly to 75,307 for 1928 (IRS, 1921; 1966; 1970). Estimates of speakeasies operating during this period were 500,000 (Lee, 1963). Circumventing the law, doctors earned about $40 million (not adjusted for inflation) for whiskey prescriptions during this period; courts convicted only about 7 percent of those charged with violations (Sinclair, 1962; Dobyns, 1940). Permits issued for sacramental wine to be used only in religious ceremony increased from 2,139,000 in 1922 to 2,503,500 in 1923 and to 2,944,700 in 1924 (Dobyns, 1940). Seizures of foreign vessels delivering liquor from Belgium and Holland increased from 134 in 1923 to 236 a year later; the Department of Commerce estimated that liquor valued at $40 million (1920 dollars) was illegally entering the U.S. on an annual basis (Sinclair, 1962).

Other unintended consequences of Prohibition were that more women started drinking alcohol, and doing so in public, while at the same time a similar signifi- cant increase was noted for the first time among youth with an alarming number admitted to hospitals with alcohol psychosis (Brown, 1932). Alcohol consumption increased during Prohibition by 11.64 percent per capita (Tillitt, 1932), and the bootleg activity fueled corruption and violence among mobsters that led to indi- vidual groups aligning together into larger and more powerful crime families which the U.S. government would then spend years trying to dismantle (Lerner, 2007).

Before prohibition, alcohol as a commodity was regulated mainly by local social and cultural morés (social control) and the economic model (economic control) where legally available. The economic model historically tends to minimize the social concerns and consequences in order to minimize waste and maximize profit. Prior to 1914, cocaine was legal in this country; today it is not. Alcohol (of the intoxicating variety) is legal in the United States today; from 1920 to 1933 it was not. Prostitution is legal in some parts of Nevada today; in the other forty-nine states it is not. All these goods — sex, alcohol, and drugs — have at least one thing in common: the consumption of each brings a willing seller together with a willing buyer followed by an act of mutually desirable exchange (at least in the opinion of the parties involved). Partly because of this consensual trade, attempts to proscribe the consumption of these goods have (1) met with less than spectacular success, and (2) yielded some peculiar patterns of production, distribution, and usage (Benja- min, Miller, and North, 2001).

Prior to Prohibition, the alcohol industry had evolved into a vertically inte- grated enterprise that found most outlets "tied" to a supplier or manufacturer. This cut acquisition costs to the retailer and guaranteed a return to the supplier in order to capture a particular market. Whether legally or simply by association, retailers were "owned" by certain brands (Fosdick & Scott, 1933, p. 48). Vertical integration describes a style of ownership and control defined by the extent to which a firm owns its upstream suppliers and its downstream customers. Vertically integrated companies are united through a hierarchy and share a common owner. Usually each member of the hierarchy produces a different product or service, and the products combine to satisfy a common need in contrast to horizontal integration wherein a single company controls each of these production elements. Whereas horizontal integration can result in a backlog, vertical integration is one method of avoiding delays in production and is sometimes referred to as a vertical monopoly (Perry, 1988).

Configuring the production and sale of alcohol as a commodity like all others is the source of concern for many citizens. "The profit motive is the core of the problem. Unless that profit motive is divorced from the retail sale of spirituous liquor, unless society as a whole can take over this business in the protection of its citizens, the future, at least in America, holds out only the prospect of an endless guerrilla warfare between a nation fighting for temperance and a traffic that thrives on excess" (Fosdick and Scott, 1933). As it was in 1933, so it is today: profit is the motive for any business. Yet unlike in 1933, the stakes are much higher today.

Alcohol in 2007 is a $452 billion industry that generates $71 billion in tax revenue for the states. Alcohol sales account for over 40 percent of the annual profits accrued by many retail accounts.

The most significant post-Prohibition regulations aimed to prevent direct interaction between the suppliers and the retailers of alcohol. Many of the alleged evils of the pre-Prohibition era involved excessive promotion of alcoholic indulgence by the suppliers and retailers of alcohol, who were often one and the same entity. Suppliers sometimes owned retail establishments directly. They also used enticements such as free equipment and interest-free loans to induce retailers to sell the suppliers' brands exclusively (Barsbay, 1999). The perception was that such "tied house" arrangements encouraged the promotion of alcohol consumption beyond acceptable limits: "Besides pressuring retailers to handle only their brands, suppliers pushed retailers to increase sales whatever the social cost" (Barsbay, 1999; Whitman, 2003).

After the repeal of the 18th Amendment, every state in the union was faced with the complex decision of how to regulate alcohol products based on the new authority granted them in the 21st Amendment. Control was given to the respective legislators, whose only source of objective information was contained in the text, *Toward Liquor Control* (Fosdick and Scott, 1933). A research-based public policy compendium which suggested how government, through law, could effectively control the consumption of alcohol, in reaction to what was viewed as a direct failure of federal intervention. How does a free enterprise system control the normal economics of supply and demand? To do this, one must alter the dynamics of the normative economic model wherein an organization can only increase profit by either charging more for the product or selling more of it. Fosdick and Scott (1933, p. 52) suggested following the Rhode Island model under which price control provisions were imposed upon the wholesaler rather than the retail trade. Such a reconfiguration of the profit incentive model is offered by Taber et al. (2003): "In recent years, public discussion of alcohol policies has too often ignored or downplayed the need to understand both the nature of the agent and its harmful properties, with an implicit acceptance of the idea that alcohol is only an ordinary commodity like any other marketable product. The validity of this assumption is questioned by evidence showing that alcohol effects on various organ systems are key mechanisms linking alcohol consumption to a wide range of adverse consequences."

The research study conducted in 1933 by Fosdick and Scott was not requested by the industry. The report was commissioned by John D. Rockefeller, a teetotaler, successful businessman and humanitarian. He selected Raymond Fosdick, a practicing attorney with a research background in criminal justice and other social issues, and Albert L. Scott, an engineer whose avocation was the intensive study of social and religious movements. The 1933 study was a science-based, data driven project.

The research of Fosdick and Scott identifies the paradox of alcohol as a commodity providing many acceptable outcomes which at the same time can be the causes of tremendous social strife. Because alcohol is a legal commodity, the challenge for government is to provide a realistic system for its accessibility while at the same time attempting to limit its abusive consumption through controlled access. By far the most notorious approach to control alcohol was the ill-advised and ill-fated 18th Amendment. By all accounts, Prohibition, given the known impact of the vertically integrated system coupled with the fact that it was a reactive approach to alleviating social disorder during that time period, was a complete failure, fostering the professionalization of expansive crime networks (Thornton, 1991). Albert Einstein, as early as 1921, realized the inevitable failure of the federal government's belief that it could pass a law that would capture the respect of most Americans and to which they would be obedient. Soon after the implementation of prohibition he said, "The prestige of government has undoubtedly been lowered considerably by the prohibition law; for nothing is more destructive of respect for the government and the law of the land than passing laws which cannot be enforced. It is an open secret that the dangerous increase of crime in this country is closely connected with this" (Einstein, 1921).

Control Given to States by the 21st Amendment

When the responsibility for alcohol control was deferred to the states it was clear to those with a broader perspective that there would be problems, as delineated in the Fosdick and Scott text (1933). The first and foremost concern was economic control, an issue in the U.S. since the introduction of trusts and the concentration of economic power in large corporations that eventually led to the passing of the Sherman Antitrust Act (Congressional Record, 1890). In 1914, the Clayton Antitrust Act was passed by Congress with the intent to limit exclusive sales contracts, local price cutting to freeze out competitors, rebates, and interlocking directorates in corporations capitalized at $1 million or more in the same field of business and intercorporate stock holdings (Shenefield and Stelzer, 1996). Utilizing the 21st Amendment and guidance from federal laws such as the Webb-Kenyon Act and the Federal Alcohol Administration Act, states created systems to separate those who made alcohol from those who sold alcohol. The purpose was two-fold: (1) to clean up the system and (2) to rid it of its unsavory rum running association imposed by Prohibition. By creating separate licensed entities, a transparent and accountable system was created to weed out organized crime influences. For example, a wholesaler today must be licensed by both the federal and state governments and as part of this process undergoes a background check (Tax and Trade Bureau, 2007). The second part of this system allowed for the separate tiers to concentrate on their functions yet serve as regulatory pressure points on a completely free market. If applying regulatory pressure to a tier would help a state reach its proper balance for regulation, it was considered. Taxes, auditing of warehouses, and outlet limits are among the types of laws that impact the three tiers.

The framework for the post-Prohibition control of alcohol consumption began with the repeal of the 18th amendment in 1933. Ironically, antitrust action sharply declined during the Prohibition years of the 1920s. Soon thereafter President Roosevelt passed the Robinson-Patman Act in 1936, which forbade anyone engaged in interstate commerce to discriminate in price to different purchasers of the same commodity if the effect would be to lessen competition or to create a monopoly. Sometimes called the Anti-Chain Store Act, it was directed at protecting independent retailers and local "mom and pop" outlets from chain store competition, but was also supported by wholesalers eager to prevent large chain stores from buying directly from the manufacturers for lower prices (Macavoy, 1999). The same issues are being argued today in the federal courts with attempts by the big box retailer, Costco, as stated in its 2004 court filing, "Plaintiff Costco Corporation, brings this action to promote competition in the sale of wine and beer in the State of Washington. Costco seeks to create lower prices and greater choices for Washington consumers and reform an inefficient and unlawful system that permits distributors to benefit at the expense of consumers and certain wineries and brewers." Washington state operates a monopoly for distributing spirits. Costco's suit is but one example of the battle between large national chain stores and the interests of local retailers and wholesalers.

The present regulatory scheme in some states requires a minimum markup price for wholesale and retail tiers. The intention here is not to guarantee a profit to wholesale and retailers at the expense of the consumer, but to maintain alcohol at a certain price level so that it cannot become too cheap and therefore easily accessible. A legitimate public policy is currently under consideration in England about the lack of price controls and sale of alcohol as a loss leader. Many blame these "race to the bottom" pricing points for an increase in alcohol-related harm in the United Kingdom (Steele, 2007). The same theory is used to justify excise taxes (Babor et al., 2003; Fosdick and Scott, 1933). Excise taxes are often harder to raise or adjust for inflation because of various procedural obstacles and a strong antitax sentiment across the United States.

Deregulators looking at this relationship through a lens of pure economic theory miss the Fosdick and Scott (1933) proposition of intentional fractionalization using a middle tier as the monopoly. Most states have laws that attempt to thwart the vertical relationship between supplier and wholesaler which, if applied and enforced, would continue to limit the ability to become vertical and cartelized (Distilled Spirits Council, 2004). State laws that may appear to make no sense in an ordinary economic model, minimum markup, brand representation, exclusive territory, tied house and other trade issues such as prohibitions on giving a retailer something of value are easily understood within the context of what was intended in 1933, and now needs to be analyzed from a 21st amendment perspective instead of an economic one (Jurkiewicz and Painter, 2004).

The second ongoing concern in alcohol control is whether the three main types of alcoholic beverages, beer, wines, and spirits, should be treated differently under the law. "A rational approach to the problem of liquor control requires an about-face and a new viewpoint. We should start by inquiring what concentration of alcohol makes a beverage intoxicating in fact to an ordinary man. When the alcoholic content is below that point, a drink should be subject to little, if any restraint upon its use. The sale of stronger drinks should be regulated under a program which, so far as is practible [*sic*], discourages consumption with increasing strictness as the alcoholic content increases" (Fosdick and Scott, 1933). This was the basis for the next 70+ years of attempts by law and public policy to control the negative outcomes involved with the consumption of alcohol by separating it into two categories: light wines and beer versus spirits. Today's research shows increasing the alcohol content of a beverage increased consumption, while lowering content decreases consumption. Research has further concluded that lowering the drinking age results in more alcohol-related accidents, while mandatory server and retail training results in a significantly reduced number of crashes. Increased alcohol consumption per individual is concomitant with the expansion of retail hours while a reduction in hours significantly reduces consumption. School- and college-based alcohol education has also been found to reduce consumption although the number of studies in this area is minimal. Risk labels on alcohol bottles have had no discernible impact on consumption (Edwards, 1997).

The third ongoing issue regarding alcohol control, again unresolved since 1933, is social control by limiting access, maybe better described as the right to offer or not offer alcoholic beverages in a community at all. The traditional economic theory of federalism posits that more heterogeneous preferences result in more decentralized policy making (Oates, 1972; Strumpf and Oberholzer-Gee, 1999). This suggests that a state will select local option or decentralization when citizens on both sides of the legalization issue have intense preferences. In states that implement the local option, one can observe how characteristics such as demographics and religious affiliation influence the probability that a county's residents will choose to legalize liquor (Strumpf and Oberholzer-Gee, 1999). The suggested process of utilizing the state legislative process instead of the federal congressional process allows the preference of the community that has to deal with the negative outcomes of alcoholic beverage use, whether agreeable or in conflict with the economic model, to be guaranteed. Utah and its citizens have different laws from Las Vegas. People within different parts of Texas have completely different views on the propriety of alcohol as do most other parts of the United States. This is an aspect of social control.

One of the goals in this retrospective of *Toward Liquor Control* is to determine whether the models that were decided upon while the memories of the failure of Prohibition were fresh have in any way succeeded in controlling the unintended consequences of the legal manufacture, distribution, sale, and consumption of alcohol, primarily through the interjection of a reverse economic model originally intended to give the middle tier the monopoly of economic control. As authors in the original text point out, in an ever-expanding universe, the natural trend of the economic model is to move toward a vertically integrated model. The solution was to break that model for control purposes by what was called "two main classifications of government control: the license method and the public monopoly method" (Fosdick and Scott 1933, Chapters 4 and 5).

This new system in the license model makes the private wholesaler a semi-monopoly and retains the community's rights to determine access. The state control model engages the government with the responsibility of limiting access of hard liquor and spirits by becoming the monopoly while leaving beer and sometimes wine to private enterprise. It also maintains the community's right to determine access. Both systems, through local options and fair trade legislation attempt to separate the first and third tiers from becoming "tied." Louisiana wholesalers today argue the need to maintain the present controls on tied houses or the consumer will have very little brand choice when shopping. "Normal economics relationships tend to draw to the vertical with large chain retailers and barrooms wanting to offer a few brands at cheaper prices. The consumer is a fourth tier which should have the right to brand choice in the market place" (Brown, 2005).

Fosdick and Scott (1933) understood the unique opportunity the United States had in the wake of Prohibition's repeal to create a valid system of control through new theories and laws. "We have come now to the situation existing in those states in which, by repeal of the 18th Amendment, the slate has been wiped clean for a new experiment in liquor control" (p. 28).

Seventy Plus Years of State Control

A report by Licensed Beverage Industries (LBI) published in 1968 and titled "The Alcoholic Beverage Industry 1934–1968, 35 Years of Growth and Progress," proclaims in its foreword that "The nation's alcoholic beverage industry recently completed its thirty-fifth year of economic growth and social progress in the public interest. This milestone provides an appropriate vantage point for reviewing the industry's contributions to our economy and society since 1933" (p. 3). The industry's successes from 1933 to 1968 include economic development (marketing) and the changing of public attitudes toward drink and drinking. The continued growth of the industry, as this report indicates, was made possible chiefly by broadening acceptance of moderate social drinking in American life. The 1968 per capita consumption for spirits was 1.71 gallons while the consumption per customer was 3.4 to 3.8 gallons annually. Beer consumption in 1968 per capita was 17.3 gallons while wine was 1.07 gallons (USDA, 2007). From an economic growth perspective, this report authenticates that the new experiment of state control was working pretty well from the spirits industries standpoint, at least for the first 35 years, where it grew from 1934 with a Gross Industry Product of $1.3 billion to a $19.3 billion mark with an average annual increase of 8.3 percent (LBI Facts Book, 1968, p. 5–6).

The industry in 1968 predicted, "Based on forecast of an expanding population and advancing technology, it is certain that leisure time, disposable income and discretionary income will steadily increase. Accordingly, it is estimated that by the end of the next 35-year period the Gross Industry Product will total $95 billion. By 2003, distilled spirits consumption should approach 1 billion gallons with the same general rate of per consumer consumption as today, due to the substantial anticipated increase in the number of adult consumers" (LBI Facts Book, 1968, p. 8).

U.S. Census data shows that a trend from 1970 to the next 35-year mark in 2003 began with per capita consumption of spirits at 3.0 gallons with beer at 30.6 gallons and wine at 2.2 gallons. From 1970 to 2003, spirit consumption decreased to 1.3 gallons; wine was still at 2.2 gallons and beer increased to 33.9 gallons per capita annually (U.S. Census, 2000). (Note: Per capita consumption is based on legal age consumption.) The projection that spirits would reach the 1 billion-gallon mark was not achieved, with totals for 2003 being 378.4 million gallons (Adams, 2006, p. 13). Regardless of the missed mark and the decline in per capita consumption, *Adams Handbook* characterizes the spirits industry in 2006 this way: "Retail dollar sales for distilled spirits continue to grow at a much faster rate than case sales. The increased popularity of premium offerings has also led prices of cocktails to rise equally, with some libations costing upwards of $15. Total retail dollar sales for spirits reached $53.5 billion (also short of the 1968 projection of $95 billion) in 2005 for a gain of 8.2 percent. Over the past five years, spirits' retail dollars grew 7.5 percent on an annual compound growth rate compared to 2.7 percent for spirits cases. The marked increase of Americans dining out aided in the 9.5 percent gain in spirits' retail dollar sales for on-premise accounts in 2005. Consumers spent $31.0 billion on spirits in these accounts while sales increased 6.5 percent to $22.5 in off premise outlets. The on-premise accounts for 24.8 percent of case sales, but 58.0 percent of total retail dollars" (Adams, 2006, p. 7).

Fosdick and Scott (1933, p. 107–108) argued that the objective for the taxation of alcohol by state and federal governments should be for rational and effective social control and not solely to increase governmental revenue. They feared that the same greed and the need to increase consumption could affect government action if it became dependent on the revenues and the need to increase them. Today, where the alcohol distribution system is under private rather than state control, taxes, tariffs, and licensing fees generate revenue for states without restricting pricing actions at the wholesale and retail levels, although they reduce the efficiency of alcohol markets. Except to the extent that a state requires otherwise, wholesalers and retailers remain free to set prices to compete with each other, including considerable price differentiation between beverage quality classes. In some places, price fixing and minimum pricing requirements are also allowed or imposed, which further restricts pricing choices in the alcohol market. It is politically very difficult for legislatures to raise taxes. However, one way to ensure that the price of alcohol does not have a "race to the bottom" is to pass minimum markup laws and let semi-capitalism effectuate the pricing and public health goals. In Canada, for instance, minimum price levels for beer as set by the Quebec and Ontario provinces have been justified as contributing to public health and order (McCarthy, 1992; Babor et al., 2003).

Prior studies of seven U.S. states that abandoned alcohol monopolies and Nordic studies of expansions and contradictions in authority to sell alcohol show that monopolies reduce per capita alcohol consumption (Wagenaar and Holder, 1991, 1995; Makinen, 1978; Babor et al., 2003; Miller et al., 2006). The main impacts of a retail monopoly are to reduce alcohol outlet density (Nelson, 1990; Miller et al., 2006), sales hours (Zardkoohi and Sheer, 1984; Miller et al., 2006), advertising of monopoly products, and to increase diligence in not selling to underage drinkers (Giesbrecht, 1995; Miller et al., 2006). Changing outlet density is associated with same direction rate changes for violence, impaired driving, and arrest for public drunkenness (Gruenewald, Ponicki, and Holder, 1993; Norstrom, 2002; Poikolainen, 1980, Miller et al., 2006). Finally, a recent study succinctly pointed out that raising alcohol taxes is not as effective as having a wide variety of active and enforced alcohol regulations (Ponicki, Gruenewald, and LaScala, 2007).

The key question for government today is how to control alcohol while at the same time maintaining or increasing revenues (McGowan, 1997). It could be said that the same approach is required of all government-regulated industries such as airlines, banking, healthcare, and insurance, but the fact that alcohol has been the subject of two different constitutional amendments affords it a unique place in U.S. history and in public policy, as well as indicating its importance as a social concern (Tropman, 1986).

Late 1990s estimates, the most recent available, put the social cost of alcohol use at $148 billion (Cook and Moore, 2000). The World Health Organization (WHO, 2004) Web site lists the following reasons to control the consumption of alcohol: chronic liver disease and cirrhosis, injury and poisoning, auto accidents and deaths, suicide and self-inflicted injuries, alcohol psychosis, work-related injuries, and absenteeism, in addition to well-publicized concerns regarding fetal alcohol syndrome and other alcohol-related birth defects.

The positive economic benefit the alcohol industry as a major contributor to the nations' economy is reported by the Distilled Spirits Council, The Wine Institute, and the Beer Institute to be in excess of $452 billion. Collectively the industry employs over 2.5 million people (Distilled Spirits Council, 2007). One of the industry's main arguments against any increase in excise taxes is that such taxes are regressive forms of taxation that unduly target the middle class and blue collar workers, and further that these taxes place an undue burden on an industry that makes significant economic contributions to the public (McGowan, 1997). Industry totals for federal, state, and local taxes paid annually on beer, wine, and spirits exceed $71 billion (Distilled Spirits Council, Wine Institute, and Beer Institute, 2007).

Today the state stores or state monopoly systems in 18 states control all spirits and most wine wholesale sales and, in a few states, retail sales also. The other 32 states and the District of Columbia operate by private enterprise in all three tiers and state control comes from licensing and enforcement. Three firms share control of 80 percent of the beer market sales: Anheuser Busch, Miller Brewing, and Coors

(McGowan, 1997). However, the growth in the beer market is with small craft beers, with sales increasing over 12 percent in 2006 alone (Beer Institute, 2007). Consolidations of spirits suppliers have most of the market concentrated in a few houses. Diageo, Constellation, Brown & Foreman, Beam Global Spirits & Wine, Sazarac, Pernard Ricard, Bacardi, Skyy Spirits, and Heavenly Hill are the most prominent suppliers garnering easily with over 80 percent of the market share. Over 80 percent of the volume of wine is distributed by five or fewer companies (Adams, 2007).

Today, as in the past, alcohol remains a controversial and divisive topic. Its use is inextricable from concerns about health, crime, and politics. Concerns over the rising costs of healthcare coupled with advances in research linking alcohol consumption to health and behavioral outcomes (Edwards, 1997), have instigated a trend for blaming alcohol consumption for egregious public misconduct, such as that reported about Patrick Kennedy, Mel Gibson, Nicole Ritchie, Mark Foley, and Bob Ney, to name only a few. Such claims are fueling a boom in the rehabilitation industry. This, in turn and combined with other special interest groups' activism on the subject, is sowing the seeds for what some researchers and professionals believe — and fear — is another move toward prohibition and all the anticipated and unanticipated woes that would certainly ensue (Lerner, 2007). Yet the biggest challenge on the horizon will be addressing the question of whether to enforce the three-tier system or to allow for changes that would ultimately affect the consumption and control of alcohol in the U.S. far into the future.

The challenge confronting the alcohol industry is to find creative methods to address the drunk driving and healthcare issues, counter growing popular claims that "alcohol made me do it," increase public acceptance of existing and new products, encourage moderation while maintaining profits, and silence demands for excise tax increases. With two constitutional amendments covering alcohol, one would think that the United States would lead the world in alcohol consumption per capita. Russell Ash's *Top Ten of Everything* (2000), lists the United States far below the top ten of industrialized nations in spirit consumption. The top consumer nation is Portugal at 2.98 gallons per capita; Switzerland rounds out the top at number 10 with 2.43 gallons. The United States (no rank given for spirits) is at 1.74 gallons per capita. Ash lists the United States at 14th for beer consumption, while Beer Institute (2000) data shows 21.7 gallons per capita for the U.S. with the Czech Republic first with 167.85 gallons (Ash, 2000). The United States operates within a state-regulated three-tier system while most of the world's industrial nations operate within completely vertical two-tier systems. The U.S. system has allowed tremendous variety and value for American consumers, yet allowed regulators to keep a check on an unregulated alcohol market. While the exact quantity of beer labels carried by Costco varies depending upon location, the average is about 14 (Murphy, 2006). However, in the United States, 13,535 brands of beer are available to consumers (12,216 from the U.S. and Canada and 1,319 imported from the rest of the world) (Modern Brewery, 2006).

Importantly, Americans are not all alike regarding their views on alcohol. In fact, according to repeated Gallup National Polls, roughly 4 in 10 Americans do not drink alcohol (Jones, 2006). This number has remained relatively constant over many decades. Alcohol is not for everyone and nondrinkers also have a stake in this debate which regulators and legislators must consider as they try to balance public health, industry, consumer, and other issues.

Since repeal of Prohibition, alcoholic beverage regulation has been generally successful. Control of intoxicating liquors does not dominate politics as it did earlier. Because of the current control systems in place, regulatory adjustments are less exaggerated and more fine-tuned. Yet debate continues and some arguments are as intemperate as they ever were. Even now, the rhetoric of the proverbial early American politician still resonates. The balance between unrestricted consumption and control of alcohol is determined by mercurial public perceptions, as Lender and Martin (1982, in Yalisove, 2004) recall: "A congressman was once asked by a constituent to explain his attitude toward whiskey. "If you mean the demon drink that poisons the mind, pollutes the body, desecrates family life, and inflames sinners, then I am against it," the congressman said. "But if you mean the elixir of Christmas cheer, the shield against winter chill, the taxable potion that puts needed funds into public coffers to comfort little crippled children, then I'm for it. That's my position and I will not compromise."

References

Adams Handbook Advance. (2007) *The First Report on Consumption of Spirits, Wine, and Beer*, Adams Beverage Group Publications.

Adams Liquor Handbook. (2006) *Spirits Sales and Consumption*, Adams Beverage Group Publications.

Ash, R. (2000) *The Top Ten of Everything 2000*, New York: DK Publishing, Inc.

Babor, T., Barbor, T., and Caetano, R. (2003) *Alcohol and Public Policy: No Ordinary Commodity*, London: Oxford University Press.

Barsby, S.L. and Associates. (1999) *The Regulatory and Economic Basis of Wine and Spirits Wholesaling in the Alcohol Beverage Industry*, 2nd ed., Wine and Spirits Wholesalers of America, Inc.

Beer Institute. (2007) *New Study Shows Beer Industry Contributes Billions Annually to U.S. Economy*, http://beerinstitute.org/tier.asp?nid=311&archiveyear=2007&bid=10 2, accessed May 6, 2007.

Benjamin, D.K., Miller, R.L., & North, D.C. (2001) *The Economics of Public Issues*, Boston: Addison Wesley.

Brown, F.W. (1932) Prohibition and Mental Hygiene: Effects on Mental Health-Specific Disorders, *Annals of the American Academy of Political and Social Science*, 163: 61–88.

Brown, G.F. (2005) Presentation before the Louisiana Beer Wholesalers' Convention, Sandestin, Florida, July 23.

Bruun, K., Edwards, G., and Lumio, M. (1975) *Alcohol Control Policies in Public Health Perspective*, Helsinki: Finnish Foundation for Alcohol Studies.

Cherrington, E.H. (1920) *The Evolution of Prohibition in the United States of America*, Westerville, OH: American Issue Press.

Congressional Record, 51st Congress, 1st session, House, June 20, 1890, 4100.

Cook, P.J. and Moore, M.J. (2000) Alcohol, in J.P. Newhouse and A. Culyer (Eds.), *Handbook of Health Economics, Vol. 1B*, New York: Elsevier.

Costco Wholesale Corporation v. Norm Mailing et al., Washington State Liquor Control Board, and Christine O. Gregoire, Attorney General, United States District Court, Western District of Washington at Seattle, File CV 04-0360, February 20, 2004.

Distilled Spirits Council. (2004) *Summary of State Laws & Regulations Related to Distilled Spirits*, 33rd ed., Washington, D.C.

Distilled Spirits Council. (2007) *Economic Contribution of Alcohol Beverage Industry*, http://www.discus.org/economics/, accessed May 6, 2007.

Dobyns, F. (1940) *The Amazing Story of Repeal*, Chicago: Willett, Clark & Co.

Edwards, G. (1997) Alcohol Policy and the Public Good, *Addiction*, 92(3s1): 73–80.

Edwards, G. (Ed.); Anderson, Peter; Babor, Thomas F., and Casswell, Sally. (1994) *Alcohol Policy and the Public Good*, Oxford: Oxford University Press, 212–213.

Quotations and Famous Quotes of Albert Einstein. (1921) http://en.proverbia.net/citasautor.asp?auto=12258&page=16, accessed June 10, 2007.

Fosdick, R.D. and Scott, A.L. (1933) *Toward Liquor Control*, London: Harper & Brothers.

Ghalioungui, P. (1979) Fermented Beverages in Antiquity, in C.F. Gastineau et al., (Eds.), *Fermented Food Beverages in Nutrition*, New York: Academic Press.

Gruenewald, P.J., Ponicki, W.R., Holder, H., 1993. The relationship of outlet density to alcohol consumption: A time series cross-sectional analysis. *Alcohol. Clin. Exp. Res.* 17(1), 38–47.

Health, D.B. (2000) *Drinking Occasions: Comparative Perspectives on Alcohol and Culture*, Washington, D.C.: Taylor & Francis.

Institute of Alcohol Studies. (2005) *Alcohol Policies*, http://www.ias.org.uk/resources/factsheets/policies.pdf, accessed June 19, 2007.

Jankowiak, W. and Bradburd, D. (1996) Using Drug Foods to Capture and Enhance Labor Performance: A Cross-Cultural Perspective, *Current Anthropology*, 37: 717–720.

Jones, J.M. (2006) U.S. Drinkers Consuming Alcohol More Regularly, Washington, D.C., The Gallup Poll Full News Service, http://poll.gallup.com/content/Default.aspx?ci=23935&VERSION=p, accessed July 31, 2006.

Jurkiewicz, C.L. and Painter, M.J. (2004) Reducing Underage Access to Alcohol: A State Program That Works, *Journal of Public Affairs and Issues*, 8(3): 1–24.

Krout, J.A. (1967) *The Origins of Prohibition*, New York: Russell and Russell.

Lee, H. (1963) *How Dry We Were: Prohibition Revisited*, Englewood Cliffs, NJ: Prentice Hall.

Lender, M.E. and Martin, J.K. (1982) *Drinking in America: A History*, New York: Free Press.

Lerner, M.A. (2007) *Dry Manhattan: Prohibition In New York City*, Boston: Harvard University Press.

Licensed Beverage Industries Facts Book. (1968) *The Alcoholic Beverage Industry 1934–1968, 35 Years of Growth and Progress*, New York.

Macavoy, C.J. (1999) A Primer on the Federal Price Discrimination Laws: A General Review of the Robinson-Patman Act for Business Managers, American Bar Association.

Makela, K., Room, R., and Single, E.R. (1981) Alcohol, Society, and the State, Volume 1: A Comparative Study of Alcohol Control, Toronto: Addiction Research Foundation.

Makinen, H. (1978). Effects of Banning Medium Beer in Municipalities. Case Study in Five Municipalities. Helsinki: *Alkoholipoliittisen tutkimusseloste*, 122.

McCarthy, S. (1992). Ontario, Will Defy Galt on Beer, *Toronto Star*, Toronto, Ontario, Feb. 14.

McGowan, R. (1997) Government Regulation of the Alcohol Industry: The Search for Revenue and the Common Good, Westport, CT: Quorum Books.

Miller, P. and Johnson, T.H. (1963) *The Puritans*, New York: Harper & Row.

Miller, T. et al. (2006) Retail Alcohol Monopolies, Underage Drinking, and Youth Impaired Driving Deaths, *Accident Analysis & Prevention*, May 2.

Modern Brewery Age Blue Book 2007. (2006) Norwalk, CT: Business Journals.

Murphy, H.L. (2006) Costco's Challenge, *Market Watch* July/August, 28.

Nelson, J.P. (1990) State Monopolies and Alcohol Beverage Consumption, *J. Regul. Econ.*, 2(1) 83–98.

Norstrom, T. (Ed.) (2002) *Alcohol in Postwar Europe: Consumption, Drinking Patterns, Consequences and Policy Responses in 15 European Countries*, Stockholm: Almqvist & Wiskell.

Perry, K.M. (1988) Vertical Integration: Determinants and Effects, in *Handbook of Industrial Organization*, Amsterdam: North Holland.

Poikolainen, K. (1980). Increase in Alcohol Related Hospitalizations in Finland, 1969–1975. *Brit. J. Addiction*, 75, 281–291.

Ponicki, W.R., Gruenewald, Paul, J., LaScala, Elizabeth, A. (2007) Joint Impacts of Minimum Legal Drinking Age and Beer Taxes on U.S. Youth Traffic Fatalities, 1975 to 2001, *Alcoholism: Clinical and Experimental Research*, 31(5).

Shenefield, J.H. and Stelzer, I.M. (1996) The Antitrust Laws. Washington: AEI Press.

Sinclair, A. (1962) *The Era of Excess*, Boston: Little, Brown.

Steele, J. (2007) Supermarkets Where Drink is Sold Like Water, Telegraph.co.uk online. http://www.telegraph.co.uk/news/main.jhtml?xml=/news/2007/06/06/ndrink306.xml, accessed June 14, 2007.

Strumpf, K.S. and Oberholzer-Gee, F. (1999) Local Liquor Control from 1934 to 1970, in *Public Choice Interpretation of American Economic History*, Heckleman, Moorehouse, Whaples.

Taber, C. et al. (2003) *Alcohol: No Ordinary Commodity*, New York: Oxford Press.

Tax & Trade Bureau. (2007) http://www.ttb.gov/forms/f510024.pdf, accessed May 6, 2007.

Thornton M. (1991) Alcohol Prohibition Was A Failure, *Cato Policy Analysis* 157, July 17, http://www.cato.org/pubs/pas/pa-157.html, accessed September 26, 2005.

Tillitt, M.H. (1932) *The Price of Prohibition*, New York: Harcourt, Brace & Co.

Timberlake, J.H. (1963) *Prohibition and the Progressive Movement*, Cambridge: Harvard University Press.

Tropman, J.E. (1986) *Conflict in Culture: Permissions versus Controls in Alcohol Use in American Society*, Lanham, MD: University Press of America Inc.

U.S. Census 2000: http//www.allcounties.org/uscensus/238_per_capita_consumption_ of_ selected_beverages accessed May 5, 2007.

United States Code Annotated. (1987) *Constitutional Amendments 14 to end*, St. Paul, MN, West Publishing Company.

United States Department of Agriculture. (2007) Per Capita Consumption of Beer & Wine, 1966-2005, http: www.ers.usda.gov/Data/foodconsumption/spreadsheets/beverages. xls, accessed May 6, 2007.

United States Department of Agriculture. (2007) Per Capita Consumption of Selected Beverages by Type 1980 to 2004, http://www.census.gov/compendia/statab/tables 07s0201.xls, accessed May 6, 2007.

United States Internal Revenue Service. (1921) *Alcohol and Tobacco Summary Statistics*, Washington, D.C.: U.S. Treasury Department.

United States Internal Revenue Service. (1966) *Alcohol and Tobacco Summary Statistics*, Washington, D.C.: U.S. Treasury Department.

United States Internal Revenue Service. (1970) *Alcohol and Tobacco Summary Statistics*, Washington, D.C.: U.S. Treasury Department.

Wagenaar and Holder, 1991.

Wagenaar and Holder, 1995.

Whitman D.J. (2003) *Strange Brew Alcohol and Government Monopoly*, California: Independent Institute, 3.

Wine Institute. (2007) U.S. Wine, Grapes and Grape Products Contribute $162 Billion to Economy, http://www.wineinstitute.org/industry/statistics/2007/us_wine_economic_impact.php, accessed May 6, 2007.

World Health Organization. (2004) *Global Status Report on Alcohol 2004*, http://www. who.int/substance_abuse/publications/global_status_report_2004_overview.pdf, accessed February 6, 2007.

Yalisove, D. (2004) Alcohol Research: Implications for Treatment, Prevention, and Policy, Boston: Pearson Education Inc.

Zardkoohi, A., and Sheer, A. (1984). Public versus Private Liquor Retailer: An Investigation into the Behavior of the State Governments. *South Econ. J. 50*(4), 1058–1076.

Chapter 2

Taxation and the Economic Impacts of Alcohol

Doug Schwalm

Contents

Background Information on Alcohol Consumption

Trends over Time

Overall consumption of alcohol has increased since the Second World War, peaking in 1980, and then decreasing. Although this is a well-established pattern (shared by a number of other countries), there is some variation in the measurement of exact amount of consumption. One respected study has consumption at four liters per annum in 1950 to three liters per year, peaking at five liters per annum in 1980, and three liters to date.* Another compilation looking at consumption trends across the Organisation for Economic Co-operation and Development reports 1970 levels in the United States at 6.7 liters per capita, rising to 8.2 liters in 1980, and falling to 7.5 in 1990.† The former information about alcohol consumption is gathered by the government from sales records. These records report the volume of beer, wine, and spirits sold by the companies, but exclude imports or home production.

These numbers can be broken up into three components: beer, wine, and spirits. The largest volatility over time has been in spirits, the consumption of which has fallen in the United States. Countering some of the fall in liquor consumption has been an increase in the consumption of beer and wine.‡ By 1990, just over 50 percent of ethanol consumed in the United States was in the form of beer, with the rest being almost equally split between wine and spirits. To gain perspective on what actual consumption looks like, it is often useful to recall that one drink of alcohol is the amount of alcohol contained in either one 12-ounce bottle of beer, one 5-ounce glass of the average wine, or a 1.5-ounce (one "jigger") drink of 80-proof liquor. Thus a container of beer (a bottle) is one drink, whereas there are 5 drinks of wine per bottle, and 17 drinks per fifth of liquor.

Individual Heterogeneity

It is important to understand that no matter our measures of total alcoholic consumption, there is a great deal of difference between alcoholic intake from one person to another. If we took a random group of 100 people,§ fully 30 percent would be teetotalers, not consuming any alcohol. Another 30 percent would consume just under a six-pack of beer, or just over the equivalent of one bottle of wine over the course of a month (recall a 750-mL bottle of wine is about five drinks of alcohol¶),

---

* Williams et al., 1996.
† Edwards et al., 1994, Table 2.1.
‡ Edwards et al., 1994, Figure 2.1.
§ This example is based on an example by Dean Gerstein (1981), though it is designed to be slightly more understandable.
¶ A fifth of a gallon is 25.6 fluid ounces, which is about 757 milliliters, only slightly more than the 750-ml bottles sold on the market. If you are a liquor drinker, 17 jiggers make 25.5 fluid ounces, or about five drinks of wine.

roughly one and a half of a drink per person over the course of the week. The next 10 percent, however, would consume about one drink a day, and the next 10 percent roughly two drinks a day. Thus only about 20 percent of the population would be considered "moderate" drinkers. The next ten people would consume double that, quaffing four drinks from sunrise to sunset, and the highest 10 percent would tipple almost ten drinks a day.

Statistically, Edwards et al. (1994) find the distribution of alcohol consumption is usually well described by a log-Gaussian distribution, which is highly skewed. This finding applies to many different societies, both those that consume large amounts of alcohol (France, Luxembourg) and those that do not (Norway, Turkey), as well as to any country over time.

What We Know about the Demand for Alcohol

Price Elasticity

Price elasticities can be estimated either based on individual data, which allow estimates to be specific to different groups, or based on aggregate data, which summarize the average societal response to price changes. Those studies that have looked at aggregate price data have found varied estimates, but generally find that alcohol responds to prices in a normal way (the elasticities are negative), and in general are indeed price sensitive (they are inelastic, but substantially different from zero). Typical estimates, based on seven Organisation for Economic Co-operation and Development (OECD) countries, show an additional pattern that is often observed. Beer is the least price-sensitive (usually around –0.35), whereas liquor is the most price sensitive (on average, –0.98). Wine is in the middle, with an average elasticity of –0.68.[*] In comparison, Grossman et al. (1998) find an overall estimate of –0.40 based on a sample of youth.[†] An additional example, provided by Leung and Phelps (1993), give "best guesses" of –0.3 for beer, –1.0 for wine, and –1.5 for liquor.[‡]

If we consider the advertising elasticity of alcohol consumption (that is, how much the demand for alcohol would increase if advertising dollars went up by 10 percent), the available evidence can only give a rough and unreliable guide to their effects. There are many methodologic problems to be overcome when estimating such elasticities (endogeneity issues plague attempts to measure changes in alcohol advertising). However, most studies find very small or zero affects *on the margin* because of advertising. However, these studies cannot address the affect of nonincremental changes in alcohol advertising. To assess the effectiveness of

---

[*]Clements et al., 1997. The countries included are Britain, Canada, Australia, New Zealand, Norway, Sweden, and Finland.

[†]Their data, however, are based on individuals. See following section for more details.

[‡]Leung and Phelps review many studies, with differing elasticities. Their numbers are their attempt at their "best" synopsis.

an advertising ban on alcohol consumption, Saffer studied 17 different countries across a span of years. His best estimate is that a ban on liquor advertising reduced consumption by 16 percent, whereas a ban on all alcohol advertising would reduce consumption by 25 percent.* It is important to note, however, that these estimates are also plagued by endogeneity issues, and thus must be seen as upper bounds of the effect of a ban (for example, if the bans were imposed because of particularly severe problems with alcohol, or social pressures to limit drinking, which would have influenced alcohol consumption independent of legislation).

Differences by Group

Using individual level data, rather than aggregate data, allows us to measure the sensitivity to price changes by different groups in the population. Two of the most important groups of policy concern are youths and heavy drinkers (potential abusers). Most work done on the price sensitivity of youth has found that they are indeed sensitive to both money prices and "total prices" (i.e., minimum drinking age laws). Grossman et al.[10] find that the myopic price elasticity is bounded between −0.20 and −0.38 (their average, −0.29, is usually quoted the most). However, their article explores the hypothesis that youths are not myopic, but rather take into consideration the possibility that alcohol is addictive, and that current consumption may change future consumption. There is other empirical evidence that there may be habit formation in the consumption of alcohol by youths (Moore and Cook, 1995). However, separating out the statistical identification issues has proved to be challenging in this literature and precise estimates cannot be claimed to be known.

Using the methodology of rational addiction,† Grossman et al. try to provide elasticities that incorporate forward looking behavior. Their short term price elasticity is bounded from −0.18 to −0.86 (average, −0.41), whereas the long-term elasticity has an average of −0.65 (bounded between −0.26 and −1.26).‡ The difference among the three estimates can be summarized as follows. Suppose there are no addictive effects to alcohol, and it is like most other goods. Then we would take their −0.29 estimate as roughly correct. If, however, there are habit-forming effects to alcohol, we would expect that a 10 percent increase in the price of beer would decrease alcohol consumption by about 4.1 percent in the near term (say over the

---

* Total bans are reported to be 11 percent lower than the partial ban.

† Becker and Murphy's rational addiction model (1988) provides a way for stating how someone may choose to engage in activities they know will prove habit forming, such as drugs, tobacco, alcohol, or perhaps even classical music.

‡ As suggested in the prior paragraph, the skeptical reader needs to hold these estimates suspect. Their empirical results are not consistent with the theory of rational addiction, and imply that youths would have implausibly large and negative real interest rates. When they impose a real interest rate of about 5 percent in their model, their results do not differ much from the myopic estimates quoted above.

course of a year). However, allowing for newer cohorts to make the decision to start drinking or not means that the increased price would have a greater long-term effect, increasing the 4.1 percent drop to 6.5 percent over time. Given the biologic evidence that alcohol has especially harmful effects on the adolescent brain,* this may be an important finding in helping to reduce the negative effects of alcohol on society.

Another type of policy control that affects "total price" is the minimum drinking law, which severely increases the cost of drinking if the youth is caught.† Grossman et al.[10] simulate the hypothetical effect of having all states changing their age from 18 to 21, and find that consumption would have fallen by about 30 percent. Thus using their long-run estimates, a similar effect would have been obtained by increasing the price of beer by about 50 percent.

As was described previously, there is a lot of heterogeneity across people in their levels of alcohol consumption. There are two contradictory findings on how price will affect the consumption patterns of heavy drinkers. One strand of literature finds that even the heaviest drinker responds to the costs associated with having a drink. Two experiments in particular illustrate this. Mello et al. (1968) found that if effort is needed to obtain a drink, then the effort elasticity of alcohol among a group of alcoholics was about −1.0. Another experiment found that when prices dropped 50 percent during happy hour, both moderate and heavy drinkers doubled their intake.‡ However, Manning et al. (1995) found that the upper ventile does not respond to price, or even responds perversely by increasing their consumption if the price of alcohol increases. In spite of the lack of specific empirical estimates of elasticity, it does seem clear that higher prices cause lower numbers of cirrhosis cases, as will be stated in the following section.

The Effects of Taxation

Goals of Taxation

To evaluate what a good tax on alcohol might look like, we need to consider what the goal of a tax is. Should the government tax to raise revenue, or should it tax to try to restrict drinking? Different countries have engaged in different goals. The Nordic countries, for example typically have high taxes to help restrict alcohol consumption, whereas Europe's grape-producing countries tend to have lower taxes. We have seen that most populations are responsive to changes in taxation, and so

---

* See Spear, 2000, 2002.
† A common way of thinking about crime is to model the cost of an action as the cost of conviction times the probability of conviction. This allows us to think of minimum drinking laws as an additional type of tax imposed upon those affected.
‡ Babor et al., 1978.

the scope for both revenue creation as well as paternalistic behavior modification exists.

Indeed, if there are negative externalities to the consumption of alcohol, then there is even a nonpaternalistic call for the government to institute Pigouvian taxes to correct for the externality. Certainly most findings on the extent of alcohol's long-term effects on heavy drinkers, as well as its effect on traffic accidents and violent assaults call to possibility that such taxes may be proper.

Given that taxation is deemed proper, we can then ask what the right type of tax might look like. Today, taxes on alcohol are based on the volume of ethanol in the product, regardless of the price of the alcohol. Although there is a proportional relationship between the amount spent on alcohol and income, there is no relationship between the volume of ethanol consumed and income (Cook and Moore, 2000). This means that because a poor household tends to drink on average as much as a rich household, the poor and rich will pay roughly the same amount in alcohol taxes. This then implies that the poor are paying a higher proportion of their income in alcohol taxes, making it a regressive tax.

Countering the undesirability of the regressiveness of the tax is that such a tax is more or less imposed as a fee for drinking. Given that more than half of all alcohol consumption occurs in less than 10 percent of the population,[*] the current excise tax is an effective way to impose most of the cost of the negative consequences of alcohol consumption on those who drink the most. However, it may not be enough to optimally change their behavior. The ideal Pigouvian tax (externalities tax) is one that changes the marginal cost of an action to reflect the full society cost of that action. The current excise tax does not seem to be even 50 percent the size needed to do so. A study by Manning et al. (1989) found that a drink imposes an extra social cost of about 30 cents,[†] which is more than twice the amount that states and the federal government impose.

Furthermore, their study studiously defined external costs as those outside the household. There are at least two further steps of "external" costs that could be added onto their estimates.

Drinking often causes severe problems on family dynamics, and can lead to spouse abuse, child neglect, pregnancy complications, and marital dissolution. Using taxation to try to curtail these activities may or may not be justified depending on the willingness of policy makers to intervene into family life.

In addition, there is an argument to be made to intervene on the well-being of the individual. Although economics has a tradition of allowing for consumer sovereignty, it is also based on the assumption that people have transitive preferences, even across time. This is often violated in the case of goods such as alcohol (and other cases in which uncertainty enters into decision making).[‡] Should policy

---

[*] See numbers from Individual Heterogeneity.
[†] They find that an ounce of ethanol has an external cost of about $0.48.
[‡] Camerer, 1999.

makers choose that the government has a role in helping consumers prevent predict-ably regrettable decisions, then the excise tax should be even higher. The suggestive evidence by Grossman and others about the higher long-term elasticity given habit formation underlines the possible justification for such taxes.

Overall Consumption vs. Binge Drinking

An additional consideration must be made on the way and timing that alcohol consumption takes place. There is a major difference in the costs imposed on soci-ety by those who engage in binge drinking (which can lead to risky behavior), and those who drink moderately at one to two drinks a day, even if their total alcohol consumption is the same. To tax by overall volume would provide no differences in incentives between the two types of behavior. To date, there are no good ex-ante ways to differentiate between the two behaviors. To the extent that laws and penalties exist to punish behavior that can stem from binge drinking, there is a differential in the price of the two activities, although the salience of the difference is probably close to zero, and thus ineffective in deterring or preventing the more risky binge-drinking behavior.

The Overall Economic Impact of Alcohol

Reductions in Mortality

Deaths from alcohol are the most severe impact on both the U.S. economy as well as the families of those killed. Estimates of such deaths range from about 5 to 7 percent of all deaths per year. In 1987, for example, the Centers for Disease Control reported 105,000 deaths (4.9 percent of all deaths that year) (1990). A more recent estimate for the state of New Jersey between 1996 and 1998 gives an age-adjusted mortality rate of 23.7 per 100,000 from alcohol, 5.1 percent of all deaths in that state. The National Vital Statistics Report from 2004 reports that the number of alcohol-induced deaths was about 6.9 percent per year between 1999 and 2002. McGinnis and Foege (1993) studied the causes of death by age group that had iden-tifiable sources and summed them up by their actual cause, and found the estimated number of deaths in 1990 to be 100,000, or about 5 percent of total deaths, third only to tobacco and diet/activity.

Deaths also cut across socioeconomic lines, affecting approximately 1,400 stu-dents ages 18–24 in 1998 (Hingson et al., 2002). Alcohol-related injuries affected a half million students (6.25 percent), and 7.5 percent were assaulted by a drunk. Fully 25 percent of students had driven while under the influence.

How effective can economic policy be in reducing mortality rates from alcohol? Most studies look at the direct (or reduced form) of tax rates or other alcohol-control policies (such as minimum age drinking laws or compulsory insurance laws) and mortality rates. This is valid only if there are causal links between higher taxes, and lower alcohol consumption, and then lower alcohol consumption causing less of the behavior that leads to mortality. However, efforts to estimate structural relationships are plagued with measurement error and statistically insignificant results.

Most studies find that higher taxes do affect motor vehicle fatalities, and, in particular, Ruhm finds that taxes are the most robust of all the various policies used.[*] He finds that for 18–20 year olds, the beer tax elasticity of traffic deaths to be –0.17, and that overall, a 78 percent increase in the beer tax would result in about a 7 percent decrease in traffic fatalities (saving around 3,500 lives annually). He further points out that the scope of many policies, such as minimum age drinking laws, is limited in the ability to yield further declines in fatalities, whereas the beer tax has actually declined in real terms, and thus presents a viable option for intervention.

Medical Expenses

Interestingly there is little direct evidence that drinking is directly related to higher medical expenses. Manning et al. (1991) found that former drinkers and abstainers use more medical care than current drinkers, whereas there is no statistically discernible difference between heavy drinkers and moderate drinkers. This is possibly the result of unobserved influences (bad health) that have caused the individual to stop drinking.

Indeed, if we consider the relationship between alcohol consumption and liver failure, we see that there is a direct link. During the major wars of the 20th century, most alcohol was diverted from the populace; as a result, there were dramatic drops in the rate of cirrhosis in the affected countries (Brunn et al., 1975; Cook and Moore, 2000). Cook and Tauschen (1982) found that taxes on spirits led to an immediate reduction in cirrhosis rates (Cook and Moore, 2000). These findings suggest that there may indeed be saving to be had by restricting alcohol consumption. However, other findings on the positive effects of alcohol on the circulatory system (at least when consumption is moderate) may lower medical expenditures.

---

[*] The effect of many policies may not be measured well due to unobserved (omitted) variables that confound the results. For example, if DUI laws were first implemented voluntarily by those states with high sentiments against drunk driving, then they may show to be effective. However, it is not clear whether it would have been the DUI laws or the sentiment that was causal. Furthermore, if DUI laws are later enacted due to federal pressure, then only those states that had not passed such laws prior to federal action would be affected. In such states, there may be weak sentiments against drunk driving, and this may undermine the (average) effectiveness of such laws. Ruhm finds evidence that many policies do not have robust estimates, possibly due to such unobserved influences. However, his findings on beer taxes are fairly robust.

Less work has been done on this by economists, but Camargo et al. (1997) is widely cited for having found that moderate drinking lowers the risk of heart disease, whereas abstinence and heavy drinking have higher rates.

Lost Productivity

Similar to the findings on medical expenses, there are no major findings of large deleterious effects of drinking on productivity. Indeed, at a cursory level, it seems that drinkers earn more than abstainers (Zarkin et al., 1998). Kenkel and Ribar (1994) looked at a sample of young adults ages 24–32 and found that there were no effects on the number of days that a person had drank in the past month and his or her current earnings. Indeed, they seemed to actually increase a woman's earnings slightly. Even heavy drinking (defined as the number of days where six or more drinks were consumed during the last month) did not have an effect on women's earnings, though there was a small negative effect on men's.

Although such findings may be influenced by statistical problems such as omitted variables, it seems unlikely that there is a link between alcohol consumption and lower direct effects on working capacity or productivity. However, as noted previously, this does not imply that there may be indirect effects. Alcohol can play a major deleterious role in the ability of adolescents to learn and successfully gain skills that will later make them productive. Speer (2000) documents some of these effects. Mullahy and Sindelar (1989) find that if an adolescent is reported as becoming alcoholic before age 19, then (other things being constant) he or she is 11 percent more likely to drop out of high school. High school dropouts have significantly reduced incomes compared with high school graduates, and this lack of schooling is a significant detriment to productivity.

Crime

Not much work has been done by economists on the effects of alcohol on crime. Cook and Moore (1993) find two complementary links between alcohol and crime. Using aggregate data from 1979 to 1988, they find that in those states that had higher alcohol consumption (holding other things constant*), there were higher rates of rape, assault, and robbery. Similarly, in those states with higher beer taxes, there were lower incidences of rape and robbery.

---

*They use a fixed-effect model that holds constant anything particular about a state, and also accounts for particular things that may have happened during the year that affects all states.

Summary

The ability of society to change an individual's behavior, even when it comes to addictive substances such as alcohol, is significant. The call to do so, however, needs to be well thought out. In a liberal society, the government should leave to its citizens the decisions that affect their own lives, and allow the individual to learn how to best cope with life's challenges.

However, when it is clear that individuals may not take the consequences that their own actions have on others into consideration, there may be a call for government intervention. Certainly the regulation of alcoholic beverages among youth is called for if for no other reason than that the biologic evidence of long-term harm is large and mounting, and that social influence can play a large and self-reinforcing role in levels of alcohol consumption. In addition to the prevention of developmental harm, reducing adolescent drinking has significant effects on traffic mortality rates, potentially saving thousands of lives a year.

Further intervention may even be justified if citizens want their government to participate in helping them mitigate decisions that they know they will come to regret. Because of the habit-forming qualities of alcohol, short-term decisions may not be consistent with long-term desires, and the ability of individuals to maintain self-control is more heterogeneous in such circumstances. Higher tax rates (higher even than normal Pigouvian tax rates) could possibly help mitigate such inconsistencies in personal choice.

However, it is also important to weigh the cost of such intervention. There is always going to be those who can maintain or develop methods to find ways to consume alcohol where they do not impose external costs either on others or on their future selves. Higher taxes are simply an excess burden for such individuals, and so the efficiency properties of higher taxes must therefore be weighed against the distribution effects of taking welfare away from those who can best control their actions.

References

Babor, et al. "Experimental Analysis of the 'Happy Hour': Effects of Purchase Price on Alcohol Consumption." *Psychopharmacology* 58 (1978): 35–41.

Becker, G. and K. Murphy. "A Theory of Rational Addiction." *Journal of Political Economy* 96:4 (1988): 675–700.

Brunn, et al. *Alcohol Control Policies in Public Health Perspective*, Aurasen Kirjapaino, Finland, 1975.

Camargo, et al. "Prospective Study of Moderate Alcohol Consumption and Mortality in U.S. Male Physicians." *Archives of Internal Medicine* 157:1 (1997): 79–85.

Camerer, C. "Behavioral Economics: Reunifying Psychology and Economics," *Proceedings from the National Academy of Sciences of the United States of America* 96:19 (1999): 10575–7.

Center of Health Statistics, New Jersey. "Alcohol Related Mortality, 1996–1998." *Topics in Health Statistics*, 2001. Available online at: http://www.state.nj.us/health/chs/topics 0105.pdf

Centers for Disease Control. "Alcohol-Related Mortality and Years of Potential Life Lost— United States, 1987." *Morbidity and Mortality Weekly Report* 39 (1987): 11.

Chaloupka, F. J., M. Grossman, and H. Saffer. "The Effects of Price on Alcohol Consumption and Alcohol-Related Problems." *Alcohol Research and Health* 26:1 (2002): 27–34.

Cook, P. and M. Moore. "Economic Perspectives on Alcohol-Related Violence." In *Alcohol-Related Violence*. Bethesda, MD: NIH Publication 93-3496, 1993.

Cook, P. and M. Moore. "Alcohol." In *The Handbook of Health Economics*. Elsevier Science, 2000.

Cook, P. and G. Tauchen. "The Effect of Liquor Taxes on Heavy Drinking." *Bell Journal of Economics* 13:2 (1982): 379–90.

Edwards, G., et al. *Alcohol Policy and the Public Good*. New York: Oxford University Press, 1994.

Gerstein, D. R. "Alcohol use and consequences." In *Alcohol and Public Policy: Beyond the Shadow of Prohibition*, eds. Mark Moore and Dean Gerstein, 182–224. National Academy of Sciences, 1981.

Grossman, M., F. J. Chaloupka, and I. Sirtalan. "An Empirical Analysis of Alcohol Addiction: Results from the 'Monitoring the Future' Panels." *Economic Inquiry* 36:1 (January 1998): 39–48.

Hingson, R., T. Heeren, R. C. Zakocs, A. Kopstein, and H. Wechsler. "Magnitude of Alcohol-Related Mortality and Morbidity Among U.S. College Students aged 18–24." *Journal of Studies on Alcohol* 63:2 (2002): 136–44.

Kenkel, D. and D. Ribar. "Alcohol Consumption and Young Adults' Socioeconomic Status." *Brookings Papers on Economic Activity-Micro* (June 1994): 119–61.

Leung, S. and C. Phelps. "My Kingdom for a Drink …?" In *Economics and the Prevention of Alcohol-Related Problems*, edited by Hilton, M. E., and G. Bloss. Bethesda, MD: NIAAA Research Monograph 25, NIH 93-3513, 1993: 1–32.

Manning W., et al. "The Taxes of Sin: Do smokers and drinkers pay their way?" *Journal of the American Medical Association* 261 (1989): 1604–9.

Manning, W., et al. *The Costs of Poor Health Habits*. Harvard University Press, 1991.

Manning, W., et al. "The Demand for Alcohol: The Differential Response to Price." *Journal of Health Economics* 14:2 (1995): 123–48.

McGinnis, J. M., and W. H. Foege. "Actual Causes of Death in the United States." *Journal of the American Medical Association* 270:18 (1993): 2207–12.

Mello, et al. "Drinking Patterns of Chronic Alcoholics: Gambling and Motivation for Alcohol." *Clinical Research in Alcoholism*, edited by Cole. Washington, DC: APA, 1968.

Moore, M. and P. Cook. "Habit and Heterogeneity in the Youthful Demand for Alcohol." NBER Working Paper no. 5152, 1995.

Mullahy, J. and J. Sindelar. "Life Cycle Effects of Alcoholism on Education, Earnings, and Occupation." *Inquiry* 26 (1989): 272–82.

National Center for Health Statistics. *National Vital Statistics Report* 53:9 (2004). Table 24.

Ruhm, C. "Alcohol Policies and Highway Vehicle Fatalities." *Journal of Health Economics* 15:4 (1996): 435–54.

Saffer, H. "Alcohol Advertising Bans and Alcohol Abuse: An International Perspective." *Journal of Health Economics* 10:1 (1991): 65–79.

Spear, L. "The Adolescent Brain and Age-Related Behavioral Manifestations." *Neuroscience Biobehavioral Review* 24 (2000): 417–63.

Spear, L. "The Adolescent Brain and the College Drinker: Biological Basis of Propensity to Use and Misuse Alcohol." *Journal of Studies on Alcohol* 14 (2002): 71–81.

Williams, et al. "Apparent Per Capita Alcohol Consumption: National, State, and Regional Trends, 1977–1994." *Surveillance Report #39.* Rockville, MD: NIAAA, 1996.

Zarkin, et al., "Alcohol Use and Wages: New Results from the National Household Survey on Drug Abuse." *Journal of Health Economics* 17:1 (1998): 53–68.

Chapter 3

The Future of the Three-Tiered System as a Control of Marketing Alcoholic Beverages

Evan T. Lawson

The majority of states have modeled their method of controlling the sale of alcoholic beverages on licensing private enterprise within a "three-tiered system," which divides the industry into the supplier, wholesaler, and retailer levels through statutes and regulations. The logic of the three-tiered system is that, by keeping the distribution levels separate and independent, the forces that promote intemperance in alcohol consumption will be tamed as the incentives to excesses are minimized. Justice Oliver Wendell Holmes, Jr., taught that the "life of the law has not been logic: it has been experience."[1] The American experience reveals that legal restrictions on alcohol must be compatible with prevailing social and economic conditions if the goal of promoting temperance is to be accomplished.[2] In looking to the future of alcohol control in the 21st century, we must first see where we have been.

The Puritans "looked upon the liquor traffic as an honorable and lucrative trade."[3] They punished the drunkard, not the one who supplied the drink. In Rhode Island in 1649, a law was enacted giving Roger Williams the exclusive right to sell alcoholic beverages to the Indians. "It is granted unto Mr. Roger Williams to have leave to sell a little wine or stronge water to some natives in theare sickness."[4] Five years later, an ordinance was passed that forbade providing alcoholic beverages to Indians, and permitted anyone finding an Indian in possession of alcohol to confiscate it.[5] So began liquor control in America.

From the Colonial period through the institution of national Prohibition with passage of the 18th Amendment, liquor control focused on either an outright ban on liquor sales or laws regulating the conduct of those trafficking in or using beverage alcohol. Although there was no attempt to force the liquor industry into "tiers," first the Colonies and then the States licensed and taxed producers and retail sellers in a variety of ways. There were laws to proscribe the proper times for the sale of alcohol ("It is ordered, that no house of entertainment shall suffer any person to tipple after nine of ye clock at night; except they can give a satisfactory reason to ye constable of magistrate," March 1656[6]). Other laws prohibited the amount of alcohol that can be sold to particular classes of people (e.g., Indians were limited to a quarter of a pint per day).[7]

One of the first Sunday sales prohibitions was enacted in 1673, not for reasons of religious conviction, but to keep people from drinking too much on a day that most people did not work. Because most people considered Sunday a holy day and therefore gave their employees and family this day off, they "soe spend it in debaistness or tipplinge and unlawful games and wantonness . . ."[8]

Rather than prohibiting drinking, the colonists sought to license the sale of alcohol. Indeed, drinking establishments were encouraged. For example, in 1654, Rhode Island towns were ordered to license "one or two howses for ye entertainment of strangers, and to encourage such as shall undertake to keepe such howes."[9]

Until the early 20th century, state liquor control waxed and waned between outright prohibition and licensing systems, with some states experimenting with local control, as the public grappled with the effects of beverage alcohol on public health and welfare.[10] Before Prohibition, the alcoholic beverage industry was divided essentially into suppliers and retailers. Except for parts of the beer industry, there were no wholesalers.[11] The suppliers were able to exercise tremendous influence over those retailers that they did not directly control through ownership by extending credit and other financial incentives. The resulting fierce competition was perceived as forcing drastic increases in consumption, which led to drunkenness and financial ruin, impoverishing the working man and his family. In an era of debtor's prisons, when women were unable meaningfully to enter the workforce, the family of a drunkard quickly became a public charge. The supplier/retailer combine used its financial strength to corrupt political power to protect itself from building public outrage. The combination of social cost with political corruption was the "tied-house evil" that Prohibition sought to sweep away.

Prohibition did not work; instead, it made the alcohol problem worse. Because it was illegal, liquor took on an aura of glamor. The speakeasy was the place to be. Increased profitability led to more aggressive marketing and murder became a method of competition. Those who liked to drink refused to be told they could not, so many otherwise law-abiding citizens became criminals. The illegal product was unregulated, untested, and thus frequently dangerous to drink because it became much more potent and adulterated. The sale of beverage alcohol was even more lucrative as an illegal enterprise, so organized crime was strengthened, if not created. Corruption of public officials increased. Government was deprived of tax revenue at the same time that it had to spend more to enforce and cope with the damaging effects of Prohibition.[12] Prohibition could not last.

When it became clear that the experiment with national prohibition had failed and the 18th Amendment would be repealed, it was obvious that the responsibility for controlling the sale of alcoholic beverages would fall to the states. John J. Rockefeller, Jr., a lifelong teetotaler concerned about the consequences of alcohol legalization, commissioned a study by Raymond B. Fosdick, a lawyer, and Albert L. Scott, an engineer, to develop a program of "carefully laid plans of control."[13] Fosdick and Scott concluded that the best method of control was through state management of the distribution and sale of alcoholic beverages. However, they recognized that many states would reject public monopoly of distribution in favor of licensing private enterprise, so they presented both monopoly and licensure as alternative methods.[14] Fosdick and Scott postulated that it was central to regulation by license that "[t]he 'tied house,' and every device calculated to place the retail establishment under obligation to a particular distiller or brewer, should be prevented by all available means."[15]

Fosdick and Scott's work was very influential in shaping the states' efforts to enact liquor control. A minority of states adopted variations of the monopoly model, whereas the states that chose regulation by license created detailed systems to avoid the "evil of the tied house." As of 2000, eighteen "control" states maintained some form of monopoly based on alcohol content and market segment: New Hampshire, Pennsylvania, and Utah control wholesale and retail sale of moderate and high alcohol content beverages (wine, fortified wine, and spirits); Idaho, Michigan, Montana, North Carolina, Ohio, Oregon, Vermont, and Washington control wholesale and retail sale of high alcohol beverages spirts (fortified wine and spirits); Mississippi and Wyoming control wholesale of moderate and high content beverages; and Alabama, Iowa, Maine, Virginia, and West Virginia control wholesale of high content beverages (Figure 3.1).[16]

The states that rejected monopoly selected licensing along the model of Fosdick and Scotts' "three-tiered system," interposing a wholesaler level between the supplier and retailer, as the best method of correcting past abuses, establishing an orderly system of distribution and control of alcoholic beverages and preventing the evil of the "tied house." The wholesaler was intended to be a local, almost exclusively family-owned business that would spend years and a great deal of capital developing its business marketing brand name alcoholic beverages in its community. With all its capital at risk, the wholesaler has a strong incentive to avoid regulatory sanctions. Wholesalers protect their interest by being good corporate citizens and becoming politically active. In addition, the states are able to collect taxes at the wholesaler

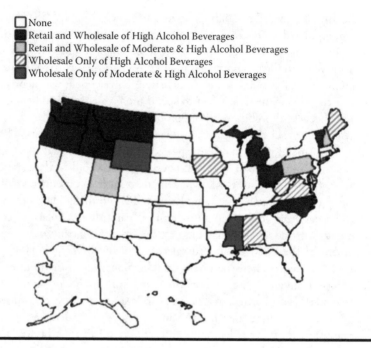

☐ None
■ Retail and Wholesale of High Alcohol Beverages
▢ Retail and Wholesale of Moderate & High Alcohol Beverages
▨ Wholesale Only of High Alcohol Beverages
■ Wholesale Only of Moderate & High Alcohol Beverages

Figure 3.1   Alcohol content and the states' control over market segment.

level, which provides the states with an efficient, reliable, and cost-effective revenue source that is easy to police. But the three-tiered system means more than just a division of distribution functions among supplier, wholesaler, and retailer. Other restrictions were thought necessary to restrain the natural capitalist drive toward increased profit and growth. The license states frequently adopted other regulatory measures to promote temperance by keeping the retail segment fragmented and weak, such as restrictions on "inducements," the number of off-premise consumption outlets that can be owned or controlled, and even price controls. Nonetheless, protecting each tier of the industry from domination by the other is vital to maintaining the three-tiered system.[17]

The 21st century presents a far different economic environment from that in which the states crafted their methods of alcohol control based on the Fosdick and Scott method. The combination of social, economic, and technologic changes typified by deregulation, economic consolidation, and mass communication are discussed in detail elsewhere in this work. For the purpose of this chapter, it is sufficient to note that 1) public attitudes toward consuming alcoholic beverages have been shaped by sophisticated advertising; 2) deregulation of business is the norm if not the goal of today's political system; 3) systems for ordering, transporting, and delivering all products are much more efficient; and 4) perhaps most significantly, there is an inexorable trend toward consolidation at every level of the industry that mocks the goal of fragmented, weak players that will be unable to wield political and marketing power.

A prime example of consolidation at the supplier level, now dominated by gigantic multinational corporations, occurred in 1998. Bacardi purchased the Dewars and Bombay brands from Diageo plc. The Federal Trade Commission had ordered Diageo to divest those brands because, as a result of its creation by consolidation, Diageo was so enormous that it would be a violation of federal antitrust laws to retain them.[18] Indeed, as shown in Figure 3.2, in 1999, five of the top 100 suppliers accounted for 41.8 percent of the sales volume, with $22.92 billion in sales of distilled spirits, and just ten of the top 100 spirits marketers account for more than 50 percent of total sales volume, with more than $32.25 billion in sales.[19]

In another example, the array of brands that had been controlled by the Joseph Seagram Companies was transferred to other suppliers, including Diageo and Pernod Ricard. The disappearance of Seagram altered the arrangement of the world's top five distilled spirits marketers giving the top five companies a 43 percent world market share (Figure 3.3).[20]

Most recently, Pernod Ricard has bought the wine and spirits business of Allied Domecq, exponentially concentrating the supplier tier.

Occasionally, the top management of suppliers will reveal an agenda that is contrary to the purpose of the three-tiered system. For example, in a 1999 interview, UDV's chief executive Jack Keenen made a statement calculated to keep wholesalers on edge.

Q: Are you satisfied with current arrangements at the U.S. wholesale tier, or might there be future change?

A: We haven't finished our value chain work. There's clearly opportunity for distributors and brand owners to do things more effectively and determine more clearly who does what. Chuck Phillips will be looking at key states and determining the right moves for UDV and our distributors. ...[21]

More recently, the chief executive of Kendall-Jackson Wine Estates was less subtle in announcing his company's agenda with respect to the "value chain."

Q: Speaking of the value chain, have you taken a look at the issues regarding distribution in this market?

A: Yes. My position is this: Distributors will continue to be very important to us, but they're not the only way that wine will reach the consumer. We need to understand that, and so do our distributors.[22]

Company	# of Brands	Sales Volume Cases × 10^6	Retail Value $ × 106	Share of Top 100	
				Sales Volume	Retail Value
UDV (Diageo)[23]	13	55.5	$8,785	10.2%	17.9%
The Seagram Co. Ltd.	8	20.3	4,130	3.7	8.4
Allied Domecq	8	22.2	3,775	4.1	7.7
VAO Sojuzplo-doimpor	3	105.6	3,545	19.4	7.2
Bacardi Ltd.	3	24.0	2,690	4.4	5.5
Total Top 5	**3**	**227.5**	**22,920**	**41.8**	**46.8**
Pernod Ricard	6	16.2	2,180	3.0	4.5
Suntory Ltd.	7	12.6	2,035	2.3	4.2
Brown-Forman	4	11.8	1,985	2.2	4.1
Moet-Hennessy (LVMH)	1	2.8	1,670	0.5	3.4
V&S Vin & Spirit AB[24]	2	7.8	1,495	1.4	3.1
Total Top 10	**55**	**278.7**	**32,285**	**51.2**	**65.9**
Jinro Ltd.	2	47.2	1,450	8.7	3.0
William Grant & Sons	2	4.6	1,190	0.9	2.4
Remy Cointreau SA	2	2.5	1,050	0.5	2.1
Polmos/ Agros Trading	2	8.8	865	1.6	1.8
Takara Shuzo Co. Ltd.	2	14.0	840	2.6	1.7
Total Top 15	**65**	**355.9**	**37,680**	**65.4**	**76.9**
Other companies	35	188.5	11,305	34.6	23.1
Total Top 100[25]	**100**	**544.3**	**$48,985**	**100.0%**	**100.0%**

Figure 3.2   100 Top distilled spirit brands worldwide at retail by marketer through 1999.

It is not surprising then that similar consolidation has been occurring at the wholesale level. In 1975, there were some twenty-five major alcoholic beverages wholesalers of wines and spirits in Massachusetts. In 2004, there were three, which operate regionally in New England and elsewhere. Nationally, the top twenty wine

Millions of Nine-Liter Case Depletions

	BEFORE			AFTER	
Rank	Company	Volume	Rank	Company[26]	Volume
1	UDV (Diageo)	98.8	1	UDV (Diageo)	112.8
2	Allied Domecq	43.6	2	Allied Domecq	43.6
3	Seagram Co.[27]	41.9	3	Seagram Co.	41.6
4	Bacardi Ltd.	34.2	4	Bacardi Ltd.	34.2
5	Pernod Ricard	27.8	5	Fortune Brands	23.2
	Total Top 5	**246.3**		**Total Top 5**	**255.4**
Top 5 Companies' World Market Share[28]		**41%**	**Top 5 Companies' World Market Share**		**43%**

Figure 3.3   World's top five distilled spirits marketers[29] (before and after the Seagram sale). *Source: Impact* **Newsletter, January 1, 2001, p. 15 (M. Shanken Communications, Inc. New York, NY).**

and spirits wholesalers controlled 67.9 percent of the entire U.S. market. The top wine and spirits wholesaler, doing business in more than twelve states, had a 17.2 percent market share.[30] Now that wholesaler has bought an interest in one of the three New England regional wholesalers, increasing its overall market share and geographic reach.

Off-premises retailers and chain retailers are challenging state restrictions on entering the market.[31] To the concern of wholesalers, Costco has brought suit in federal court in Washington to force the state to allow it to bypass the three-tiered system and deal directly with suppliers.[32]

As social, economic, and technologic changes have evolved to undermine the three-tiered system, changes in constitutional doctrine have undermined its legal foundation, which depends on giving the states virtual carte blanche to fashion liquor control.

The three-tiered system was intended to suppress the natural drive of business to increase profits by increasing consumption. But, as the industry has evolved after Repeal, the federal Constitution has been the instrument by which the most aggressive actors in the alcoholic beverages industry have overcome the tight regulation required to maintain the logic of the three-tiered system. State price controls that required suppliers to sell in state at the best price offered anywhere in the county were stricken as violative of the Commerce Clause.[33] State mechanisms for controlling wholesale prices through private price posting arrangements have also fallen.[34]

Governmental attempts to dampen demand by restricting advertising have fared no better. The First Amendment has been found to protect commercial speech concerning alcoholic beverages in spite of federal regulation.[35] And notwithstanding the 21st Amendment, the states' power to regulate advertising has similarly been curtailed.[36] Indeed, the states have not been able to implement an effective ban on billboard advertising.[37]

The conflict between the economic forces at work in the alcoholic beverage industry and the three-tiered system as envisioned by Fosdick and Scott will be resolved politically either through legislation or litigation. The leading edge of that resolution is the Supreme Court's decision of the direct shipping cases, which present the forces working against the traditional three-tiered system in microcosm. Direct shipping of alcoholic beverages from suppliers to consumers, and its cousin, direct dealing of suppliers with retailers, anathema to the three-tiered system, is the result of inexorable social, economic, and technologic forces. The consumer culture spawned by advertising and facilitated by mass retailing and Internet commerce is based on choice and price, neither of which is a friend of strict control under a rigid three-tiered system. Within the recent past, states, responding to economic forces and perceived popular will, or effective lobbying, have passed laws liberalizing parts of their alcohol regulatory schemes by bypassing the three-tiered system. In particular, states have allowed in-state wineries to sell or ship wine directly to consumers in their state, while prohibiting out-of-state wineries from doing the same. Out-of-state wineries protested these laws as discriminatory in violation of the Commerce Clause of the U.S. Constitution. The states responded that it was within their power under the 21st Amendment. As a result, federal courts across the country have had to resolve the tension between the "dormant" aspect of the Commerce Clause and the 21st Amendment, but the proponents of direct shipping make their case by presenting the tension as existing between modern, dynamic, innovative free enterprise and anachronistic concerns with the long-banished "evils of the tied house."

Section 2 of the 21st Amendment prohibits "[t]he transportation or importation into any State, Territory or possession of the United States for delivery or use therein of intoxicating liquors, in violation of the laws thereof..." Although Section 2 directly authorizes state control over imports, "dormant" Commerce Clause jurisprudence concludes that the grant of power to Congress to regulate interstate commerce implies a limitation on state authority over the same subject. Initially, the Supreme Court afforded the states nearly limitless power to regulate alcohol under the new amendment.[38] However, as early as the 1960s, the Supreme Court signaled a break with this line of reasoning. In *Hostetter v. Idlewild Bon Voyage Liquor Corporation*,[39] a case involving the prohibition of liquor sales to departing international airline travelers, the Court observed:

> To draw a conclusion from this line of decisions [*Ziffrin, Young's Market*, etc.] that the Twenty-first Amendment has somehow operated to "repeal" the Commerce Clause whenever regulation of intoxicating liquors is concerned would, however, be an absurd oversimplification. If the Commerce Clause has been pro tanto "repealed," then Congress

would be left with no regulatory power of interstate or foreign commerce in intoxicating liquor. Such a conclusion would be patently bizarre and is demonstrably incorrect. ...Both the Twenty-first Amendment and the Commerce Clause are parts of the same Constitution. Like other provisions of the Constitution, each must be considered in the light of the other, and in the context of the issues and interests at stake in any concrete case.[40]

In *Capital Cities Cable v. Crisp*,[41] although not a liquor importation or Commerce Clause case, the Supreme Court found that a state ban on alcohol advertising conflicted with regulations of the Federal Communications Commission. The Supreme Court applied a balancing test to determine "whether the interests implicated by a state regulation are so closely related to the powers reserved by the [Twenty-first] Amendment that the regulation may prevail, notwithstanding that its requirements directly conflict with express federal policies."[42] The Supreme Court concluded that the federal interest must prevail because the state's banning of alcohol advertising did not directly relate to the core concerns of the 21st Amendment (i.e., to exercise "control over whether to permit importation or sale of liquor and how to structure the liquor distribution system").[43]

Shortly after *Capital Cities* was decided, the Supreme Court issued *Bacchus Imports v. Dias*,[44] in which out-of-state wholesalers challenged a Hawaii excise tax exemption for certain locally produced alcoholic beverages. The state argued that the statute advanced legitimate state interests, that it imposed no patent discrimination against interstate trade, and that the effect on interstate commerce was minimal.[45] The Supreme Court rejected these defenses, finding that "the legislation constitutes 'economic protectionism' in every sense of the phrase,"[46] and noting that "one thing is certain: The central purpose of the [Twenty-first Amendment] was not to empower States to favor local liquor industries by erecting barriers to competition."[47] Instead, the Supreme Court considered "whether the principles underlying the [Twenty-first] Amendment are sufficiently implicated by the [tax exemption] to outweigh the Commerce Clause principles that would otherwise be offended."[48] In *Bacchus*, the state did not contest that the law's purpose was "to promote a local industry," so the Supreme Court did not have to engage in the normal Commerce Clause analysis of whether the law was sufficiently closely related to the promotion of lawful interests to vitiate its discriminatory effect. Instead, the Supreme Court held that the law discriminated against interstate commerce in violation of the Commerce Clause and was therefore unconstitutional.

Thus, although the Supreme Court has observed that "the State has 'virtually complete control' over the importation and sale of liquor and the structure of the liquor distribution system," and that "the States have the power to control shipments of liquor during their passage through their territory and to take appropriate steps to prevent the unlawful diversion of liquor into their regulated intrastate markets,"[49] it also clarified that it would be an "absurd oversimplification" to conclude that the 21st Amendment shields all state regulations from the reach of the Commerce Clause. "It is well settled that the Twenty-first Amendment did not entirely remove state regulation of alcohol from the reach of the Commerce Clause....Rather the Twenty-first Amendment and the Commerce Clause 'each must be considered in light of the other and in the context of the issues and interests at stake in any concrete case.'"[50]

An alternate method of analysis holds that all components of the "dormant" Commerce Clause doctrine govern unless a "core concern" of the 21st Amendment is implicated. Case law recognizes several core concerns of the 21st Amendment, including temperance, raising revenue and "ensuring orderly market conditions."[51] When a core concern is implicated, the 21st Amendment empowers the state to regulate in a way that affects interstate commerce as long as it demonstrates that it genuinely needs the regulation to effectuate its proffered core concern. Accordingly, the federal courts had to decide whether the 21st Amendment authorizes the discriminatory impact on interstate commerce caused by statutes prohibiting out-of-state direct shipping by applying either the "core concern" analysis or considering the 21st Amendment "in light" of the Commerce Clause. The results were mixed, with a conflict in the federal circuits that was resolved by the Supreme Court. The Supreme Court's resolution of the direct shipping cases presents a challenge to the validity of the three-tiered system.

The Court found the circuits in conflict in cases from Michigan and New York. In Michigan and New York, as in all three-tiered system states, wineries are required to distribute their wine through a local wholesaler. Both states, as many others, have made exceptions for in-state wineries. In Michigan, in-state wineries may obtain a "winemaker" license, allowing them to directly ship to in-state consumers. Out-of-state wineries cannot obtain a "winemaker" license, but rather must obtain a license that only allows them to sell to wholesalers in Michigan. In New York, in-state wineries may obtain a license allowing them to ship directly to consumers so long as the winery's grape volume consists of at least 75 percent New York–grown grapes. Out-of-state wineries may ship directly to consumers so long as they establish "a branch factory, office or storeroom within the State of New York" (Granholm, p. 6).

In *Heald v. Engler*,[52] Michigan wine connoisseurs, wine journalists, and one small California winery that ships its wines to customers in other states claimed that Michigan's alcoholic beverages control law discriminated between in-state and out-of-state wineries in violation of the Commerce Clause because it prevents out-of-state wineries from shipping wine directly to Michigan consumers, which in-state wineries are allowed to do. After providing a brief history of the Supreme Court decisions on the tension between the 21st Amendment and the dormant Commerce Clause, the 6th Circuit held that the Michigan regulations were not a "benign product of the state's three-tier system" and the facial discrimination of the regulations eliminated the immunity afforded by the 21st Amendment. Thus the proper inquiry was whether the regulations advance a legitimate local purpose that cannot be adequately served by reasonable nondiscriminatory alternatives. The 6th Circuit saw no evidence of this on the record. The case was remanded for entry of summary judgment against the State.

In *Swedenburg v. Kelly*,[53] two out-of-state wineries and several New York consumers filed an action against the chairman of the New York State Liquor Authority requesting that the Court declare a New York statute that prohibits direct shipping[54] unconstitutional, void, and of no effect. Differing from other state statutes, this statutory scheme also forbade certain advertising of lawful products, challenged by all plaintiffs as restriction of the free flow of communications guaranteed by the 1st Amendment.[55] Although the state attempted to argue that in-state wineries are receiving no preferential treatment, the federal district court disagreed holding that in-state wineries can bypass two tiers in the three-tier system under the statute, constituting a "cut and dry example of direct discrimination against interstate commerce."[56] Further, the court held that the statute provides an "impermissible economic benefit and (protection) to only in-state interests."[57] The state contended that out-of-state wineries could very easily obtain a license by maintaining an office or presence in New York. The district court found this unreasonable.

When faced with the secondary analysis under the 21st Amendment, the district court was not entirely convinced that the collection of taxes is, in and of itself, a core concern of the 21st Amendment. Instead, the court weighed heavily on the state to show that the exceptions for in-state wineries were not enacted to provide an economic benefit for local farmers, coined "economic protectionism."[58] The court found that the state failed to meet this burden because it did not establish that its legitimate goals cannot be accomplished without discriminating. The district court also mentioned that recent federal legislation has authorized direct shipment of wine for personal use.[59] Relying on the method of analysis employed by a number of other federal courts in similar challenges, the district court first found that the New York regime directly discriminated against interstate commerce.[60] The court then held that the 21st Amendment did not save the ban on direct shipment by out-of-state wineries.

On appeal, the 2nd Circuit[61] disagreed with the District Court, affirming in part and remanding in part. Specifically, the 2nd Circuit agreed that the portion of the statute restricting advertising was overbroad and violated the 1st Amendment because it "encompasse[d] a broader prohibition than the solicitation of orders by unlicensed, out-of-state wineries for direct shipment of wine to New York consumers."[62] However, the appellate court upheld the statute as constitutionally authorized by 21st Amendment. The 2nd Circuit found that the "two-step approach used by the [other] circuit courts in invalidating anti-direct-shipping laws [was] flawed because it has the effect of unnecessarily limiting the authority delegated to the states through the clear and ambiguous language of section 2."[63] This was the "core concern" approach. Instead, the 2nd Circuit employed the alternate mode of analysis that considers "both the Twenty-first Amendment and the Commerce Clause…in the light of the other, and in the context of the issues and the interests at state in any concrete case."[64] This analysis led the 2nd Circuit to conclude that the "constitutional grant of authority [in Section 2] should not…be subordinated to the dormant Commerce Clause inquiry when the two provisions conflict, as they do here."[65] The 2nd Circuit reversed the District Court holding that the New York statute was a proper exercise of the power granted to the states in Section 2 because "the Supreme Court has consistently recognized only that, under Section 2, a state may regulate the importation of alcohol for distribution and use within its borders, but may not intrude upon federal authority to regulate *beyond* the state's borders or to preserve fundamental rights."[66]

On May 24, 2004, to resolve the conflict in the circuits, the Supreme Court granted certiorari limited to the question: "Does a State's regulatory scheme that permits in-state wineries directly to ship alcohol to consumers but restricts the ability of out-of-state wineries to do so violate the dormant Commerce Clause in light of Sec. 2 of the 21st Amendment?" On May 16, 2005, by the slimmest of margins, the Supreme Court declared a victory for wineries across the nation in *Granholm v. Heald*,[67] ruling that State laws discriminating against out-of-state wineries for directly shipping to consumers are unconstitutional. In a major break with traditional doctrine, the Court held that the 21st Amendment did not immunize the states from enforcement of the dormant Commerce Clause against laws regulating the importation and possession of alcoholic beverages that discriminated against out-of-state interests. Consequently, as long as a state allows in-state wineries to ship wine directly to consumers, wineries in other states must be given equal treatment.

In rejecting the states' argument that the 21st Amendment allowed them unfettered regulation of alcoholic beverages, including the right to discriminate against interstate commerce, the majority imposed the laissez-faire economics espoused by Adam Smith that it found embodied in the Commerce Clause on the regulation of alcoholic beverages. The Court rejected the deeply ingrained conventional wisdom that beverage alcohol has a special potential for evil, that is, the "tied-house evil," that requires giving the states the widest possible latitude in control. We call that conventional wisdom the "demon rum" model.

Before *Granholm v. Heald,* it was commonly held that the 21st Amendment constitutionalized the "demon rum" model. In rejecting the "demon rum" model as a basis for determining the scope of the 21st Amendment, the Court has made a "paradigm shift" in which, in the words of Thomas Kuhn, "one conceptual world view is replaced by another."[68]

An intoxicating blend of Adam Smith's 18th century economic theory and today's e-commerce influenced the majority to conclude that impediments to the direct shipment of wine disrupts the flow of commerce between the states and unnecessarily burdens consumers. That New York and Michigan discriminated between in-state and out-of-state wineries prevented consumers from purchasing wine produced by small wineries, deemed by Justice Anthony Kennedy writing for the Court to be an "otherwise emerging and significant business."[69] The Court portrays small wineries as an industry with a desirable product, which is helpless and immobilized by the three-tiered system, pointing to the power of wholesalers to control consumer access to wine. The Court states that small wineries cannot find wholesalers to distribute their products and, further, that "the wholesaler's markup would render shipment through the three-tier system economically infeasible."[70]

The Court begins its constitutional analysis by quoting and citing to an array of cases that hold state laws in violation of the Commerce Clause if they favor in-state economic interests while burdening interstate commerce. Adam Smith's economics prevailed as the Court held that these discriminatory laws "deprive citizens of their right to have access to the markets of other States on equal terms."[71] However, the Court does not mention that none of these cases concern alcoholic beverages. The Court then addresses its history regarding the sale of alcoholic beverages. Before Prohibition, there was another direct shipping controversy resulting in the Court holding "that the Commerce Clause prevented States from discriminating against imported liquor," citing *Scott v. Donald*, 165 U.S. 58 (1897); *Walling v. Michigan*, 116 U.S. 446 (1886); and *Tiernan v. Rinker*, 102 U.S. 123 (1880).[72] In *Scott*, the Court stated:

> The evils attending the vice of intemperance in the use of spirituous liquors are so great that a natural reluctance is felt in appearing to interfere, even on constitutional grounds, with any law whose avowed purpose is to restrict or prevent the mischief. So long, however, as state legislation continues to recognize wines, beer, and spiritous liquors as articles of lawful consumption and commerce, so long must continue the duty of the federal courts to afford to such use and commerce the same measure of protection, under the constitution and laws of the United States, as is given to other articles.

The *Scott* Court declared that the law at issue "was not intended to confer upon any state the power to discriminate injuriously against the products of other states." Therefore, in the prelude to Prohibition, as the nation's view of beverage alcohol became increasingly disapproving, the Court still did not treat alcoholic beverages specially, and discrimination against interstate commerce in beverage alcohol was not tolerated.

Before Prohibition, the individual states' goal was to prevent all alcoholic beverages from being sold within their borders, not to favor local interests. *Leisy v. Hardin*, 135 U.S. 100 (1890), by holding that the Commerce Clause protected alcoholic beverages that traveled in interstate commerce so long as they remained in the original package, thwarted the states and caused Congress to pass the Wilson Act (27 U.S.C. § 121), which mandated that, on arrival in a state, alcoholic beverages were subject to the same restrictions as if they had been produced there, and could not be held exempt under the Commerce Clause merely because they arrived in their original packaging. According to the Wilson Act, after alcoholic beverages came within state borders, they were considered to have originated in the state, regardless of where they were produced. The Wilson Act allowed states to regulate alcoholic beverages passing through interstate commerce to the same extent as those produced in the state. Although the Wilson Act was a response to direct shipping, the factual setting is the opposite of today's direct shipping issue. Before Prohibition, states wanted to keep all alcoholic beverages out of the hands of their citizens, but could only regulate in-state alcoholic beverages, allowing alcoholic beverages from other states to enter unregulated. The Wilson Act allowed both in-state and out-of-state producers to be regulated. Today, the states want alcoholic beverages to be sold within their borders, but have tried to afford in-state producers a less rigid and burdensome distribution system than the three-tiered system.

The majority in *Granholm v. Heald* interprets the Wilson Act to forbid discrimination, but ignores that its purpose was to give the states the authority over alcoholic beverages that they requested. Instead, the Court reasons that the Wilson Act banned discrimination using that "history" to find that the states may not discriminate against wine producers in other states.

The Wilson Act did not stop direct shipping. An industry arose that directly shipped alcoholic beverages into dry States for "personal" use. Ultimately, in *Rhodes v. Iowa*, 170 U.S. 412 (1898), the Supreme Court held that the Wilson Act applied only to liquor being sold for commercial use. Thus the states still had to contend with regulating out-of-state producers who sold alcohol directly to consumers for personal consumption. Under even more primitive conditions of communication and transportation, a bourgeoning direct shipping industry was created. In response, Congress passed the Webb-Kenyon Act (27 U.S.C. § 122) in 1913 to grant the states the power to regulate all imported alcohol, regardless of whether it was for personal or commercial use. The states' intention was to keep alcohol out on their own terms.

New York and Michigan argued to the Supreme Court that the Webb-Kenyon Act restored the states' power to regulate alcoholic beverages, including discriminatory regulations. The distinction between the Wilson Act and the Webb-Kenyon Act divided the Court in *Granholm v. Heald*. The majority holds that the Wilson Act has not been repealed and the two Acts must be construed to exist simultaneously and harmonized because the Webb-Kenyon Act did not expressly reject the anti-discriminatory message of the Wilson Act. Therefore, "discrimination against out-of-state goods is disfavored."[73]

The Court moves into its discussion of the 21st Amendment by asserting that the 21st Amendment followed the Wilson Act and the Webb-Kenyon Act and did not authorize discrimination. However, the 21st Amendment does not prohibit discrimination. Section 2 appears straightforward: "The transportation or importation into any State, Territory, or possession of the United States for delivery or use therein of intoxicating liquors, in violation of the laws thereof, is hereby prohibited."

Although it is correct that the Wilson Act, the Webb-Kenyon Act, and the 21st Amendment are all in effect, how do we rationalize their purposes when a strict reading of the 21st Amendment provides the states with unfettered control over intoxicating liquors? The Court's decision in *State Bd. of Equalization of Cal. v. Young's Market Co.*, 299, U.S. 59 (1936) appears to support such a strict reading of the 21st Amendment. However, the Court disposes of this argument by stating that "[i]t is unclear whether the broad language in *Young's Market* was necessary to the result because the Court also stated that 'the case [did] not present a question of discrimination prohibited by the commerce clause.'"[74]

In its analysis, the Court reminds us of its cases where "state laws that violate other provisions of the Constitution are not saved by the Twenty-first Amendment," citing *44 Liquormart, Inc. v. Rhode Island*, 517 U.S. 484 (1996) (the 1st Amendment); *Larkin v. Grendel's Den, Inc.*, 459 U.S. 116 (1982) (the Establishment Clause); *Craig v. Boren*, 429 U.S. 190 (1976) (the Equal Protection Clause); *Wisconsin v. Constantineau*, 400 U.S. 433 (1971) (the Due Process Clause); and, *Department of Revenue v. James B. Beam Distilling Co.*, 377 U.S. 341 (1964) (the Import-Export Clause).[75] However, because none of these cases dealt with state laws that directly concerned the importation or transportation of alcohol, which is the obvious target of the 21st Amendment, the Court relies on *Bacchus Imports, Ltd. v. Dias*, 468 U.S. 263 (1984), in which it held that a Hawaiian import tax on all liquor, where one type of locally produced pineapple wine was exempted, violated the commerce clause because it favored a local industry, and was not saved by the 21st Amendment. In *Bacchus*, the Court centered on taxation and in response to Hawaii's admission that the tax's purpose was to promote a local industry stated: state laws that constitute mere economic protectionism are therefore not entitled to the same deference as laws enacted to combat the perceived evils of an unrestricted traffic in liquor (*Id.* at 276).

The *Bacchus* Court specifically distinguished between laws that generally concern alcohol and laws that specifically concern the importation and transportation of alcohol, which are apparently immunized from scrutiny by the 21st Amendment. Regardless, the *Granholm v. Heald* majority finds *Bacchus* fatal to the New York and Michigan statutes. Indeed, the states had conceded the point, asking the Court to overrule or limit *Bacchus*.[76] This concession may have been unnecessary and unwise. If the states' argument had focused on whether the law concerned the importation and transportation of alcohol, *Bacchus* might have been distinguished in the mind of at least one member of the majority.

Last, in the required final inquiry, the Court rejects the states' arguments, citing sales to minors and tax collection as major concerns, as well as the inability to police direct shipments by out-of-state wineries, that a "legitimate local interest" is served by New York's and Michigan's "discriminatory" laws. The Court found those arguments not compelling because it saw the same problems arising from in-state direct sales. Neither the states nor their supporters were able to prove that the problems they relied on were real and that the direct shipping ban served any legitimate purpose. In conclusion, the Court holds that the states must allow the direct shipment of wine on "evenhanded terms" and that the New York and Michigan regulations unconstitutionally "disadvantage[d] out-of-state wine producers."[77] To the majority, the direct shipping cases are strictly about economic protectionism, which cannot be tolerated in light of the values represented by the Commerce Clause. Adam Smith would be proud.

The Court did not split along its usual ideologic lines. The four dissenters were Justice Stevens, usually considered among the most liberal; Justice O'Connor, a conservative moderate; and two of the most conservative Justices, Chief Justice Rehnquist and Justice Clarence Thomas. However, the premiere conservative Justice, Antonin Scalia, joined the majority. If he had agreed with his usual ideologic brethren, direct shipping and the interesting implications of *Granholm v. Heald*, would be a dead issue. Why didn't Justice Scalia vote to affirm plenary state power over alcoholic beverages? It must be that he saw more harm to the nation in abridging Adam Smith's economics as embodied in the Commerce Clause than from unsupported reliance on the evils of demon rum. Perhaps he agreed with the conclusion of the New York State Moreland Commission on the Alcoholic Beverage Control Law in 1964 that excessive control "serve[s] merely to insure the profit margins of the various segments of the industry."[78]

Before examining the reasoning of the minority, consider how Americans went from embracing alcoholic beverages to despising demon rum. Professor David J. Hanson has followed "The American Whiskey Trail" to discover some revealing examples of the importance of beverage alcohol in American history.

- The Puritans loaded more beer than water onto the Mayflower before they cast off for the New World.
- Although there wasn't any cranberry sauce, mashed potatoes, sweet potatoes, or pumpkin pie to eat at the first Thanksgiving, there may have been beer, brandy, gin, and wine to drink.
- A brewery was one of Harvard College's first construction projects so that a steady supply of beer could be served in the student dining halls.
- The early colonists made alcohol beverages from, among other things, carrots, tomatoes, onions, beets, celery, squash, corn silk, dandelions, and goldenrod.
- The production of rum became early colonial New England's largest and most prosperous industry.
- Tavern owners enjoyed higher social status than did the clergy during part of the Colonial period.
- The laws of most American colonies required towns to license suitable persons to sell wine and spirits and failure to do so could result in a fine.
- Colonial taverns were often required to be located near the church or meetinghouse.

- Religious services and court sessions were often held in the major tavern of Colonial American towns.
- A traveler through the Delaware Valley in 1753 compiled a list of the drinks he encountered; all but three of the 48 contained alcohol.
- The first Kentucky whiskey was made in 1789 by a Baptist minister.
- Thomas Jefferson wrote the first draft of the Declaration of Independence in a tavern in Philadelphia.
- George Washington, Benjamin Franklin, and Thomas Jefferson all enjoyed brewing or distilling their own alcohol beverages. George Washington was one of the country's first large commercial distillers.
- The Colonial Army supplied its troops with a daily ration of four ounces of either rum or whiskey.
- The heavy taxation of whiskey led to the first test of federal power, the Whiskey Rebellion (1794).
- In the 1830s, the average American age 15 or older annually consumed more than seven gallons of absolute alcohol (resulting from an average of 9.5 gallons of spirits, a half gallon of wine, and 27 gallons of beer), a quantity about three times the current rate.
- Abraham Lincoln held a liquor license and operated several taverns.[79]

The groundswell of public condemnation that led to Prohibition came from the effect of alcohol abuse on a society that had no organized social welfare system and was undergoing a major transformation from rural to urban and agrarian to industrial. Although Carrie Nation attacked the saloons with her Bible and her axe, the supplier/retailer combine used its financial strength to corrupt political power to hold off the building public outrage. The "tied-house evil" was perceived as a real and immediate threat to society.

In his five-page dissent, Justice Stevens reminds the nation of the time when the tied-house evil was seen as a serious concern. Based on his "understanding (and recollection) of the historical context,"[80] Justice Stevens criticizes "younger generations" (the majority Justices?) for regarding "alcohol as an ordinary article of commerce,"[81] and forgetting "the moral condemnation of the use of alcohol.[82] Plainly, Justices Stevens and O'Connor accept the traditional view that because it is susceptible to abuse, the states must be given extraordinary scope to regulate beverage alcohol.

Although Justice Thomas, joined by the Chief Justice, bases his dissent on more intellectual and historical analyses, it is apparent that the underpinning of his opinion is acceptance of the "demon rum" model. Justice Thomas aggressively captures the mood of the minority that "[t]he Court today seizes back" from the states the power of the 21st Amendment, implying that prior to this decision the states had absolute control over alcoholic beverage importation.[83] Beginning with the Webb-Kenyon Act, Justice Thomas finds that the regulation of liquor importation has been consistently "exempt from judicial scrutiny under the negative Commerce Clause, as this Court has long held."[84] Therefore, he argues that the New York and

Michigan statutes are within the terms of the Webb-Kenyon Act. Interestingly, he relies on the pre-Prohibition Webb-Kenyon Act, rather than the 21st Amendment. There is no explanation for this reliance, other than a statement that the Webb-Kenyon Act was reenacted in 1935 "without alteration."[85]

Also without explanation, Justice Thomas sweeps aside the issue of discrimination against interstate commerce, likening the state law upheld in *McCormick & Co. v. Brown*, 286 U.S. 131 (1932), to the New York and Michigan laws, albeit acknowledging that "*McCormick* did not discriminate against out-of-state products" and finding this inconsequential as "*McCormick* applies equally to state laws that so discriminate."[86] His failure to address the significance of discrimination against interstate commerce means that he does not directly challenge the force of the Court's opinion on economic protectionism. Instead, he argues that the Webb-Kenyon Act does not mention discrimination and, therefore, was intended to allow states to discriminate. Further, he supports the idea that the Webb-Kenyon Act allows discrimination by arguing that *Clark Distilling Co. v. Western Maryland R. Co.*, 242 U.S. 311 (1917), authorized the states to discriminate. In *Clark Distilling*, the Court corrected the "misconception of the text of the Webb-Kenyon Act" by clarifying that the Act "did not simply forbid the introduction of liquor into a State for a prohibited use, but took the protection of interstate commerce away from all receipt and possession of liquor prohibited by state law" *Id.* at 325. Therefore, the Webb-Kenyon Act "overturned" the Court's nondiscrimination principle.[87] Unlike the cases referenced by the majority, *Clark Distilling* dealt with the importation and transportation of alcohol and confirmed the states' right to control the movement and receipt of alcohol in interstate commerce. This competent support for the New York and Michigan laws did not move the majority.

Attempting to resolve the tension between the Wilson Act and the Webb-Kenyon Act on the issue of discrimination and prove that the Webb-Kenyon Act implied repeal of the Wilson Act, Justice Thomas points out notations in the Senate Report for the Webb-Kenyon Act stating:

> The effect of [allowing direct shipment of alcohol for personal use was] to throw down all the barriers erected by the State law, in which she is protected by the Wilson bill, and allow the untrammeled importation of liquor into the State upon the simple claim that it is for private use. S. Rep. No. 151, 55th Cong., 1st Sess., 5 (1897) [internal quotation marks omitted].[88]

Justice Thomas asserts that the Webb-Kenyon Act would have "amended the Wilson Act to grant States 'absolute control of...liquors or liquids within their borders, by whomsoever produced and for whatever use imported.'"[89] However, he does not specifically rebut the majority's argument that because the Webb-Kenyon Act did not expressly repeal the Wilson Act, they must be interpreted to exist in harmony.

In his dissent, Justice Thomas intuitively identifies a possible consequence of the Court's opinion because the Webb-Kenyon Act covers "any person interested therein." He argues that "[a] wine manufacturer shipping wine directly to a consumer is an interested party, just as an out-of-state liquor wholesaler is."[90] Thus Justice Thomas warns that, despite the majority's words of approval, the future of the three-tier system is in jeopardy because of the decision. How are wholesalers any different than manufacturers in directly shipping to a consumer? This opinion may create an opening for out-of-state manufacturers and wholesalers to ship directly to retailers and consumers.

Finally, Justice Thomas addresses the 21st Amendment, beginning boldly by stating that "[t]here is no need to interpret the Twenty-first Amendment because the Webb-Kenyon Act resolves these cases."[91] Despite this opening, he asserts that the 21st Amendment "mirrors the basic terminology of the Webb-Kenyon Act," arguing that "its language is broader, authorizing States to regulate all 'transportation or importation' that runs afoul of State law." Reverting to his previous contention, Justice Thomas attributes this broader language to "naturally encompass discriminatory state laws." He aptly recognizes that the New York and Michigan laws at issue are specifically in the scope of Section 2 because they concern "transportation and importation." Justice Thomas highlights that the Court in *Young's Market* has previously resisted narrowing the broad language of the 21st Amendment because "the Amendment is clear." He praises *Young's Market* as having "properly reasoned that the text of our Constitution is the best guide to its meaning. ...[and] requires sustaining the state laws that the Court invalidates."[92]

Justice Thomas emphasizes that an effective three-tiered system requires the states to be free from the dormant Commerce Clause and free to discriminate against interstate commerce, allowing them to monopolize and license alcohol with immunity. "The requirement that liquor pass through a licensed in-state wholesaler is a core component of the three-tier system."[93] Thus, allowing the direct shipment of wine begins the destruction of the three-tier system because the wineries bypass the wholesale tier.

In addressing the final inquiry of his opinion, Justice Thomas maintains his strong stand on the importance of the three-tiered system, maintaining that "the direct shipment of liquor was of 'clear concern' to the framers of the Webb-Kenyon Act and the Twenty-first Amendment."[94] This is a dramatic contrast to the majority's insistence that neither taxation nor sale to minors were worthy as "core concerns." As New York and Michigan argued, Thomas finds that *Bacchus* is based on unpersuasive reasoning, implying that it should be overturned because, without *Bacchus*, the Court has no authority for finding the New York and Michigan laws invalid. In a powerful conclusion, Justice Thomas observes that "the Court. ... believes that its decision serves this Nation well," but he finds that the Court has done the "Nation no service by ignoring the textual commands of the Constitution and Acts of Congress."[95]

The Supreme Court may be narrowly divided between Adam Smith's economics and fear of demon rum, but where does the nation stand? Are alcoholic beverages, or at least wines, seen as just another part of daily life, "an ordinary article of commerce," by a majority of Americans? The direct shipping cases of the 19th century were prompted by an irresistible popular demand to ban beverage alcohol. The laws that gave rise to the current direct shipping cases were passed in various states because of public acceptance of beverage alcohol, particularly wine. It was this "modern" attitude toward wine that motivated the states to allow in-state wineries to bypass their three-tiered systems. Therefore, it is not clear that the majority of the Court is leading, rather than following, public opinion.

Powerful economic forces have already reshaped the alcoholic beverages industry, thereby challenging the rationale for the three-tiered system. The 21st century presents a far different economic environment from that in which the states crafted their methods of alcohol control in 1933. The combination of social, economic, and technologic changes typified by deregulation, economic consolidation, and mass communication coupled with an inexorable trend toward consolidation at every level of the industry mocks the three-tiered system's goal of fragmented, weak players unable to wield political and marketing power. The direct shipping cases came about because the three-tiered system conceived by Fosdick and Scott and implemented by the state legislatures in 1934 does not fit well with contemporary notions of a modern, dynamic, innovative free enterprise system. Indeed, the three-tiered system may already have been rendered ineffective for its intended purpose. The suppliers today are mostly huge multinational corporations whose must-have brands are essential for wholesalers and retailers. The wholesale tier is tending toward large national or regional firms. Big chain retailers are penetrating the retail tier as quickly as they can. The concept of promoting temperance by limiting local sale of alcoholic beverages to local businesses that are sensitive to the needs of their community and impervious to pressure to increase sales because of the separation of the tiers, if it was ever viable, no longer applies. There is an inherent contradiction in a system that tries to distribute alcoholic beverages through a capitalist system with the objective of limiting growth. Even the control state model for promoting temperance has succumbed to the states' need to increase revenue by increasing sales of alcoholic beverages with more aggressive marketing tactics in state liquor stores. Indeed, faced with a need for more revenue, Maine recently privatized its wholesale function by auctioning it to raise money.[96]

The majority view in *Granholm v. Heald* seems more in tune with the current popular attitude toward beverage alcohol. There is more than a little irony in the alcoholic beverages industry raising the "demon rum" model of seventy years ago to preserve its competitive position within the three-tiered system today. The wineries and big retailers will not go down quietly, and the public is becoming more and more accustomed to today's e-commerce, wide choices, and competitive pricing.

Some states will experiment with a more accommodating approach. Direct shipping will not be stopped; instead, it will be licensed, regulated, and taxed. This path will legitimize direct shipping, and in so doing will raise the question of why sound regulation needs a three-tiered system. Licensing some direct shipping will likely pave the way for more direct shipping, substantially weakening wholesalers by eroding profit margins. Every exception to the three-tiered system is a potential discrimination case. The three-tiered system will be irretrievably unbalanced and thus more vulnerable.

As Adam Smith would happily tell you, it is inevitable in our capitalistic system that businesses will push toward any source of profit. Somewhere a wholesaler will try to sell to retailers or consumers in an adjoining state, and claim local licensing discriminates against interstate commerce. Somewhere else a supplier will try to sell to retailers in an adjoining state because a local winery can, arguing that local licensing unconstitutionally discriminates against interstate commerce. It may be that these capitalistic pushes will go so far that the *Granholm v. Heald* majority will not hold and teeth will be restored to the 21st Amendment. It will be crucial for supporters of the three-tiered system to provide proof that it is an effective means to the goal of temperance, notwithstanding the trend in public opinion and Justice Scalia's rejection of the "demon rum" model. For now, the Supreme Court has eliminated the comfortable space within which alcoholic beverages regulation was believed to exist under the 21st Amendment. Whether leading or following, the majority has set a tone against the "demon rum" model. Beverage alcohol is moving closer to being just "an ordinary article of commerce."

The three-tiered system as a form of distribution will not vanish. Suppliers will continue to need wholesalers to service thousands of small retailers, although the suppliers would like to deal directly with the mega-retailers. The giant wholesalers will continue to be powerful in the industry. Small retailers will bear the burden of consolidation, as they have in most industries. The very large retailers will not be subservient to either large wholesalers or suppliers, but neither will they be content with low sales growth. Marketing restrictions and other traditional efforts to dampen consumption will be constrained by the First Amendment, the states' need to increase revenue and, ultimately, consumer demand. Even if we see the shadow of the evil of the tied house in current market trends, it is likely that we have come to the end of believing in the three-tiered system as a panacea for promoting temperance. In order to have effective alcohol control in the 21st century, we must reevaluate what is meant by the goal of temperance and fashion a regulatory scheme that is directly tailored to accomplishing it while withstanding constitutional scrutiny.

References

1. Holmes, Jr., O.W. *The Common Law* 1. Boston: Little, Brown, and Company, 1881.
2. Fosdick and Scott. *Toward Liquor Control* 5-6. Harper & Brothers, 1933.

3. Howie, Wendell D. "Three Hundred Years of the Liquor Problem in Massachusetts." *Massachusetts Law Quarterly* 18 (1933) 79–248.

4. Stiness, John H. "A Sketch of Rhode Island Legislation Against Strong Drink." Sidney S. Rider (1882), 6, citing, R.I. Col. Rec., I., p. 219.

5. Id.

6. Id., citing, R.I. Col. Rec., I., p. 330.

7. Id., citing, R.I. Col. Rec., I., p. 338.

8. Id., citing, R.I. Col. Rec., II., pp. 500–4.

9. Stiness, John H. supra, citing, R.I. Col. Rec., I., p. 280.

10. Fosdick and Scott, supra at 1–5.

11. For a general overview, see Denning, Brannon P. "A Brief History of the Creation of the Three-Tier System," located online at http://www.nbwa.org/public/gov_industry _issues/3_tier_sys/index.aspx.

12. Thornton, Mark. "Alcohol Prohibition Was A Failure." *Cato Policy Analysis* No. 157 (July 17, 1997).

13. Fosdick and Scott, supra, viii.

14. Id. at 18.

15. Id. at 43.

16. Alcohol Policies in the United States: Highlights from the 50 States. Alcohol Epidemiology Program, University of Minnesota, 10–11 (2000). In 2004, Maine privatized wholesaling of high-content beverages to raise revenue by selling the wholesale distribution rights to the highest bidder. See 28-A M.R.S. §88.

17. See James J. Sullivan, Inc. v. Cann's Cabins, Inc., 309 Mass. 519, 521 (1941); Opinion of the Justices, 368 Mass. 857, 861–62 (1975); Black v. Magnolia Liquors Co., 355 U.S. 24, 25–26 (1957); Affiliated Distillers Brands Corp. v. Gills, 56 N.J. 251, 256, 265 A.2d 809, 811–812 (1970); Delaware Alcoholic Beverages Control Commission v. B-F Spirits, Ltd., 429 A.2d 975, 977–78 (Del. Supreme Ct. 1981).

18. See FTC complaint, In re Guinness PLC, et al. and FTC press release (12/15/97).

19. In fact, the chart substantially understates Diageo/UDV's strength in the U.S. market since the number 4 marketer sells almost exclusively in Eastern Europe and the former Soviet Union.

20. Impact newsletter, January 1, 2001, p. 15. New York: M. Shanken Communications Inc. Preliminary ranking by 1999 depletions, including agency brands.

21. Impact newsletter, April 15, 1999, p. 11.

22. Impact newsletter, August 1 and 15, 2000, p. 14.

23. Excludes brands sold in 1999.

24. Includes Aalborg Aquavit, acquired in 1999.

25. Addition of columns may not agree due to rounding.

26. Includes Captain Morgan (litigation pending).

27. Includes Absolut (not included in sale).

28. Based on global total, excluding local, traditional spirits.

29. Preliminary ranking by 1999 depletions, including agency brands.

30. Impact newsletter, May 1, 2004.

31. The First Circuit has rejected an attempt by supermarket chains to invalidate a restriction on the number of retail outlets that may be controlled by a single entity or "combination of persons." Massachusetts Food Association v. Massachusetts Alcoholic Beverages Control Commission, 197 F.3d 560 (1st Cir. 1999).

32. Costco Wholesale Corp. v. Maleng, et al., U.S. District Court for the Western District of Washington (Seattle), filed on Feb. 20, 2004.

33. Healy v. Beer Institute, 491 U.S. 105 (1989). Although a law guaranteeing low prices to wholesalers might seem contrary to promoting temperance, it prevented suppliers from using price discrimination as a tool to manipulate wholesalers. Such laws are generally part of an overall price stabilization scheme. See, for example, Mass. Gen. Laws c. 138 §§25, 25A, 25B, 25C and 25D. However, such comprehensive plans are being dismantled. See next endnote.

34. See Canterbury Liquors & Pantry v. Sullivan, 18 F. Supp. 2d 41 (D. Mass. 1998). In addition, Massachusetts' attempt to fix minimum retail prices, see Mass. G.L. c.138 §25C, has been ineffective since 1968 when the attorney general ruled that it could not be enforced because the Alcoholic Beverages Control Commission lacked the resources properly to determine what the minimum price should be. Op. Atty. Gen. October 8, 1968, 45. Massachusetts has not seen fit to allocate resources to fix minimum prices since, and surely will not in the future.

35. Rubin v. Coors Brewing Co., 514 U.S. 476 (1995).

36. 44 Liquormart, Inc. v. Rhode Island, 517 U.S. 484 (1996).

37. See Eller Media Co. v. City of Cleveland, Ohio, 2003 U.S. App. LEXIS 7425, affirming 161 F.Supp.2d 796 (2001). The only opportunity for a blanket ban on advertising appears to be when it is targeted at particularly sensitive locations. See Lorillard Tobacco Co., et al. v. Reilly, et al., 533 U.S. 525, 121 S.Ct. 2404, 150 L.Ed.2d 532 (2001).

38. See, for example, Ziffrin, Inc. v. Reeves, 308 U.S. 132, 138 (1939). ("The Twenty-first Amendment sanctions the right of a state to legislate concerning intoxicating liquors brought from without, unfettered by the Commerce Clause."); Indianapolis v. Brewing Co. v. Liquor Control Comm'n, 305 U.S. 391, 394 (1939). ("Since the right of the Twenty-first Amendment... the right of a state to prohibit or regulate the importation of intoxicating liquor is not limited by the Commerce Clause..."); State Bd. of Equalization v. Young's Market Co., 299 U.S. 59 (1936).

39. Hostetter v. Idlewild Bon Voyage Liquor Corp., 377 U.S. 324 (1964).

40. Id. at 324, 331–2 (1964).

41. Capital Cities Cable v. Crisp, 467 U.S. 691 (1984).

42. Id. at 714.

43. Id. at 715 (quotation omitted).

44. Bacchus Imports v. Dias, 468 U.S. 263 (1984).

45. Id. at 270.

46. Id. at 272.

47. Id. at 276.

48. Id. at 275.

49. North Dakota v. U.S., 495 U.S. 423, 431 (1990) (plurality opinion) (quoting California Retail Liquor Dealers Ass'n v. Midcal Aluminum, Inc., 445 U.S. 97 (1980).

50. Brown-Forman, 476 U.S. at 584 (quoting Hostetter, supra at 332).

51. North Dakota v. US, 495 U.S. 423 (1990).

52. Heald v. Engler, 342 F.3d 517 (6th Cir. 2003).

53. Swedenburg v. Kelly, 232 F.Supp.2d 135 (S.D.N.Y. 2002).

54. N.Y. Alco. Bev. Cont. Law §§ 102(1)(a), (c), and (d) (2003).

55. See ABC Law § 102 (1)(a).

56. Id. at 145.

57. Id.

58. Id. at 148.

59. Under traditional dormant Commerce Clause analysis, a state regulation is unconstitutional if it "affects interstate commerce in a manner either that (i) discriminates against interstate commerce, or (ii) imposes burdens on interstate commerce that are incommensurate with putative local gains." Brown & Williamson Tobacco Corp. v. Pataki, 320 F.3d 200, 208 (2nd Cir. 2003).

60. Swedenburg, 232 F.Supp.2d at 145.

61. Swedenburg v. Kelly, 358 F.3d 223 (2nd Cir. 2004).

62. Id. at 241.

63. Id. at 231.

64. Id., citing, Hostetter v. Idlewild Bon Voyage Liquor Corp., 377 U.S. 324, 332 (1964).

65. Id. at 233.

66. Id.

67. Granholm v. Heald, 544 U.S. 410, 125 S.Ct. 1885 (2005).

68. Kuhn, The Structure of Scientific Revolution, 10 (University of Chicago Press 1962).

69. Granholm v. Heald, 125 S.Ct. at 1892.

70. Id. at 1893

71. Id., at 1895.

72. Id., at 1898.

73. Id., at 1901.

74. Id., at 1903.

75. Id., at 1903–4.

76. Id., at 1904.

77. Id., at 1907.

78. Report and Recommendations 3 (January 21, 1964): 18.

79. http://www2.potsdam.edu/alcohol-info/Controversies/references/1106164274.html.

80. Granholm v. Heald, at 1909.

81. Id., at 1908.

82. Id., at 1908.

83. Id., at 1909.

84. Id., at 1910.

85. Id., at 1910.

86. Id., at 1911.

87. Id., at 1913.

88. Id., at 1914.

89. Id., citing, 30 Cong. Rec. 2612 (1897).

90. Id., at 1912.

91. Id., at 1919.

92. Id., at 1920.
93. Id., at 1921-1922.
94. Id., at 1924.
95. Id., at 1927.
96. See 28-A M.R.S. §88

Chapter 4

Contents Under Pressure: Regulating the Sales and Marketing of Alcoholic Beverages

Susan C. Cagann[1]

Contents

The debate over state power to regulate interstate shipment of wine reached the Supreme Court in 2004 in the form of *Granholm v. Heald*. State regulators, consumers, wineries, wholesalers, and many pundits entered the fray and debated a state's right to limit access to the direct to consumer trade channel to in-state businesses. Stories appeared monthly in major U.S. newspapers. Law review articles digested the history of beverage alcohol law. Those who view wine as a commodity such as cheese or shrimp sharpened their wits against regulators and wholesalers raising America's pre-Prohibition history with liquor as a shield. Extremists on both ends of the spectrum predicted the demise of the three-tier system separating the manufacture, distribution, and retail tiers. In the end, the Supreme Court nodded to state power to structure a distribution system, but tempered that power, breathing vigor into the battle to modernize federal and state control of alcohol sales.

To absorb the import of the recent decision and what it portends for the current systems of alcohol distribution, this chapter examines the current alcohol[2] market, its stakeholders, and the evolution of its regulation since repeal of Prohibition in 1933. Alcohol has been treated differently than other consumer products throughout the last century. It is the only consumer product that is the subject of two constitutional amendments. Alcohol's manufacture, marketing, distribution, and sale are regulated like no other beverage or food. The confounding question is whether current regulatory constraints efficiently accomplish their goals in today's global, consolidating market.

Alcohol is a popular, profit-generating product.[3] This is a constant since our nation's founders arrived with casks of liquor and planted vineyards in Virginia. Today, retail sales of alcohol are a $155 billion industry.[4] In 2004, the volume of wine sales climbed to a record 278,000,000 cases—an expansion of 105 million cases since 1991.[5] As of 2002, wine contributed $45 billion to California's economy adding 207,550 full-time jobs and 14.8 million visitors to its wineries.[6] The United States is home to more than 1,800 brewers, 60 distilleries, and 3,000 wineries.[7] United States imports exceed $3 billion in distilled spirits, and $2 billion each in beer and wine.[8] Americans consume on average 21.6 gallons of beer, 1.3 gallons of distilled spirits, and 2.2 gallons of wine per capita.[9]

The players in today's market differ greatly from their counterparts before, during, and just after repeal of Prohibition. Global spirits companies report annual revenues in the billions.[10] Global retail chains have thousands of stores worldwide.[11] Restaurant and hotel chains hold hundreds of on-premise licenses throughout the country. Wholesalers do business in dozens of states. As of 2004, the ten largest wholesalers had a 67.9 percent share of the U.S. market and cumulative sales revenue of $21.7 billion.[12]

Governments, as well as the private sector, profit from alcohol sales. Alcohol taxes are a steady source of funding for federal and state coffers. The Federal government collected $6.8 billion in federal excise tax for beer, wine, and distilled spirits in 2003.[13] Annual revenues from alcohol trade reported for 27 states exceeded $2.1 billion in 2004.[14] Texas led the pack with revenues from alcoholic beverage taxes of $600 million for fiscal 2004.[15] In California, revenues from beer, wine, and distilled spirits excise tax exceeded $300 million for fiscal year 2003–2004.[16] New York and Illinois reported revenues from alcohol as $140 million and $190 million, respectively.[17]

Although the market has changed considerably since 1933, most state regulations have not.

Prohibition's legacy is a fractionalized beverage alcohol market keenly stressed by today's global economy. The evils of "tied houses," bootlegging, and criminal domination of the market motivated lawmakers to constrain the marketing and sale of alcohol. Pre-Prohibition excess is legend. Suppliers dominated saloons—creating the tied house. Tied houses would sell beer or ale and offer a free lunch to attract customers. Tied houses were the font of excessive consumption and gave birth to the phrase, "there is no such thing as a free lunch." Retailers were weak, single-store businesses. Booze was cheap and easily obtained. Pre-Prohibition annual consumption of distilled spirits was as high as 7.5 gallons per capita as compared with 1.36 gallons in recent years.[18] In as early as 1810, there were more than 14,000 distillers in the United States with an estimated production of 33,000,000 gallons.[19] Abuses by manufacturers and excessive consumption fueled temperance activism and led to the passage of the 18th amendment prohibiting almost all legitimate trade in alcohol in the United States.

Prohibition failed. Prohibition did not render America dry; rather, illegitimate enterprises dominated by organized crime flourished. Bootleggers and gangsters took over liquor trafficking.[20] Large numbers of Americans defied the laws. In 1932, John D. Rockefeller, Jr. wrote to proponents of a plank in the Republican National party platform:

> When the Eighteenth Amendment was passed I earnestly hoped … that it would be generally supported by public opinion and thus the day be hastened when the value to society of men with minds and bodies free from the undermining effects of alcohol would be generally realized. That this has not been the result but rather that drinking has generally increased; that the speakeasy has replaced the salon … that a vast army of lawbreakers has been recruited and financed on a colossal scale; that many of our best citizens … have openly and unabashed disregarded the Eighteenth Amendment; that as an inevitable result respect for all law has been greatly lessened; that crime has increased to an unprecedented degree—I have slowly and reluctantly come to believe.… In my judgment it will be so difficult for our people as a whole to agree in advance on what the substitute should be, and so unlikely that any one method will fit the entire nation, that repeal will be far less possible if coupled with an alternative measure. For that reason I the more strongly approve the simple, clear cut proposition you are proposing to recommend and which I shall count it not only a duty but a privilege to support. …[21]

With the passage of the 21st Amendment repealing prohibition and prohibiting the transportation in, or importation of, intoxicating beverages to any state in violation of its laws, America warily opened the spigot on re-legitimizing the alcoholic beverage trade. Since Repeal, states developed trade zones, sanctioned monopolies, and anticompetitive practices, and created unique and disjointed market systems for alcohol sales.

Consumers in Massachusetts, Pennsylvania, and California each uniquely experience the impact of the market system in their own state when purchasing a bottle of wine. A California consumer buys wine from a local retailer. The retailer may be owned by the winery. The wine may have been sold directly from the winery to the retailer or the winery may have sold the wine to a wholesaler who sold it to the retailer. The Pennsylvania consumer visits a state-operated store to purchase a bottle. The wine was sold by the winery to the Pennsylvania government by a broker the winery is required to use as a middle tier. The Massachusetts consumer buys wine from a retailer—not a chain retailer. (In Massachusetts, a retailer cannot hold more than three retail licenses.) The winery must sell the wine to a local wholesaler. The wholesaler then sells the wine to the retailer. Only the California consumer has the option to purchase the wine directly from a California winery. To understand the rhyme and reason behind these different consumer experiences, we must examine how the sale and marketing of alcohol has been controlled since Repeal.

Creation of Control and License Distribution Systems

In designing systems to address the evils of "demon rum," evil influence was presumed to flow down from powerful manufacturers to wholesalers and from wholesalers to local retailers. In drafting the rulebooks, practices that would be considered anticompetitive restraints on commerce in any other product are tolerated or championed as the means to create orderly markets and promote temperance. Checks and balances were imposed on production, marketing, and sale of alcoholic beverages. The resulting systems are vulnerable to challenges to the extent their checks and balances are not tailored to—or exceed the mandate to—promote temperance, restrict access to minors, create orderly markets, and protect revenues.

Federal Regulatory Framework

After repeal, the federal government retained power to regulate the manufacture, labeling, and sale of alcohol. Presently, the Tax and Trade Bureau of the Department of Treasury (TTB) is the federal agency primarily responsible for governance of the alcohol industry.[22] TTB is the successor of several Treasury Department agencies or units responsible for administering beverage alcohol laws. Congress passed the Federal Alcohol Administration Act (FAA Act) in 1935 creating a federal administrative unit in the Treasury Department.[23] Ultimately, a bureau was created within the Department of Treasury, the Bureau of Alcohol, Tobacco, and Firearms (BATF).[24] With the reorganization of the Department of Treasury under the Homeland Security Act of 2002, the BATF functions were split and beverage alcohol regulation and enforcement was posited in the TTB. TTB's mission is "to collect … excise taxes, to ensure that these products are labeled, advertised and marketed in accordance with the law, and to administer the laws and regulations in a manner that protects the consumer and the revenue, and promotes voluntary compliance."[25]

TTB administers excise tax statutes under the Internal Revenue Code[26] and regulates alcohol under the FAA Act.[27] Pursuant to the FAA Act, the government established a permit system for manufacturers of wine and spirits, importers and wholesalers of distilled spirits, wine or malt beverages, and a registration system for beer producers. The permitting process was established to combat the evils of Prohibition by ensuring that permits are kept out of the hands of persons with criminal convictions or with financially unstable businesses. To operate a distillery, winery, or import business, the owner of the business must apply for a federal basic permit. In that process, one's background and financial stability is checked. All permits are conditioned on compliance with federal and state laws relating to alcoholic beverages. The federal government also enforces violations of state alcohol laws under the Webb-Kenyon Act.[28]

State Regulatory Framework

The 21st Amendment gave each state the power to regulate the importation and distribution of alcohol within its borders. This power included the right to go wet or dry; and the right to control the distribution and sale through state oversight and management. States used this power to establish a system of licenses with unique privileges for each tier of the industry—supply, wholesale, and retail. State responses to Repeal varied. There was consensus in avoiding the return to the social evils fed by tied houses. States grappled with the issue of whether to adopt private licensing systems or state-controlled systems in which sale or distribution would be performed by the state. Equally contentious issues arose in how to tax and distribute revenue from the newly legitimized industry. Ultimately, eighteen states opted to control the sale of all or some alcoholic beverages. Twelve states control retail off-premise sale through government operated package stores or designated outlets. These include Alabama, Idaho, Iowa, Maine, Michigan, Mississippi, Montana, New Hampshire, North Carolina, Ohio, Oregon, Pennsylvania, Utah, Vermont, Virginia, Washington, West Virginia, and Wyoming. By 1949, forty-five of the forty-eight states had legalized the sale of beverage alcohol in some form.

Control States

Control states set up varied systems that have evolved since Repeal. Response time to the end of national Prohibition varied. Oregon, Montana, and Kansas illustrate different paths chosen by control states to keep tight reigns on the industry.

Oregon became a hybrid state. In Oregon, the Legislative Assembly held a special session that culminated in the establishment of the Oregon Liquor Control Commission just four days after repeal of national prohibition.[29] The Commission's mission is "to effectively regulate the sale, distribution, and responsible use of alcoholic beverages to protect Oregon's public health, safety and community livability." Oregon's Liquor Control Act of 1934 gave the state the exclusive rights to sell distilled spirits and fortified wine.[30] Oregon authorized its Commission to establish a license system for the sale of beer and table wine (less than 14 percent alcohol) on- and off-premise by private enterprise. By the end of 1934, Oregon operated 22 stores staffed by state employees and issued contracts to 117 sales agencies for operating contract liquor stores.[31] In the 1970s, some retail permittees were authorized to sell wine up to 20 percent alcohol by volume. Today, the Commission oversees 236 contract agent retail liquor stores selling packaged distilled spirits.[32]

Montana also responded quickly by establishing the Montana Liquor Control Board for purchasing, pricing, and selling liquor in the state. By 1935, 115 state-owned retail stores were in operation.[33] In 1937, liquor by the drink was legalized. By 1995, the State Legislature directed the conversion of all state stores to privately owned agencies. These agencies own their liquor inventory and set retail price. Montana sets the price for liquor sold at wholesale and runs the wholesale distribution operation.

Kansas took a bit longer. Officially dry since 1880, Kansas again rejected the opportunity to legalize alcohol in 1934.[34] Illegal trade in alcohol continued in that state. In 1937, the Kansas legislature enacted a law permitting the sale of a category of products with low alcohol content—cereal malt beverages—by excluding these products from the definition of intoxicating liquor. In 1948, Kansas passed legislation authorizing the sale of package liquor, but the sale of liquor by the drink in public places was prohibited. The next year, Kansas enacted a Liquor Control Act and created the Division of Alcoholic Beverage Control for enforcement of its new laws.[35] Kansas had trouble enforcing its prohibition of on-premise sale and consumption of alcohol. Speakeasy bars sold liquor illegally. Other establishments came up with creative systems for consumers "brown bagging" their own products and even purchasing coupons for brands that were then purchased by the establishment as the consumer's agent. In response, Kansas passed a Private Club Act in 1965 to provide for licensure and regulation of these establishments.[36] The Act required consumers to pay a $10 fee and wait ten days before buying their first drink. Consumers could join multiple clubs.[37] Liquor by the drink did not become legal in Kansas until 1986 and then only by a 59.9 to 40.1 percent margin.[38]

Control states herald their choice as an effective way to corner the profit on alcohol sale and use such revenue for the community and to promote temperance. And control states profit handsomely from their decision. The following results were reported by control state chief executives in the "Control States Executive Forum" published by the Adams Beverage Group.[39] In 2003, Alabama shared $161,400,000 in revenue from the sale of alcohol with the State General Fund, Mental Health, Education, and other state and local agencies. In 2004, Idaho had a record-breaking year; sales totaled $86 million. Iowa reported a 28 percent increase in net revenue in 2003. Michigan is championing its Internet-ordering system. In its pilot year, Michigan received 2,000 orders in a month. In Montana liquor sales reached an all-time high in fiscal 2004—total dollar sales were $70,827,000. This resulted in revenues for Montana of $20,913,826. Montgomery County, Maryland, reported over $168 million in total sales for fiscal year 2004, resulting in a transfer of $20,501,030 unencumbered to the Montgomery County General Fund. New Hampshire also reported strong sales with an increase of more than $26 million over fiscal year 2003 sales. As sales flourish, regulators must be mindful of their commitment to further core goals of their mission to temper trade and promote temperance while enriching state coffers. Control states must walk the tightrope of a fox guarding the hen house as their financial success increases.

License States

States that allowed private enterprise came to be known as "license states." License states issue licenses and sharply define privileges and restrictions for each license type. The license system complements the federal permitting system. Licensing enables state agencies to evaluate the character, fitness, and financial responsibility of each license applicant.[40] Several states impose residency requirements on licensees in all or some tiers.[41] The goal of many states in enacting residency requirements was to address concerns over organized crime influencing the legitimate industry. States also enacted laws to prohibit persons convicted of a felony or crime involving liquor laws, gambling, prostitution, or other crimes against morality from holding direct or indirect interests in a license. Several states prohibit a retailer from employing anyone with a felony conviction. State licensing authorities may take into account proposed locations of premises and may limit the concentration of licenses. Licensing also provides a means by which states can enforce their limitations on business hours and other restrictions on operations. Licensing provides a key control mechanism in checking abuses including illegal sales to minors.

Licensing also is a mechanism by which a state can limit vertical integration among the tiers. Many states chose to prohibit a supplier from owning an interest in an on-premise retailer—the classic "tied house," and some prohibit a supplier from owning an interest in off-premise retailer or any wholesaler. Within these state regulatory schemes, not all alcohol is treated equally. Vertical integration may be permitted for those with interests in wineries or breweries, but not for those with interests in distilleries. A few states have no constraints on cross-tier common ownership for those with interests in certain types of alcohol licenses such as wine.

License privileges differ vastly from state to state. This can hinder or help the success of a tier within a given state. Some states with powerful interests in, or focus on, a particular sector have passed progressive laws with expansive privileges for that sector. In the winery context, California, Colorado, New York, Pennsylvania, Oregon, Virginia, and Washington have granted wineries great flexibility in their ability to market and sell wine. In each of these states, there has been phenomenal growth in the number of local wineries. The expanded privileges can include the wineries right to: serve as their own distributors; sell direct to consumers at retail onsite and through the Internet; own off- and on-premise businesses; sell at farm markets; and hold events serving food and their winery locations. In 2002, Wine America commissioned a study of winery privileges and compared the privileges conferred across the fifty states.[42] For example, all fifty states permit tasting room sales to consumers and samples. Thirty to forty states permit sales to retailers, sales by the glass, restaurant privileges, signs on highways, and operation of viticulture faculty. Twenty or more states permit sales of other in-state wineries' wines, more than one tasting room, special event licenses, and direct shipment. Greater privileges for wineries have enhanced the local wine industry. As discussed in the following section, some of these privileges—if not afforded to out-of-state interests—may run afoul of the dormant Commerce Clause.

Trade Practice Regulation

Permitting and licensing systems were augmented by laws designed to promote core policy concerns—temperance, orderly markets, and revenue collection.[43] Federal and state trade practice laws place acute constraints on the relationship between the supply and wholesale tiers. In addition to prohibiting the owner of a supplier from holding an interest in wholesaler or retailer, states established exclusivity mandates, minimum price margins, constraints on termination rights, and privilege exclusivity. Many states prohibit discrimination by a trade member toward members in another tier even with legitimate business justification, such as quantity discounts. Others compel "transparency" by requiring price posting, disclosure of private contracts, brand registration, and price-posting laws. Laws, and in particular exceptions to the laws, have evolved as market strength waxes or wanes in a particular tier.

Legislatures prohibited numerous trade practices to avoid evils perceived to be inherent in the distribution of alcohol absent governmental control. The FAA Act is the platform from which state trade practice laws follow. Section 105 of the Act deems certain acts a "means to induce" and renders such behavior unlawful if it has an exclusionary effect on trade. The prohibited acts include exclusive outlets, tied houses, commercial bribery, and consignment sales. In addition, each state adopted legislation governing trade practices. Unlike federal prohibitions that require an exclusionary impact, state laws forbid practices for which a trade member is strictly liable regardless of intent or effect. In general, regulatory schemes feature general prohibitions, eroded by legislative exceptions. At play are the terms of sale—cash vs. credit; level of services—stocking and category management; pricing—quantity discounts, depletion allowances, equipment, signage, and product advertising and promotion.

Unlawful inducements by a supplier under the federal "tied house" prohibitions include: holding a direct interest in a retail licensee or the property of a licensee; furnishing things of value to licensee; paying a retailer for display space or advertising; or guaranteeing loans, extending credit, or requiring quota sales.[44] Federal regulations then enumerate exceptions to the unlawful means to induce. These include: product displays of less than $300 per brand; point of sale advertising materials; selling equipment of supplies at cost; a finite number of samples; newspaper cuts; combination packaging, educational seminars; consumer tastings; consumer promotions such as coupons, prizes, and refunds; category management (e.g., stocking and rotation services); and outside signs not exceeding $400 in costs.[45]

Each state likewise prohibits a manufacturer from providing an item of value to a retailer. Although all states begin at the same place—a desire to avoid tied houses or detrimental inducements to the retail tier, the paths to achieve the goals widely diverge on a trade practice by trade practice basis. Louisiana succinctly sets forth its rationale in its regulations:

> Prohibitions against exclusive outlets and tied house arrangements with respect to the marketing and sale of alcoholic beverages in Louisiana has stabilized the industry and prevented unlawful and unfair inducements for the retail purchase of alcohol and unlawful coercion, bribery, kickback demands, and other unfair and unlawful business practices. It is in the best interest of the state's citizens that fair business dealings and unfettered competition govern the alcohol beverage industry ... that it remains an industry dominated by fairness and integrity and safeguarded against the threat of corrupt and unfair business practices.[46]

Louisiana regulations prohibit exclusive outlets and tied house arrangements and then define exceptions to this general prohibition. California's Alcoholic Beverage Control Act likewise defines its tied house restrictions by requiring discrete ownership interest in on- and off-premise sale licensees and providing items of value directly or indirectly to such licensees. These prohibitions are followed by thirty-seven statutory exemptions.[47] California and Louisiana provide just a glimpse into the means by which states constrain manufacture tier influence over the retail tier.

This patchwork of local rules presents a compliance quagmire for licensees, particularly out-of-state suppliers. Following are some examples of rules applied to popular promotional vehicles. In each instance, the practice is allowed at the federal level. Laws regulating sweepstakes illustrate the challenge. Most states permit sweepstakes in beverage alcohol marketing campaigns. Some states require prior approval with significant lead time; others prohibit alcoholic beverages as prizes and almost all require the winner to be of legal drinking age. California limits the value of the prize for a sweepstakes related to the promotion of alcohol to twenty-five cents for beer, one dollar for wine, and five dollars for distilled spirits.[48] Texas permits a sweepstakes if it is national in scope and offered in at least thirty states simultaneously.[49] Louisiana has no restrictions on prizes, but does not allow winning names to be drawn on a licensed premise.[50] Couponing presents another challenge. Rules differ state by state as to whether mail-in coupons, instant redeemable coupons, or coupons with purchase of alcohol are allowed. California permits all three forms with no-dollar-value limit. Texas prohibits all three forms of coupons. Louisiana permits mail-in coupons for wine, but prohibits instantly redeemable coupons.[51] Some states forbid a supplier from visiting a retailer to provide education regarding products and their attributes if a wholesaler is not present. Other states have no restrictions on supplier educational visits to retail accounts.

These are just a few examples of the state departures from federal general trade practice laws. Although some states simply adopt the federal rules, the majority of states impose greater restrictions. This begs the questions as to whether core policy concerns could be achieved by resisting the temptation to expand on federal prohibitions in the interest of developing a consistent, predictable regulatory framework across the United States for alcohol marketing and sales.

It is the stated intent of many state laws to create "fair and efficient three-tier systems of distribution."[52] Regulators in some states support price posting systems as a means to create a level playing field. Although price posting schemes vary, most require suppliers and wholesalers to file schedules of prices to which they must adhere for a specified period of time with the Alcoholic Beverage Control Board or other regulatory agency. Price-posting schemes have been challenged on antitrust grounds and have been upheld only where a state clearly communicates a policy to regulate the market for a legitimate end, and the state actively supervises the regulated market.[53] In addition to requiring price posting, some states also control other aspects of pricing.

For example, Washington has the following rules for beer and wine manufacturers and wholesalers:

■ Product must be sold at least 10 percent above acquisition cost;
■ Quantity discounts are prohibited;
■ Prices must include delivery to retail premises;
■ Prices must be posted in advance and not changed for a set period of time; and

■ No credit may be offered to retailers.[54]

A major retailer challenged these rules as well as those allowing it to purchase beer and wine directly from in-state suppliers while forbidding it to purchase directly from out-of-state suppliers.[55] This challenge was mounted on the theory that the pricing constraints violate antitrust laws and that the differential treatment of in-state and out-of-state producers violates the Commerce Clause.

The Court followed the recent Supreme Court decision in *Granholm* and found laws favoring in-state suppliers unconstitutional. Washington legislature then passed legislation to "level up" the rules and permit out of state suppliers to sell direct to trade as well; see further discussion in the following sections.

State rulebooks were not written to forbid upward pressure on the chain of distribution. Some tied house laws have unintended consequences. Though designed to protect retailers, today they offer protection to suppliers and wholesalers from the demands of powerful retailers. For example, the rules prohibit a supplier from paying a "slotting fee" for premier, or for that matter, any real estate on a retail shelf or wine list and also prohibit a supplier from paying a retail licensee for advertising. Suppliers and wholesalers find themselves using the trade practice rules as a shield against powerful retailer's demands. From the large retailer's perspective, they do not need protection from supplier dominance. In a low margin business why not demand a slotting fee from a supplier of beer, wine, and spirits as is the practice with other consumer products.

Washington litigation over price posting may be the harbinger of other challenges to the myriad rules constraining alcohol trade. If the retailer is successful there, alcohol will be one step closer to being treated like other commodities. Large retailers would welcome this change as a means to compete in price and enhance distribution efficiencies. Retailers then could exert their market clout to extract greater discounts from suppliers for large-quantity purchases. Ultimately, large retailers could seek the ability to purchase alcohol like other products at the national level and warehouse and self-distribute the product. The victors in this provocative scenario would be large retailers and suppliers. Its success would jeopardize the viability of the middle tier—wholesale—and would put further pressure on the vitality of small producers and retailers.

The Middle Tier and Franchise Protection

In the recent Supreme Court battle over direct shipping, wholesalers were vocal participants. They staunchly defended a state's right to regulate liquor sales and to do so without regard to the Commerce Clause's prohibition on discrimination.[56] Wholesalers urged the Court to support strict state and local control over retail outlets to foreclose an unrestrained distribution scheme. Wholesalers advocated for a state's right to require a local presence to qualify for a privilege—selling direct to consumers via the Internet or mail order. In so doing, wholesalers were defending their turf. Wholesalers have sought and received statutory protection at the state and even local level. Many states and one county have passed some form of legislation known as "franchise regulations" governing formation and conclusion of the relations between suppliers and wholesalers. The purpose underlying these protections was ostensibly to check the power of suppliers over local wholesalers. Absent such regulations, the supplier-wholesaler relationship is established by the parties and may or may not be evidenced by a written contract. As with any other contract, the respective bargaining power of the parties dictates how terms favor their respective positions. If a dispute should arise, the parties would resolve the dispute in court or arbitration under generally applicable contract laws. Franchise laws enhance wholesaler bargaining power and impose additional protections.

Generally, franchise laws require the formal appointment of a wholesaler, notification to the state of such appointment, and permission from the state to terminate the relationship. In many franchise states, a supplier cannot "dual," that is appoint two or more wholesalers in a specific geographic area.[57] Twenty-one states, the District of Columbia, and Puerto Rico have adopted laws that provide additional protection for termination of a beverage alcohol distributor. Many of these states require that a franchise fee be paid if a supplier terminates a wholesaler without "good cause" or completely forbids a termination without good cause absent quite narrow exceptions such as discontinuance of a brand. Although franchise laws are not limited to the Eastern seaboard, the laws of Connecticut, Massachusetts, New Jersey, and North Carolina exemplify these protections in varying degrees.

Connecticut requires a manufacturer or out-of-state shipper selling alcoholic beverages to establish "just and sufficient cause" to terminate a wholesaler.[58] Connecticut provides that a wholesale relationship of greater than six months duration may be terminated only if: 1) there is a written agreement signed by both the wholesaler and supplier agreeing to the change and the change is approved by the Department of Consumer Protection or 2) the supplier sends written notice to the wholesaler and the Department of Consumer Protection. The termination will not become effective if there is not just and sufficient cause as determined in a hearing. "Just and sufficient cause" means circumstances in which a reasonable person considering the equities would determine that termination should take place.[59]

Massachusetts also requires good cause to terminate.[60] Under Massachusetts law, a supplier may not refuse to sell to a wholesaler, except for good cause shown, any item that has a brand name if the parties have made regular sales of the brand in the preceding six months. A supplier must give notice in writing to the wholesaler and Commission providing at least 120 days' notice of intent to terminate. The Commission then determines if there is good cause. "Good cause" means product disparagement; unfair preference of a competitor's items; failing to exercise best efforts in sales and promoting a brand item; engaging in illegal trade practices; or failing to comply with the parties' terms of sale.[61]

North Carolina likewise requires good cause to terminate. A supplier there may not amend, cancel, terminate, or refuse to renew an agreement unless good cause can be shown. Good cause does not include a change of ownership of a winery. Good cause does include: revocation of wholesaler's license; a wholesaler's bankruptcy or insolvency; assignment for the benefit of creditors; or the wholesaler fails to substantially comply with material requirement of the supplier without reasonable excuse or justification.[62]

New Jersey has an "antidiscrimination" law. If a supplier refuses to sell alcoholic beverage (other than malt beverages) to a wholesaler, the wholesaler can petition the director for specific enforcement of the appointment. The director will assess whether the refusal to sell is discriminatory. Discrimination is not deemed to include refusal to sell because of the bankruptcy of the wholesaler, the suspension or loss of the wholesaler's federal or state license to do business for more than sixty days, product disparagement, favoring a competitor's product, or the material breach of a material term of the agreement between the wholesaler and supplier.[63]

Franchise regulation unquestionably benefits the middle tier. In franchise states, it may be easier to divorce a spouse than end a distribution relationship. The arguments for franchise protections are most persuasive in the context of a small local distributor seeking protection from unexpected terminations by a large national supplier. As distributors consolidate and grow in market power, franchise protection seems a rather potent weapon for a state to confer on one private party to wield against the small and large supplier alike. A few states do exempt very small suppliers from the orbit of franchise protection. However, those states that tried to do so only for in-state suppliers faced and lost constitutional challenges. Suppliers successfully challenged franchise regulations in Illinois and Washington where local suppliers were exempt from their purview.[64]

The question as to whether franchise protections are appropriate expressions of state power over private parties' contractual relationships is oft asked by suppliers. In the consolidating industry franchise laws often confound global companies when attempts are made to streamline or align distribution networks after mergers and acquisitions. Many state laws do not include a change in control in the supplier or distributor as "good cause" to terminate. Larger companies may find themselves required to deal with several distributors in a given geographic area. And, as distributors consolidate, many brand owners find themselves captive in distribution houses where a competitor has more influence or attention. In a franchise state, the brand owner generally cannot change distributors without litigating the issue of good cause or paying a fee to leave. Suppliers sometimes question the validity of the rationale for leveling the playing field through franchise regulations when the party protected may have more clout than the supplier.

Direct to Consumer Sales and Other Pressures on the System

In the last decade, consumers have embraced the Internet and mail-order businesses as a viable channel of trade. Small wineries have gravitated to the direct to consumer channel as a profitable means by which to market their goods. As of 2005, twenty-nine states allowed interstate wine shipments in some form to local consumers. Several states permitted in-state wineries to ship to consumers, but did not confer such privileges on out-of-state wineries. Challenges were brought against the laws of two of those states—Michigan and New York. Michigan permitted in-state wineries the privilege to ship to in-state consumers. New York permitted in-state wineries and out-of-state wineries with "a branch, factory, office or storeroom" within New York to ship directly to New York consumers.[65] The cases were consolidated and presented to the Supreme Court. In 2005, the Supreme Court declared that such differential treatment between in-state and out-of-state wineries constitutes explicit discrimination against interstate commerce and found such regulations unconstitutional under the Commerce Clause in *Granholm v. Heald*, 125 S. Ct 1885 (2005).

How did a case about small New York and central California wineries wind up in front of the Supreme Court for the 2005 term? In the last decades, while the big grew bigger, small producers expanded. From 800 wineries in 1975 the number of wineries has grown to more than 3,000 in all fifty states. California is home to more than 2,000 wineries.[66] In Pennsylvania, New York, Colorado, Virginia, Washington, and Oregon, the number of wineries increased from 91 in 1975 to 806 in 2002. Many mom and pop retailers appear to be on the endangered list. Large distributors and larger retailers wanted a decent portfolio of wines, but certainly not thousands from small suppliers. Large suppliers with multiple wine brands present an attractive efficient business partner. The little guys were squeezed and the Internet was their answer. They combined forces with bigger wineries and launched a strategy to open as many markets to direct shipping as possible.

Wineries formed a "Coalition for Free Trade" and began a "Free the Grapes" campaign.[67] The Wine Institute of California and Family Winemakers of California added strong voices to the direct shipping debates.[68] In general, wholesalers were staunch supporters of state laws restricting direct shipping and the Wine & Spirits Wholesalers of America led the counterattack.[69]

The debate was carried to statehouses across the country. Direct shipping legislation was passed in dozens of states. Others imposed restrictions on direct shipping to all but local wineries. As a result, several direct shipping cases have been winding their way through the federal court system.[70] The national press seemed fascinated with the battle. *The New York Times* published op-ed pieces sporting titles such as "Let It Flow."[71] In the fall of 2004, the debate was heard by the justices of the U.S. Supreme Court. During the course of the debate, stakeholders, judges, and the media examined the state regulatory framework of the alcohol trade and considered the intersection between state and federal power over alcohol.

The Court concluded that "the [Twenty-First] Amendment did not give states the authority to pass nonuniform laws in order to discriminate against out-of-state goods, a privilege they have not enjoyed at any earlier time."[72] The Court described the Michigan law as obviously discriminatory and found the New York in-state premise requirement "contrary to our admonition that States cannot require an out-of-state firm 'to become a resident to compete on equal terms.'"[73] The Court concluded that the discriminatory laws faced a "virtually *per se* rule of invalidity.[74] The Court found that such discriminatory laws did not fall within the power conferred upon the states under the 21st Amendment. The Court defined the purpose of the 21st Amendment as permitting the states "to maintain an effective and uniform system for controlling liquor by regulating its transportation, importation, and use" as long as it was done in a non-discriminatory manner.[75] In so doing, the Court played down the import of post-Prohibition jurisprudence in favor of the more "modern" line of caselaw.[76] The Court posited the modern cases in three categories—those holding state laws violating another section of the Constitution—First Amendment, Establishment Clause, Equal Protection Clause, Due Process Clause, and Import-Export Clause—were not saved by the 21st Amendment[77]; those holding that the 21st Amendment did not operate to repeal the commerce clause for alcoholic beverages[78]; and those finding that state regulation of alcohol is limited by the no-discrimination principle or dormant Commerce Clause.[79] The Court gave short shrift to arguments that either discriminatory law was demonstrably justified.

The Court stated that its ruling did not call into question the validity of the three-tier system. It acknowledged the power conferred by the 21st Amendment included the authority to "assume direct control over liquor distribution ... or to funnel sales through the three tier system."[80] However, it does call into question residency requirements, license privileges conferred on each tier and not conferred on out-of-state licensees, physical premise requirements for licensee status, and reciprocity laws. The Court commented on reciprocal direct shipping laws as potentially generating the trade rivalries and animosities that the Commerce Clause forbids. The Court characterized "the current patchwork of laws—with some States banning direct shipments altogether, others doing so only for out-of-state wines, and still others require reciprocity— ... as the product of an ongoing, low-level trade war."[81]

Each side claimed victory. The Wine & Spirits Wholesalers of America (WSWA) press release is titled "Supreme Court Upholds States' Broad Authority to Regulate Alcohol,"[82] although Wine America describes the outcome as "favorable" and a landmark decision.[83]

Who won? The immediate impact of *Granholm* is on those states with laws discriminating in favor of local wineries by permitting them to ship direct to consumers. These states will need to level up by allowing all direct shipment or level down by prohibiting all direct shipment. In other words, the battle has shifted back to the statehouses. The reach of *Granholm* may extend far beyond wine shipping.

As pointed out by the dissent in *Granholm*, "[t]here is not warrant in the Act's text for treating regulated entities differently depending on their place in the distribution chain: the act applies in undifferentiated fashion to 'any person interested therein.'"[84] Viewed expansively, *Granholm* could stand for the proposition that as long as a state permits any player to sell alcohol without a face to face transaction, a state must allow anyone to exercise this privilege. To consummate the transaction, the seller may need to obtain a state license, but *Granholm* appears to say that a state cannot require a bricks and mortar presence within the state or require residency once the state has opened the door to a virtual transaction. Other state laws that discriminate against out of state alcohol products, suppliers, wholesalers, and retailers may be in jeopardy. The reach of *Granholm* will be interpreted by legislature and tested by courts in the years to come.

The first of such tests was decided by a federal district court in Washington,[85] where a major retailer challenged state law restrictions on trade in alcoholic beverages. The court held Washington laws permitting in-state wineries to sell direct to retailers while denying such privileges to out-of-state wineries violated the Commerce Clause and that such restraints were not a valid exercise of state power under the 21st Amendment. Then the Court held that the following state restraints *are preempted* by the Sherman Act and *not* saved by the 21st Amendment: post and hold requirements; requirements that beer and wine distributors charge uniform pricing to retailers; credit prohibitions; volume discount prohibitions; policies that require the same "delivered price" to retailers regardless of costs; central warehousing prohibitions; and mandatory minimum markups from producers to wholesalers and from wholesalers to retailers. The Court did dismiss the challenge on laws banning retail to retail sales. As in Washington, courts and regulators in Minnesota and Texas are heeding the message of *Granholm* and ending other exercises of state power to regulate alcohol sales and advertising.[86]

These courts are nodding to state power under the 21st Amendment to regulate the structure of importation and distribution of alcohol. In other words, a three-tier system preventing or limiting vertical integration can be imposed by states under the Constitution. However, a state cannot carve out exceptions to its system to benefit in-state interests. Likewise, states cannot overregulate or micromanage the sale and distribution of alcohol if such laws do not further the purposes underlying the 21st Amendment—temperance and orderly markets—and where a restraint's relevance to such goals cannot be substantiated. As a result, many similar state restraints on alcohol trade practices likely will be challenged in the coming months and years.

Conclusion

All stakeholders agree that regulation is needed to prevent sales to minors, reduce alcohol abuse, and create orderly systems of importation and distribution of alcohol and collect revenue. The vibrancy of current laws and regulations is under pressure from changing times and changing guards in the industry. Will the state power fade as a new generation of regulators, business owners, and consumers examine the rules without the vivid memory of the excesses that led to Prohibition? Will global businesses and consolidating tiers put sufficient pressure to bear on the system to force a more homogenized set of rules? Ultimately, will alcohol be marketed and sold like other commodities? The debate over direct shipment showed that profound change is not at hand, but that pressures are changing the contours of the trade in alcohol.

References

1. Linda Spath, librarian, contributed significantly to this effort. Additional support was provided by Karen Valter.
2. "Alcohol" will be used to generally refer to beer, wine, and spirits and beverages defined by federal and state law as intoxicating liquor in lieu of the more awkward expressions "beverage alcohol" or "alcoholic beverages."
3. Alcohol also is the cause or a contributing factor to significant harm to individuals, families, and society. The scope of this chapter does not include an analysis of such harm.
4. Beverage Dynamics (March 2005).
5. Gomberg, Frederickson, & Assoc. "2005 Report to Unified Symposium" (January 2005).
6. Motto, Kryler, and Fisher. "Report to California Association of Winegrape Growers and the Wine Institute" (2002).
7. "Brewer's Almanac." Beer Institute. http://www.beerinstitute.org.pdfs/production _of_ malt_beverages_ in _US.pdf (October 5, 2004). Production dropped significantly in the late 1980s. Id.
8. U.S. Dept. of Commerce, Bureau of Foreign & Domestic Commerce.
9. Calculated from data reported in Supermarket News (July 19, 2004) and U.S. 2002 Census population numbers. Note: This figure should be higher for imbibers because the average was not adjusted for the number of teetotalers.
10. 2004 revenues for Brown-Forman, Allied Domecq, PLC, and Constellation Brands, Inc., exceeded $2.5 billion, $5.8 billion, and $3.5 billion, respectively. DCA, February 28, 2005, Allied Domecq Plc; Hoover's Online Report Builder-Constellation Brands, Inc. (2004).
11. See e.g., Wal-Mart with 3,600 stores worldwide as of 2004 and 7-Eleven with 5,800 stores worldwide. Wal-Mart reported revenues of 258,681,000 in fiscal year 2004. Available online at: http://walmartstores.com (April 6, 2005); http://www.7_eleven.com (April 27, 2005).
12. "Top U.S. Wholesalers Keep Expanding as Big Changes Loom." Impact April 15, 2004 at 1, cited in Petitioner's Brief at 6, *Swedenberg v. Kelly* No. 03-1274.

13. Federal Excise Tax Reported to or Collected by the IRS, Fiscal Years 1996-2004." Available online at: http://www.taxpolicy center.org/TaxFacts/TFDB/Content/GIF/excise_type_2004.gif (June 16, 2005).

14. Based on data reported for Alaska, Arizona, Arkansas, California, Colorado, Connecticut, Delaware, the District of Columbia, Hawaii, Illinois, Indiana, Iowa, Kentucky, Massachusetts, Missouri, Montana, Nevada, New Hampshire, New York, Ohio, Pennsylvania, South Dakota, Texas, Utah, Vermont, Washington, and Wyoming.

15. Stryhorn, C. "Window on State Government."

16. Available online at: http://www.ca.gov. (June 14, 2005).

17. Illinois Dept. of Revenue. "2004 Annual Report." Available online at: http://www.ILtax.com (June 14, 2005). New York State Department of Taxation and Finance, "Annual Statistical Report—2003-2004 New York state Tax Collections" (March 2005).

18. USDA, 2007. ERS/USDA Data: Food Consumption (per capita) data system. Last updates Feb. 15, 2007.

19. Id.

20. Id.

21. Kobler, J. Ardent Sprits: The Rise and Fall of Prohibition. New York: G.P. Putnam's Sons, 1973: p. 350–1.

22. The FDA has concurrent jurisdiction over alcohol labeling. In a November 30, 1987, Memorandum of Understanding, the agencies clarified their roles. 52 Fed. Reg. 45502. The memorandum described the jurisdictional overlap between the FDA's authority to prevent adulteration in the food supply under the FDCA and the [TTB's] more general broadly worded mandate under the FAA Act. [TTB] agreed to promulgate labeling regulations "when FDA has determined that the presence of an ingredient in food products, including alcoholic beverages, poses a recognized public health problem." The agencies also agreed to "consult on a regular basis concerning the propriety of promulgating regulations concerning the labeling of other ingredients and substances for alcoholic beverages."

23. Congress was not in session when the states ratified the Twenty-first Amendment. President Roosevelt acted by executive order to create Federal Alcohol Control Administration pursuant to the National Recovery Act. Exec. Order No. 6474, December 4, 1933. This Act was declared unconstitutional by the Supreme Court. Schechter Bros. Poultry Corp. v. U.S. 295 U.S. 495 (1935).

24. In 1936, the Liquor Administration Act was passed creating an independent agency, but the Act never took effect because the triggering event—appointment of agency members by the President—never occurred. In 1940, the Agency was abolished and its functions transferred back to Treasury. From that time until 1972, the unit was within the Internal Revenue Service of the Department. 37 Fed. Reg. 11696 (June 10, 1972).

25. Available online at http://www.ttb.gov. (June 14, 2005).

26. 26 U.S.C.§§ 5001–5691 (1970).

27. 27 U.S.C. §§ 201-211 (1970).

28. 27 U.S.C. § 122 (1970).

29. Oregon Liquor Control Commission (OLCC) Administrative Overview, http://arcweb. sos.state.or.us/recmgmt/sched/special/state/overview/20010010olccadov.pdf accessed 7/31/2007.
30. Id.
31. Id.
32. Id.
33. Department of Revenue. "Learn About Liquor Distribution in Montana." Available online at http://mt.gov/revenue/forbusinesses/liquordistribution/learnaboutliquor distribution.asp accessed 7/31/2007.
34. Kansas Department of Revenue. "Alcoholic Beverage Control History of Alcoholic Beverages in Kansas." Available online at http://www.ksrevenue.org/abchistory.htm. accessed 7/31/2007.
35. Id.
36. Id.
37. Id.
38. Id.
39. Adams Beverage Group. "Control States Executive Forum." Available online at http://www.beveragenet.net/sw/2004/0409/0409exf.asp. (May 31, 2005).
40. See, e.g. 9 N.Y.Comp. Codes R & Regs. § 48.7 (CCH 2002).
41. See, e.g. Florida: 17 Fla. Stat. Ann. § 561.24 (1997) (prohibiting out of state manufacturers from obtaining a wholesale license); Massachusetts: 4B Ann. Laws of Mass., ch. 138 §§18, 18A (2003) (residency requirements).
42. Nelson, B. "A Model Winery Law" (2002). Available online at http://www.american wineries.org/issues/modellaw.descrip.pdf. (June 15, 2005).
43. In addition to licensing requirements and trade practice regulation, federal and state laws govern alcohol labeling and advertising. The FAA Act makes it unlawful to sell, ship, or receive any distilled spirits or wine unless such products are bottled, packaged, and labeled in strict conformity with the federal labeling regulations. 27 U.S.C. § 205 (e). A supplier must obtain prior approval of labels. Under federal laws, advertising of alcoholic beverages is unlawful unless the advertising meets regulatory standards for labeling and furthermore does not contain any statement inconsistent with the product labels. 27 U.S.C. § 205(f). Prior approval of advertisements is not required at the federal level. A supplier or wholesaler cannot stop at federal compliance. Thirty states require a supplier to register its labels. The majority of states require suppliers to file monthly reports or tax returns.
44. 27 U.S. C. 205 (b) (1970); 27 C.F.R. § 6.21-6.72 (1995).
45. 27 C.F.R.§ 6.81-6.102 (1995).
46. La. Reg. Title 55 Chapt, 3. § 317(B)(4)(5) (2002).
47. Cal. Bus. & Prof. Code §§ 25502-25503.37 (2001).
48. Cal. Code Regs. Tit. 4, Art. 16, Rule 106 (1998).
49. Tex. Alco. Bev. Code § 102.07(c) (1999).
50. La. Reg. Title 55 Chapt, 3. § 317 (2002).
51. Id.
52. See, e.g. Wash. Rev. Code § 66.28.180(1) (2004).
53. *California Retail Liquor Dealers Ass'n v. Midcal Aluminum, Inc.* 445 U.S. 97 (1980).

54. See, Wash. Admin. Code §§ 314-24-190(2004); 314-20-100 (2004). Wash. Rev. Code § 66.28.180 (2004).

55. *Costco Wholesale Corp. v. Maleng.* Case No. CV04-0360. Trial is scheduled for spring of 2006.

56. See, "Brief for the Wine and Spirits Wholesalers of America et al." filed in *Granholm v. Heald.*

57. Dual distributor appointments are prohibited in Alabama, Arkansas, Connecticut, Georgia, Idaho, Kansas, Maine, Maryland, Nevada, New Hampshire, North Carolina, Ohio, Tennessee, Vermont, and Virginia.

58. Conn. Gen. Stat § 30-17 (2004).

59. Id.

60. N.J Admin. Code tit. 13, § 13:2-18:1-18.8 (1995).

61. Id.

62. N.C. Gen. Stat. § 18 B-1201 (1983) (applies to wineries with more than 1,000 cases per year in local sales).

63. Id.

64. *Mt. Hood Beverage Co. v. Constellation Brands, Inc.*, 63 P.3d 779 (2003); *Kendall-Jackson Wine Estates, Ltd. v. Branson, et al.* 212 F. 3d 995 (7th Cir. 2000).

65. N.Y. Alco. Bev. Cont. Law §3(37) (2004).

66. Wine Institute. Available online at http://www.wineinstitute.org/californiawineimpact. pdf (last accessed August 31, 2007).

67. See, http://www.freethegrapes.org. (June 10, 2005).

68. See, http://www.wineisntute.org and http://www.family winemakers.org. (June 10, 2005).

69. See, http://www.wswa.org. (June 10, 2005)

70. See, e.g. *Dickerson v. Bailey*, 336 F. 3d 388 (5th Cir. 2003); *Bainbridge v. Bush*, 48 F. Supp. 2d (1306 (M.D. Fla. 2001), vacated and remanded sub nom by *Bainbridge v. Turner*, 311 F. 3d 1104 (11th Cir. 2002); *Bridenbaugh v. Freeman-Wilson*, 227 F. 3d 848 (7th Cir. 2000); *Beskind v. Easley*, 325 F. 3d 506 (4th Cir. 2003).

71. Hargrave, L. "Let It Flow." The New York Times, June 5, 2005.

72. *Granholm v. Heald*, 125 C. Ct. 1885, 1902 (2005).

73. Id., at 1897 quoting *Halliburton Oil Well Cementing Co. v. Reily*, 373 U.S. 64, 72 (1963).

74. Id., at 1902 quoting *Philadelphia v. New Jersey*, 437 U.S. 617, 624 (1978).

75. Id., at 1897.

76. Id., at 1904. The Court described State Bd. Of Equalization of *Cal. v. Young's Market Co.*, 299 U.S. 59 (1936) as "inconsistent" with the view that the 21st Amendment did not authorize discrimination.

77. Id., at 1904. See 44 *Liquormart, Inc. v. Rhode Island*, 517 U.S. 484 (1996) (First Amendment); Larking v. Grendel's Den, Inc., 459 U.S. 116 (1982) (Establishment Clause); Craig v. Boren, 429 U.S. 190 (1972); (Equal Protection) *Wisconsin v. Constineau*, 400 U.S. 433 (1971) (Due Process); and *Department of Revenue v. James B. Beam Distilling Co.*, 377 U.S. 341 (1964) (Import-Export).

78. Id., citing *Hostetter v. Idlewild Bon Voyage Liquor Corp.*, 377 U.S. 324 (1964).

79. Id., citing *Bacchus Imports, Ltd. v. Dias*, 468 U.S. 263 (1984) (Bacchus held that a Hawaiian excise tax on out of state producers that exempted local pineapple wine was discriminatory and unconstitutional).

80. Id. at 1897.

81. Id. at 1896.

82. Available online at http://www.wswa.org/public/media/20050516.html (May 16, 2005).

83. "Supreme Court Issues Favorable Decision on Direct-to Consumer Wine Shipping." Available online at http://www.wineamerica.org (May 16, 2005).

84. *Granholm v. Heald.* (J. Thomas dissenting), 125 S. Ct at 1918.

85. *Costco Wholesale Corp. v. Hoen, et al.* Case No. C04-360P (U.S.D.C. W.D. Wash. April 21, 2006).

86. *Wine Country Gift Baskets.com et al. v. Steen.* Case NO. 4:06-CV-232-A (U.S.D.C N.D. Tex. May 22, 2006).

Chapter 5

Policy, Regulation, and Legislation

Terrel L. Rhodes

Contents

I was born a teetotaler and I have been a teetotaler on principle all my life. Neither my father nor his father ever tasted a drop of intoxicating liquor. I could hope that the same might be true of my children and their children. It is my earnest conviction that total abstinence is the wisest, best, and safest position for both the individual and society. But the regrettable failure of the Eighteenth Amendment has demonstrated the fact that the majority of the people of this country are not yet ready for total abstinence, at least when it is attempted through legal coercion. The next best thing — many people think it a better thing — is temperance.

–**John D. Rockefeller, Jr.**
(1933, Toward Liquor Control, p. vii)

Nothing is more attractive to the benevolent vanity of men than the notion that they can effect great improvement in society by the simple process of forbidding all wrong conduct, or conduct that they think is wrong, by law, and of enjoining all good conduct by the same means.

–**James Coolidge Carter as quoted in Fosdick (1933)**

Part of the ability of the nation to reverse course on the prohibition of alcohol manufacture and sales was the realization by powerful individuals such as Rockefeller that government could have only a limited impact on the behavior of citizens, especially when it came to regulating behavior that was widely accepted. In reality, it was a realization that law in and of itself cannot succeed without popular acceptance of the underlying principles associated with the law. As the authors of the *Toward Liquor Control* report declared in their first chapter, "We have labored under a belief that law could be used as a short cut to a desired end and that the agencies—for example, the home, the school, the church—could be subordinated to a speedier process" (Fosdick & Scott, 1933, p. 6).[2]

Although the authors, and Rockefeller, admitted the failure of Prohibition and the lawlessness or increased disregard for the law that it engendered, they still worked to develop model liquor control laws as a substitute for prohibition. The model laws developed by the Rockefeller supported Institute for Public Administration and published through the National Municipal League continue to form the basis for current legislation, regulation, and policy in the United States. The shifts in the national approach to the liquor "problem" have resulted in partial success for some of the objectives of the 1934 reformers, but in other ways have witnessed limited impact for other important aspects of alcohol control. The model laws have restored widespread acceptance and compliance with liquor control laws and policies, but have done little to enhance public health and temperance.

The language of the 18th Amendment only prohibited the "manufacture, sale or transportation" of "intoxicating liquors," not the possession, consumption, or home production. Introduced in 1917, adopted in January 1919 by Congress, and implemented in 1920, the 18th Amendment was in force for thirteen years.

States enjoyed concurrent enforcement powers over liquor control with the federal government.

Signifying the shifting political scene, Franklin Roosevelt campaigned against Prohibition in the 1932 presidential election. The 21st Amendment to repeal the 18th (Prohibition) Amendment was adopted as part of the Constitution in 1933 through 35 state referenda passed by vote of the people by three to one average vote margins. It is noteworthy that the repeal of Prohibition, which at the time was broadly disregarded, was accomplished through referenda in the states, not by state legislative action, thus permitting elected state legislators to avoid going on record either for or against repeal. The referenda, as with *Toward Liquor Control,* were consummate recognition of political realities.

Although Prohibition did not intrude on personal *behavior* per se in that it did not prohibit individual manufacture of alcohol, its possession, or consumption, the law did have a substantial unintended impact on the behavior of many in society. The laws on the control, manufacture, sale, and transportation of alcohol created monetary incentives for law breaking that ultimately lead to its repeal. So it was no mistake that the 1934 report had two objectives: 1) The abolition of lawlessness and 2) the focusing of all the forces of society on the development of self-control and temperance in the use of alcoholic beverages (Fosdick and Scott, p. ix).

With repeal of the 18th Amendment, "alcohol control" became the political and policy catchwords. The federal government would control the legal production of spirits, wine, and beer, and regulate the purity and alcoholic content of beverages. Primary regulatory powers would eventually be placed in the U.S. Treasury Department's office of Alcohol, Tobacco, and Firearms, recognizing the revenue as well as the enforcement components of alcohol control at the federal level. At the state level, power devolved for the creation of local option laws, retail monopolies, and taxation. State Alcohol Control Boards were created to oversee regulation in each state (Levine 1980).

Since Prohibition, policy and legislation have largely focused on regulation of access and distribution and taxes to raise revenue, not necessarily on controlling drinking.

Beer, Wine, and Spirits

The model alcohol control laws that grew out of the recommendations of the *Toward Liquor Control* report and disseminated by the National Municipal League, still form the basis for current law and policy. A particular recommendation of the report and the model laws was to treat beer, wine, and spirits differently. Beer was defined as "regular strength" malt beverages with an alcohol content between 3.9 and 6 percent alcohol by volume. Beer was the least intoxicating form of alcohol and was the most common and widely available. Wine was referred to as "table wine" with an alcohol content between 7 and 14 percent alcohol by volume. This moderately intoxicating alcoholic beverage occupied the middle ground in the new lexicon of regulation. Spirits referred to distilled spirits and fortified wines with a high alcohol content between 26 and 50 percent alcohol by content. Spirits had become the major source of profits for bootleggers under Prohibition and continued to reserve the primary concern of the new approaches to controlling alcohol consumption after repeal.

As the alcohol content decreased, the seeming importance of control of the beverage also decreased. Beer was viewed as the least troublesome alcoholic beverage and the most readily available at the lowest cost. Beer became the alcohol choice of the working class, whereas spirits and wine were often more expensive and preferred by the economic and social elites that had formulated the policies. The new, more pragmatic approach to the control of alcohol reflected the drinking habits of the population more than any overriding presumptions about moral behavior. The difference in type of alcoholic beverage and the realities surrounding its manufacture, transportation, and clientele were reflected in the development of each sector of the control systems that emerged across the country.

In the years immediately following repeal of the 18th Amendment, the distilled liquor (spirits) industry became quickly concentrated in a handful of large corporations that operated on a national and international scale. Spirits were more easily transported and preserved for long periods and over long distances and not as subject to changes in climate and temperature. Beer, on the other hand, was typically locally produced and required more immediate shipment because it was often not pasteurized and was subject to deterioration from temperature change and movement over long distances. Multiple regional brewers developed, but these large regional firms tended to force out smaller brewers with less capability to produce and distribute quantities of beer. Wine was a relatively small portion of the alcoholic beverage market in the early to mid twentieth century because most wine was imported from abroad or manufactured in small quantities as "sweet" wines. As the domestic wine industry grew and established itself on both coasts of the country, it gained in market share through the introduction of a broad range of low cost wines in addition to high-end varieties.

What Is Happening at the State Level?

Alcohol policy and legislation over the last third of the twentieth century has centered on four major areas: distribution systems, purchase and sales of alcohol, taxation, and drinking and driving. In a comprehensive study of all fifty states, the University of Minnesota's Alcohol Epidemiology Program examined state session laws, statutes, case law, and regulatory laws between 1968 and 2000. The study did not examine local ordinances (Wagenaar 2000).

Although there is variation in the particulars of regulations and policies among the states, primary policy activities have involved regulation of alcohol distribution (accounting for close to half of all policies) and regulation of drinking and driving (accounting for approximately one quarter of alcohol control policies). In contrast, alcohol prevention programs accounted for only 4 percent and taxation and fees for only 3 percent of policy activity in the states during the last thirty years of the twentieth century.

The largest arena for state legislation pertains to issues related to distribution. *Distribution systems* are regulated in two ways: either through what is termed *control* or through *licensure.* Some states directly control the pricing of alcoholic beverages through operating state or agency stores or through establishing retail prices—these states are considered to be *control* states; whereas states that operate indirectly to control alcohol distribution and sales through private businesses typically sell licenses to private providers.

Only eighteen of the fifty states and the District of Columbia are classified as *control* states. Seven of the eighteen—Alabama, Iowa, Maine, Mississippi, Virginia, West Virginia, and Wyoming—exercise control at the wholesale market level for moderate or high alcohol content beverages. The other eleven *control* states involve *both* wholesale and retail sales of moderate (wine) and high (spirits) alcohol content beverages (New Hampshire, Pennsylvania, and Utah) or *only* high alcohol content beverages (Idaho, Michigan, Montana, North Carolina, Ohio, Oregon, Vermont, and Washington). The remaining states and the District of Columbia are *licensure* states.

Studies have found that when states move from a *control* system to a *licensure* system that overall sale of alcoholic beverages increases significantly (Toomey et al., 1993; Toomey and Wagenaar 1999). The state *control* system does seem to exercise a degree of restraint in the availability of alcoholic beverages (e.g., it is not viewed as desirable for the state when it exercises substantial direct control to advertise spirits or to be too actively engaged in encouraging "sinful" behavior). Licensure of private establishments, on the other hand, allows private enterprise to seek profits through lengthened store hours, lower prices, more outlets, and increased marketing and advertising of alcoholic beverages and hence greater availability to consumers.

Drinking and driving laws are probably the most visible and discussed aspect of liquor control policy and the second most frequent area for legislation and policy proposals. Drinking and driving regulations revolve around blood alcohol content (BAC) standards. In 1968, most states allowed BAC limits of 0.14 g/dL to 0.09 g/dL. In 1991, Congress began to offer monetary incentives for states to lower acceptable BAC levels by offering supplemental highway grants to those who lowered BAC for youths to 0.02 g/dL (23 USCA 410). In 1994, Congress made 5 percent of a state's highway transportation grant contingent on adopting laws by 1998 setting youth BAC at 0.02 g/dL or lower (23 USCA 161). With the passage of the U.S. Transportation Appropriations bill S.2720 in the year 2000, all states were given until 2004 to reduce BAC limits for adults to 0.08 g/dL or face reduced federal transportation funding in their states.

The focus on limiting BAC is based on years of study by the National Highway Transportation Administration (2000) and others confirming that an individual's balance, vision, and intellectual functioning are significantly impaired at BAC levels of 0.08 g/dL and higher. The evidence further suggests that reducing BAC levels to 0.02 g/dL for youth significantly reduced fatal and nonfatal traffic accidents, especially when coupled with educational and public information campaigns (Blomberg 1992; Hingson 1994).

Although substantially smaller as a proportion of alcohol control activity in recent years, the *purchase and sales* of alcohol still occupy attention even though the basic rules surrounding purchase and sales are broadly set and accepted. These laws are usually associated with who can buy alcohol when and where (e.g., legal drinking ages, hours of operation, type of establishment, presence or absence of food, types and amounts of beverages). The stated intent of controlling purchase and sales has not been to end consumption of alcoholic beverages, but rather to limit the usage by restricting the amount and availability of beverages. In recent years, legislation and policy in this area has focused on keg registration and server training.

Although local ordinances existed in many places, Oregon in 1978 was the first state to adopt a statewide keg registration law. Approximately one fourth of the states now have keg laws and regulations. Because research studies demonstrated that youth consumption of alcohol declined with higher alcoholic beverage prices and less availability, keg registration laws were prompted by the desire to inhibit the availability of low-cost beer for youth parties, especially for off-premises consumption (Grossman et al., 1994; Jones-Webb et al., 1997). The argument was presented that by tracking the purchaser of beer kegs, the responsibility for intoxication, and underage drinking could be more readily ascertained or restricted.

Focusing on a different aspect of purchase and sales, the restriction of on-premises consumption of alcoholic beverages for legal consumers in particular has been approached in recent years through the adoption of either mandatory or voluntary server training programs. The policies surrounding serving alcoholic beverages placed a responsibility, including potential legal liability on the person serving the alcohol to another person who subsequently was involved in an accident or arrest while under the influence of alcohol. By making clear the legal consequences for the seller or supplier of serving alcohol to intoxicated individuals, the expected outcome was that less alcohol would be consumed and fewer intoxicated individuals would result, especially intoxicated drivers. Slightly fewer than half of the states have adopted server training programs, with approximately half adopting mandatory requirements and half relying on voluntary compliance as a way to limit server and seller liability.

Evidence of the effectiveness of server training programs is mixed, although the trend is for states to adopt such regulations. Toomey et al. (1998) have found that, regardless of the variation in extent and quality of server training programs, the active involvement of management was particularly important for an effective server training program to have the desired impact of fewer inebriated customers.

A final area of alcohol control policy and at times animated debate is *taxes*. Taxes have become one of the accepted components of alcohol control policy. Revenue generation from the 1934 report to today has never been the primary rationale for taxing alcohol, but it has become a frequent and widely accepted form of taxation for government. The actual price of alcohol has declined since 1970 in relation to cost of living and cost of non-alcoholic beverages.

Alcohol taxes, along with taxes on cigarettes and gambling, have been labeled "sin" taxes (i.e., assessed only against those who decide to engage in a behavior considered to be immoral by many). The argument that adults should be able to decide to engage in these behaviors or not depending on their own moral codes has been legally and politically successful. But it is also accepted that those who do engage in these activities should pay a higher price through taxes to help defray the costs of policing the provisions and the consequences of engaging in the behavior. The actual amount of tax assessed tends to depend on the type of alcoholic beverage—beer, wine, and spirits are taxed at different rates—and are calculated differently in different states (e.g., on the quantity sold or as a percentage of the sale price).

Toomey and Wagenaar (1999) and others have found that traffic accidents, violent crime, and cirrhosis of the liver decline with increased taxes and thus increased price of alcoholic beverages. Price elasticity seems to be particularly important when considering youth consumption. Despite the evidence of a direct relationship between price and consumption, states have not seemed to use taxation as a way to maintain or increase the cost of alcoholic beverages. The University of Minnesota's Alcohol Epidemiology Program found in their 2000 study of beer taxes that in most states, the adjusted-for-inflation taxes on beer have typically decreased in relation to 1968, suggesting that higher alcohol taxes have not been used as part of overall policy to restrict consumption. It is likely that the same trend holds true for wine and spirits, although it is more difficult to make the comparisons because of the differential methods of taxing and the *control* vs. *licensure* approaches to distribution systems.

State policies during the past several decades have changed as states have recognized and tried to address aspects of alcohol related issues and problems. The policy changes also highlight many of the challenges in formulating and implementing alcohol control policy. For example, the total prohibition of sale and manufacture of alcoholic beverages is not an option since the repeal of Prohibition. The ensuing efforts to control alcohol consumption have tended to focus on those areas where there is broad public support (e.g., placing limits on youth to buy and consume alcohol, but not purposefully raising the price of alcoholic beverages through taxation even when the evidence suggests that increased prices for alcoholic products, such as beer, are associated with reduced consumption). In other words, limiting the ability to purchase beer would affect all consumers, not just youth (who are not supposed to be able to buy beer anyway). Raising both the opposition of adult consumers, especially those of more limited means who may not be able to afford more expensive alcoholic beverages, as well as the manufacturers and distributors of beer who may see reduced consumption as reducing their profits, appears to have limited taxation as a primary means for alcohol control.

Federal Policy and Legislation

The 2002 National Survey on Drug Use and Health (NSDUH) conducted by the Substance Abuse and Mental Health Services Administration (SAMHSA) of the U.S. Department of Health and Human Services, reported that more than half of the U.S. population 12 and older are current drinkers of alcohol and that almost half of those reported binge drinking (five or more drinks on the same occasion) within the past thirty days. For individuals over the age of 21, approximately 60 percent are current drinkers. Any federal policy or legislation is constructed with the reality that a clear majority of the population will be affected by alcohol control legislation or regulation.

During 2002 and 2003, there were 1,639 bills and regulations adopted by the federal government and the states that in some manner directly related to alcohol policy (National Institute of Alcohol Abuse 2004). Of those, only 15 were federal regulations or laws. At the federal level, these regulations and laws ranged from the Department of the Treasury's Bureau of Alcohol, Tobacco, and Firearms' regulation to add "tannat" to the prime grape variety names for use in designating American wines, to the U.S. Congress' No Child Left Behind Act (PL 107-110) requiring each local educational agency desiring assistance to submit application to state educational agencies to permit funds to be used for:

- coordination of health and social services for individuals returning from incarceration if there is likelihood that such services, including drug and alcohol counseling, will improve likelihood these individuals would complete their education;
- requiring correctional facilities receiving funds to provide transition assistance to help youth stay in school, including assistance in accessing drug and alcohol abuse prevention programs;
- exempting teachers' limitations on liability for misconduct when under the influence of intoxicating alcohol;
- establishing toll free hotlines for students to report substance abuse; and
- providing grants to reduce alcohol abuse, including through such means as mentoring programs.

The vast majority of both federal and state policy and legislative actions related to alcohol control are minor adjustments to existing policies, regulations, and laws. Federal activity is especially modest when it comes to alcohol control, especially beyond issues related to youth drinking.

Effects of Alcohol Controls

In recent decades, a substantial literature evaluating the effects of alcohol controls has emerged. Several reviews of this literature have appeared (e.g., Smith 1988). A number of conclusions about the effects of alcohol controls emerge from these studies:

■ Under all circumstances so far measured, raising the price of alcoholic beverages reduces the consumption, when other factors are unchanged. Because alcoholic beverages, and particularly the most popular type of beverage in a given society, are often not very price elastic, raising alcohol taxes will usually both add to government revenues and modestly reduce the level of consumption. It appears that the effect on heavy drinkers' consumption is at least as strong proportionately as the effect on light drinkers' consumption.

■ Other alcohol control measures that limit alcohol's availability in terms of time, place, and manner of sale or in terms of the buyer's eligibility (e.g., minimum purchase age, alcohol rationing) often—though not always—affect the level of consumption. The effects seem to be stronger in situations of restricted availability than in situations of relatively free availability.

■ There is little concrete evidence of a positive effect of controls on the advertising or presentation of alcoholic beverages (e.g., warning labels on bottles, warning signs in stores) on levels of consumption.

■ From a policy perspective, the effects of alcohol controls on rates of health and social problems are arguably more important than the effects on consumption levels. The rates of various alcohol-related problems—alcohol-related traffic casualties, cirrhosis deaths, violent crime rates—are often affected by alcohol controls. The effect of price and availability controls on rates of alcohol-related problems is often stronger than the effects on consumption levels. This suggests that some alcohol controls may have an especially strong effect on vulnerable subpopulations (e.g., those at risk of death from cirrhosis) or may push consumption into less risky locales or forms (it may be that the main effect of raising the U.S. drinking age has been in part separating teenage drinking from driving).

Smith's conclusions are based on examination of a broadly conceived, multinational literature. Most of the study designs rely on strong research designs, studying changes over time in given societies or localities, often with a comparison of changes in control societies or localities. The limitations of the literature evaluating the effects of alcohol controls should be kept in mind.

■ Most of the studies have been carried out in societies with a strong tradition of concern about alcohol problems—notably in Nordic and English-speaking countries. These are societies in which there is a long tradition of state oversight of the alcohol supply, and in which home production of alcoholic beverages is much less important than in many developing countries. There is reason to believe that the relations of alcohol controls with some alcohol problems is affected by the cultural position of alcohol and the level of concern about drinking—e.g., the relation of consumption levels with violent crime may be stronger in societies that define alcohol as a powerful and criminogenic substance.

■ The most broad-ranging segment of the literature concerns the effects of prices and taxes on consumption levels. The literature on the effects of raising and lowering drinking ages is very well developed, but is almost entirely based on North American experience. More generally, the literature relies heavily on "natural experiments:" on studying changes in alcohol availability and controls which occur as policy decisions, rather than an experimental intervention. This means that alcohol control measures are only studied when and to the extent they are politically feasible somewhere. The general trend toward liberalizing alcohol controls in the last forty years means that, except for taxes and minimum drinking ages, there are more studies of the effects of loosening than of tightening alcohol controls. Thus, too, the literature on unpopular restrictive measures, even those, such as alcohol rationing, which seem likely to affect alcohol-problems rates, is not very developed.

■ As is true more generally for evaluation studies, studies of the effects of alcohol controls provide much stronger evidence on short-term than on long-term effects. An effect that is immediate and discontinuous is more measurable than an effect which is delayed and gradual. This limitation of the technology of evaluation tends to favor measures where the postulated connection between control and consumption is immediate and mechanical over measures where the postulated connection is more distal and diffuse. Thus, for instance, we might expect the effects of a price rise or the closing of the liquor store on the corner to be inherently more detectable than the effects of a change in advertising regulations (Smith, 1998, p. 682).

Conclusions

What have alcohol control legislation and regulation accomplished since the repeal of Prohibition and the publication of the landmark *Toward Liquor Control*?

The first objective—to reduce lawlessness—has indeed been accomplished. Alcohol control policies have reduced lawlessness—bootleggers and crime syndicates trafficking in alcohol are out of business for the most part. People accept most alcohol control policies and laws and penalties are relatively light (e.g., fines, driver's license suspensions, short jail terms). The legal drinking age is honored most of time, but not always. The off-premises sale and availability has shifted much alcohol-related behavior to the home where public control is mostly absent. In short, most laws related to alcohol control are obeyed. One major exception

Table 5.1   Alcohol Use in Lifetime among Persons Age 12 to 17 and Persons Age 18 to 25 during the Years 1966 to 2002, by Gender: Percentages, Based on 2002 National Survey on Drug Use and Health

Year	Age 12 to 17			Age 18 to 25		
	Total	Male	Female	Total	Male	Female
1966	17.9	25.3	10.9	70.5	79.1	62.9
1970	20.8	27.4	14.2	75.3	83.8	67.5
1974	29.0	36.0	22.5	79.5	87.1	72.2
1978	29.2	36.2	22.7	82.5	89.3	75.8
1982	30.3	35.6	25.1	83.9	87.9	80.0
1986	30.6	36.7	24.5	82.2	87.2	77.6
1990	28.9	34.1	24.0	80.9	85.7	76.3
1994	28.1	30.9	25.2	81.8	86.4	77.2
1998	31.2	33.4	29.0	82.0	85.2	78.9
2002	43.4	43.4	43.4	86.7	88.0	85.4

Source: Table 47.2B, Substance Abuse and Mental Health Services Administration, Office of Applied Studies, National Survey on Drug Use and Health, Washington, D.C.: U.S. Department of Health & Human Services, 2002.

Note: Percentages are calculated using a weighted ratio estimate where the numerator is the weighted sum of all lifetime users within each age group for a specific year and the denominator is the weighted sum of all persons within each age group for the same year. Lifetime drug use status and age group, for each specified year, were determined using the age, date of first use, and interview date for each respondent. See *Results from the 2002 National Survey on Drug Use and Health: National Findings.*

is the legal age restrictions, the one remaining form of prohibition, which seems to work the least well. As Table 5.1 indicates, a large and growing proportion of underage youths continue to report using alcohol.

The second objective—to encourage temperance—has not been successful. Alcohol control policies are not designed to stop drinking or abstinence, but to promote the orderly, quiet, and socially acceptable production, sale, and consumption of alcohol. Decriminalization of most alcohol consumption, production and sales, and the creation of laws that are perceived as not too restrictive has turned alcohol into a major industry with its own legitimate economic and business elite interested in maintaining order and obedience to law to preserve profits.

The 1934 report even argues that reducing habitual drinking and prevention would really have to come from other agencies/entities (e.g., home, church, family, public health professionals). The creation in 1971 of the National Institute on Alcohol Abuse and Alcoholism was a formal effort to record alcohol trends and occurrences with a goal of alcohol abuse prevention. Although there have been some efforts to promote health concerns related to alcohol consumption and there is strong popular support for some public health concerns (e.g., package labeling and drunk-driving laws), the alcohol industry typically has resisted most efforts to diminish alcohol consumption. Public support for alcohol policies to limit drinking is fairly broad but variable (i.e., 88 percent support labeling, 82 percent support more prevention, 80 percent server training, 60 percent counter ads, 43 percent more taxes, 35 percent restricted store hours, 31 percent higher drinking age [Geisbrecht and Greenfield 1999]).

Repeal did turn consumption away from hard liquor to beer. Decriminalization and regulation turned a crime-ridden problem of violence that some argued could not be changed to something that is manageable, routine, and generally accepted. The patterns of legislative activity suggest that we will see little beyond tinkering with the current alcohol control policies. More emphasis will be placed on public health, but much of any success in this arena will likely be driven by economic benefits from reducing the costs of health and insurance through further controlling alcohol consumption.

The example of alcohol control policy in this country is illustrative of the balance among competing interests. As with tobacco control, there is an age limit, excise taxes are collected, sales are regulated, and restrictions exist for sale, use, and consumption of the product. Public health campaigns for tobacco have had an impact on behavior and resulted in declining sales that have been partially offset by increased international sales. The alcohol industry is wary of public health campaigns because of the same fear of reduced sales, but without the opportunity for increased international markets because many other countries have established international and domestic alcohol industries. The approach to alcohol control might also be a promising approach to illegal drug control. Many of the same arguments for continuing the prohibition on existing illegal drugs are the same raised about alcohol (e.g., it is addictive, it destroys families, it is immoral, it will corrupt children). Prohibition policies on illegal drugs have resulted in many of the same evils found with alcohol prohibition, violence, disrespect for law, increased law enforcement costs, lack of control over purity, and spread of disease. Although addiction and destruction of families would be likely to continue as it did with alcohol, legalization and regulation might actually decrease the likelihood of these consequences through controlling the strength and availability in ways to address the negative effects of drugs. There is experience in other countries with legalized drug control, and the experience from alcohol legalization in the United States suggests that the benefits might indeed outweigh the negatives, but the political will is not there because a much smaller proportion of the population uses drugs than uses alcohol. The power of public health programs and campaigns against lawlessness can have a strong impact on legislation and policy change as witnessed through alcohol control. It is likely that any major changes in current alcohol policy will result from increased public recognition of health risks and costs that begin to affect their own behaviors in relation to alcohol.

Digital Alcohol Control Policy Resources

Federal Alcohol Law Decisions

Recent U.S. Supreme Court Alcohol Law decisions: Legal Information Institute (LII) http://supct.law.cornell.edu/supct/
Recent Appellate Court Alcohol Law decisions: LII http://www.law.cornell.edu:9999/ USCA-ALL/results.html?search=alcohol%20cigarette%20television%20pictures

U.S. Constitutional Alcohol Law Provisions

18th Amendment, Prohibition: http://www.law.cornell.edu/constitution/constitution. amendmentxviii.html
21st Amendment, Repeal of Prohibition: http://www.law.cornell.edu/constitution/constitution. amendmentxxi.html

Federal Statutes and Regulations Related to Alcohol

Liquor Traffic: U.S. Code, Title 18, Chapter 59 http://uscode.house.gov/title_18.htm
Alcohol and Drug Abuse Educational Programs and Activities: U.S. Code, Title 21, Chapter 14 http://www4.law.cornell.edu/uscode/21/ch14.html
President's Media Commission on Alcohol and Drug Abuse Prevention: U.S. Code, Title 21, Chapter 18 http://www4.law.cornell.edu/uscode/21/ch18.html
Intoxicating Liquors: U.S. Code, Title 27 http://www4.law.cornell.edu/uscode/27/
Alcohol and Tobacco: U.S. Code of Federal Regulations, Title 27 http://cfr.law.cornell. edu/cfr/cfr.php?title=27

Federal Alcohol Law Web Resources

Bureau of Alcohol, Tobacco, and Firearms: http://www.atf.gov/
Drug Enforcement Administration: http://www.atf.gov/
U.S. Department of Agriculture: http://www.usda.gov/
U.S. Department of Justice: http://www.usdoj.gov/

Alcohol Law Web Sites

Alcoholic Beverage Control Authorities: Directory of Agencies for All States: http://www. wineinstitute.org/shipwine/state_abcz/abcz.htm

Alcohol Epidemiology Program (AEP): http://www.epi.umn.edu/alcohol/default.html
  AEP Database of Enacted Alcohol Legislation for 1998, 1999, and 2000: http://www.epi.umn.edu/enacted/
  AEP Pathfinder for Research of Alcohol Law in the United States: http://www.epi.umn.edu/alcohol/pathfinder/pathfinder.html

Alcohol Law Legislation (Australian Site): http://www.murdoch.edu.au/elaw/indices/subject/827.html

Alcohol Problems and Solutions: Law and Policy: http://www2.potsdam.edu/alcohol-info/LawAndPolicy.html

Alcohol and Temperance History Group: http://www.athg.org/

American Beverage Licenses: http://www.ablusa.org/home.asp

Beer Institute: http://www.beerinstitute.org/

Beverage Net: http://www.beveragenet.net/home.asp

Brewer's Association of America: http://www.brewersadvocate.org/

Center for Substance Abuse Research (University of Maryland): http://www.cesar.umd.edu/

Coalition for Free Trade: http://www.coalitionft.org/

Direct Shipment Laws by State for Wineries: http://www.wineinstitute.org/shipwine/analysis/intro_analysis.htm

Distilled Spirits Council of the United States: http://www.discus.org/

Lawyers Specializing in Alcohol Beverage Law: http://www.wineinstitute.org/shipwine/lawyers_and_legislature/lawyers.htm

National Association of American Wineries: http://www.americanwineries.org/

State Wine Excise Tax Rates: http://www.taxadmin.org/fta/rate/wine.html

Wine Institute: http://www.wineinstitute.org/

World Association of the Alcohol Beverage: Industries http://www.waabi.org/

WSWA Direct Shipping Litigation: http://www.wswa.org/public/legal/direct.html

Related MegaLaw Resources

MegaLaw Drunk Driving Law: http://www.megalaw.com/top/drunkdriving.php

MegaLaw Tobacco Law: http://www.megalaw.com/top/tobacco.php

MegaLaw Toxic Torts: http://www.megalaw.com/top/toxtort.php

State Laws Regarding Alcohol

Alabama: Title 28 http://www.legislature.state.al.us/CodeofAlabama/1975/coatoc.htm

Alaska: Title 4 http://www.touchngo.com/lglcntr/akstats/Statutes/Title04.htm

Arizona: Title 4 http://www.azleg.state.az.us/ars/4/title4.htm

Arkansas: Title 3 http://www.arkleg.state.ar.us

California: (scroll down to Title 4) http://ccr.oal.ca.gov/cgi-bin/

Colorado: Article 12, Title 47 (searchable index) http://www.megalaw.com/co/cocode.php

Connecticut: Title 30 http://www.cga.state.ct.us/2001/pub/Title30.htm
Delaware: Title 4 http://www.megalaw.com/de/de.php
District of Columbia: Title 25 http://www.megalaw.com/dc/dc.php
Florida: Title 34 http://www.megalaw.com/fl/TitleXXXIV
Georgia: Title 3 (searchable index) http://www.megalaw.com/ga/ga.php
Hawaii (Division 1, Title 16): (searchable index) http://www.capitol.hawaii.gov/site1/docs/
   docs.asp?press1=docs percent20
Idaho: Title 23 http://www3.state.id.us/idstat/TOC/23FTOC.html
Illinois: Chapter 235 http://www.legis.state.il.us/legislation/
Montana: Title 16
Nebraska: Chapter 53
Nevada: Title 52, Chapter 597 (searchable index)
New Hampshire: Title 13
New Jersey: Title 33, Chapter 1 (searchable index)
New Mexico: Chapter 44-7-1 to 44-7-22
New York: Chapter 3B
North Carolina: Chapter 18B
North Dakota: Title 5 (PDF)
Ohio: Title 43 http://www.megalaw.com/oh/oh.php
Oklahoma: Title 37 (searchable index) http://oklegal.onenet.net/statutes.basic.html
Oregon: Chapters 471–475 http://landru.leg.state.or.us/ors/
Pennsylvania: Title 47 http://members.aol.com/StatutesP3/47.html
Indiana: Title 7.1 http://www.state.in.us/legislative/ic/code/title7.1/
Iowa: Title IV, Subtitle 1 (searchable index) http://www.legis.state.ia.us/IACODE/ 1999
   SUPPLEMENT/IV.html
Kansas: Chapter 41 http://www.ink.org/public/legislative/statutes
Kentucky: Title XX (PDF) http://www.megalaw.com/ky/ky.php
Louisiana: (searchable index) http://www.legis.state.la.us/tsrs/search.htm
Maine: Title 28 & 28A http://janus.state.me.us/legis/statutes/
Maryland: (Alcoholic Beverages) http://www.megalaw.com/md/md.php
Massachusetts: Chapter 138 http://www.megalaw.com/ma/ma.php
Michigan: Chapter 436 http://www.michiganlegislature.org/mileg.asp?page=ChapterIndex
Minnesota: Chapter 340 http://www.revisor.leg.state.mn.us/stats/
Mississippi: Title 67 http://www.megalaw.com/ms/ms.php
Missouri: Title XX
Rhode Island: Title 3
South Carolina: Title 61 http://legis.state.sd.us/statutes/Index.cfm?FuseAction=Display
   Statute&FindType=Statute&txtStatute=35
South Dakota: Title 35
Tennessee: Title 57
Texas: http://www.megalaw.com/tx/txcodefiles.php?file=http://www.capitol.state.tx.us/statutes/
   abtoc.html
Utah: Title 32A http://www.le.state.ut.us/ percent7Ecode/TITLE32A/TITLE32A.htm
Vermont: Title 7 http://www.leg.state.vt.us/statutes/sections.cfm?Title=07&Chapter=001
Virginia: Title 4.1 http://legis.state.va.us/Laws/CodeofVa.htm
Washington: Title 66 http://www.leg.wa.gov/rcw/index.cfm

West Virginia: Chapter 60 http://www.megalaw.com/wv/wv.php
Wisconsin: Chapter 125 http://www.legis.state.wi.us/rsb/Statutes.html
Wyoming: Title 12 http://legisweb.state.wy.us/statutes/sub12.htm

Bibliography

Blomberg, R. D. *Lower BAC Limits for Youth: Evaluation of the Maryland '02 Law.* Washington, D.C.: National Highway Traffic Safety Administration, 1992.

Edwards, G., et al. *Alcohol Policy and the Public Good.* Oxford: Oxford University Press, 1994.

Engs, Ruth S. (ed.) 1990. *Controversies in the Addiction's Field.* Dubuque, IA: Kendall-Hunt.

Fosdick, Raymond B. and Albert L. Scott 1933. *Toward Liquor Control.* New York: Harper & Brothers.

Giesbrecht, N. and T. K. Greenfield. "Public Opinions on Alcohol Policy Issues: Comparison of American and Canadian Surveys." *Addiction* 94 (1999): 521–31.

Greenfield, Thomas K. 2000. Alcohol Policy (lecture). Berkley, CA: The Alcohol Research Group of the Public Health Institute.

Grossman, M., F. J. Chaloupka, H. Saffer, and A. Laixuthai. "Alcohol Price Policy and Youths: A Summary of Economic Research." *Journal of Research on Adolescence* 4:2 (1994): 347–64.

Hingson, R., T. Heeren, and M. Winter. "Effects of Lower Legal Blood Alcohol Limits for Young and Adult Drivers." *Alcohol, Drugs and Driving* 10:3/4 (1994): 243–52.

Jones-Webb, J. R., T. L. Toomey, K. Miner, A. C. Wagenaar, M. Wolfson, and R. Poon. "Why and in What Contexts Adolescents Obtain Alcohol from Adults: A Pilot Study." *Substance Abuse and Misuse* 32:2 (1997): 219–28.

Levine, H. G. "On the History and Aims of Alcohol Control System: A Personal Note." Berkley, CA: Social Research Group, 1980.

Moore, M. and Gerstein, D. 1981. Alcohol and Public Policy: Beyond the Shadow of Prohibition. Washington, D.C.: National Academy Press. Alcohol and Health: Ninth Special Report to the U.S. Congress. Rockville, MD: The U.S. Department of Health and Human Services.

National Highway Transportation Administration. *Traffic Tech: A Review of the Literature on the Effects of BACs of .08 and Lower.* (May). Technology Transfer Series No. 223. Washington, D.C.: Department of Transportation, 2000.

National Institute on Alcohol Abuse and Alcoholism, U.S. Department of Health and Human Services. APIS, 2004.

National Institute on Alcohol Abuse and Alcoholism. *Ninth Annual Special Report to the U.S. Congress on Alcohol and Health.* Rockville, MD: Department of Health and Human Services. NIH Pub No. 97-4017, 1997. PL-100–690 (Labeling law), 1988

Room, Robin 1983. Legislative Strategies and the Prevention of Alcohol Problems. In *Alcohol: The Prevention Debate.* Edited by Grant, M., and B. Ritson, B. London: Croom Helm, pp.152–64.

Room, Robin. Thinking about Alcohol Controls. In *Controversies in the Addiction's Field.* Edited by Ruth C. Engs. Dubuque: Kendall-Hunt, (1990) pp. 68–75.

Smith, D.I. 1988. "Effectiveness of Restrictions on Availability as a Means of Preventing Alcohol Problems, *Contemporary Drug Problems*, 15 pp. 627–684.

Substance Abuse and Mental Health Services Administration, Office of Applied Studies. National Household Survey on Drug Use and Health. Washington, D.C.: U.S. Department of Health and Human Services, 2002.

Toomey, T., R. J. Jones-Webb, and A. C. Wagenaar. "Policy – Alcohol." *Annual Review of Addiction, Research and Treatment* 3 (1993): 279–92.

Toomey, T., J. R. Killian, J. P. Gehan, A. C. Wagenaar, and R. J. Jones-Webb. "Qualitative Assessment of Responsible Alcohol Service Training Programs." *Public Health Reports* 113:2 (1998): 162–9.

Toomey, A. R. and A. C. Wagenaar. "Policy Options for Prevention: the Case of Alcohol." *Journal of Public Health Policy* 20:2 (1999): 192–213.

23 USCA 161.

23 USCA 410.

Wagenaar, A.C. 2000. *Alcohol Policies in the United States: Highlights from the 50 States*. Minneapolis: University of Minnesota.

Chapter 6

The Repeal Program

Stephen Diamond

Prohibition has often been described as a great mistake. This conclusion often generates the further judgment that Repeal should simply have been a swift undoing of that mistake. This attitude is reflected by legal commentators who criticize the 21st Amendment for doing more than repealing the 18th Amendment. The assertion that Prohibition did not work is broad and ambiguous. Was the error in establishing one centralized law with largely decentralized enforcement? Was it in imposing a single solution to a problem for which no national solution was possible because of varying practices and values with regard to alcoholic beverage consumption? Was the problem the illegitimacy of sumptuary legislation?[1]

The harsh assessment of Prohibition helps explain the lack of attention given by later commentators to Repeal policy. First, alcoholic beverage policy was to be elaborated at the state level and, with the New Deal, focus was increasingly on Washington. The deviation of alcoholic beverage policy from this general norm was noted by contemporaries. In 1934, a political scientist, observed: "It is one of the paradoxes of American politics that we have destroyed the possibility of centralization in the field of liquor control at the same time that we have been attempting to achieve greater centralization in a number of activities hitherto believed to be completely in the field of state authority."[2] Second, there appears to have been a casual assumption that anything was better than Prohibition and little interest in the debate over what was to replace it.[3]

Those who helped develop and then implement state alcoholic beverage policies after Repeal expressed frustration with this attitude. They did not consider

97

Prohibition to have been an utter failure. Like recent historians, they acknowledged its accomplishments.[4] H. L. Mencken to the contrary notwithstanding Prohibition was in part an effort "noble in motive," as President Hoover, implicitly conceding its lack of achievement, described it. For many of the heroes in the Progressive pantheon, Prohibition was not an excrescence on their program, but a central part of it. Neither its motives nor its achievements can be summarily dismissed.

Historians have in recent years begun an at least partial rehabilitation of Prohibition. There is, as there was at the time, disputed evidence as to its effectiveness. Prohibition, it is argued, did limit alcoholic beverage consumption, and, at the margin, alcoholic beverage abuse. Higher prices, greater inconvenience of access, and continuing norms of obedience to law reduced alcoholic beverage consumption, particularly among the less well-off. Yet there was significant disobedience, especially in urban areas and among the well-to-do—cocktails at famous speakeasies were a form of conspicuous consumption—and the urban press publicized and even glamorized such behavior.

As Prohibition recedes into a past beyond the memories of all but a few, its significance for contemporary practice becomes obscure. Some breezily insist that the past should be ignored. They do not understand what Repeal was attempting to accomplish and dismiss the professed concern with the saloon as outdated and irrelevant. The Anti-Saloon League had been successful by focusing on the business of providing alcohol, rather than the act of consuming it. The emphasis on the rejection of the saloon in Repeal discourse, even in President Roosevelt's declaration to the nation upon passage of the 21st Amendment, now serves as a reminder of the Anti-Saloon League rhetoric and of the excesses of militant, legalistic prohibitionism. Moreover, it seems to trivialize alcoholic beverage control. Is the tavern simply a change of name? Are blinds or swinging doors critical components? Is exclusively male patronage? Yet the saloon, as a metaphor for the dangers of private distribution and sale of alcoholic beverages, is not trivial or outdated. By insisting that the saloon had been forever removed from the country, the architects of Repeal meant that distribution and sale would be heavily regulated to an extent unknown before Prohibition.

The fundamental concern of Prohibition and of Repeal remains with us today. Alcoholic beverages can be abused, and such abuse can be encouraged or facilitated by the unconstrained pursuit of profit. The architects of Repeal saw it as both a rejection and a continuation of Prohibition, rejecting the latter's national, overreaching, and unenforceable prohibition of a legal market for the distribution and sale of alcoholic beverages, but substituting some form of regulation of such distribution and sale. They struggled to create a policy and a practice in a nondualist world. Alcohol was not simply good or simply bad. It was not to be banned nor was it to be allowed to be manufactured, distributed, and sold in an unrestricted way. The problem is more exigent with alcoholic beverages, but is a general one: the extent of regulation in a society that rejects both a command economy and unregulated license. In effect, the problem was, and still remains, to shape and define ordered liberty for the market, or less abstractly, to harness and constrain the profit motive, to allow only that degree of entrepreneurial autonomy that comports with regulated distribution, sale, and consumption.

Liquor control after Repeal was discussed in print, but not at length. This was for several reasons. Until 1930, reformers assumed that Prohibition would not be repealed and turned their efforts consequently to discussions of modification of the Volstead Act. Charles Merz, in his history of the politics and administration of Prohibition, suggests the year 1930, when he ended his study, as a turning point.[5] As Prohibition became increasingly beleaguered, attackers stopped trying to tweak the system, which instead became the task of its defenders, who suggested that relaxation of the Volstead Act, permitting home winemaking and brewing for instance, might buy acquiescence to Prohibition's continuation.

Support for the 18th Amendment crumbled so rapidly that there was little time for discussion.[6] Congress did not spend time debating particulars of new alcoholic beverage regulatory codes. It decided, after some debate, that alcoholic beverage regulation was to be primarily a state matter and that the Constitution should, through the second paragraph of the 21st Amendment, protect state regulation from being undercut by importations, as had occurred before Prohibition.[7] The state ratifying conventions devoted almost no time at all to discussing what would emerge after Repeal. Most simply elected convention officers and then quickly voted. The Delaware convention, at more length than most, resolved "to again take up, with hope of success, a program of education and character building among young and old, that will promote true temperance." It also acknowledged the abuses that existed before and during Prohibition, "the evils which existed in connection with the old-time saloon, as well as with the prohibition speakeasy."[8] Other conventions made it clear that they anticipated strict state regulation. Since Repeal arrived more quickly than was anticipated by its supporters or feared by Prohibitionists, commentators noted that states were obligated quickly to set up alcoholic beverage regulatory systems. These were sometimes described as reflecting urgency and haste rather than systematic thought.[9] In part, this critique was simply a residue of the Progressive fantasy that true legislation should follow from dispassionate study of widely gathered facts. No law that might be enacted could ever meet the highest standards of advocates of the apolitical administrative state, who wanted law disinterestedly shaped by incontrovertible facts and undistorted by self-interest.

It is incorrect, however, to conclude that there was no effort to think through and propose a general approach to alcoholic beverage regulation. There were, in the early 1930s, a number of such ventures. The topic was sufficiently discussed to be the subject of a college debate.[10] Most of these efforts were relatively brief. They shared a common assumption that Americans wanted an end to Prohibition lawlessness, but did not want a return to what they saw as the inadequate regulation of the pre-Prohibition period. They generally insisted that the profit motive in the distribution and sale of alcoholic beverages must be eliminated or at least controlled, but there was disagreement among the commentators, and ultimately, among the states, over whether this was best achieved through state ownership of the means of distribution and sale or through licensing.[11]

As Repeal became more probable, after the presidential election, John D. Rockefeller, Jr., in January 1933, asked Raymond Fosdick and Albert Scott to head up a research team to advise the states on post-Repeal alcoholic beverage regulatory systems. Fosdick had been a trustee of the Rockefeller Foundation in 1920 and would become its president in 1935.[12]

Their work, *Toward Liquor Control*, became the most important proposal for post-Repeal regulation.[13] It was influential because it articulated commonly accepted ideas and packaged them in a form that demanded respect in a post-Progressive world, with extensive comparative survey data. This book-length treatise exemplified classic Progressive analysis of social problems. This was not surprising. Fosdick had earlier investigated police organization in Europe, a project that grew out of Rockefeller's chairmanship of a special grand jury investigating prostitution, or the social evil, as it was then delicately described.[14] Fosdick found less corruption in European than in American police departments. He explained this in large part because

> European police are not called upon to enforce standards of conduct which do not meet with general public approval ... The distinction between what is criminal and what is merely vicious is on the whole clearly drawn ... and the functions of the police are not confused with those of the church, the school, and other organizations and influences by which civilization is advanced.[15]

Similar assertions would appear in the liquor report.

John D. Rockefeller Jr.'s forward to this study expressed many of the assumptions and aims of post-Repeal thought. He wrote, "Rightly, the first objective is the abolition of lawlessness." He then continued:

> The second objective is the focusing of all the forces of society upon the development of self-control and temperance as regards to the use of alcoholic beverages. As the report aptly says, public standards as a basis for law can be improved only as private standards are improved.[16]

Rockefeller had earlier expressed the view that Repeal should be a continuation and not a repudiation of Prohibition. In his public letter of June 7, 1932, supporting Nicholas Murray Butler's proposed resolution that the Republican Party platform advocate repeal, Rockefeller wrote:

> My hope is that the tremendous effort put forth in behalf of the Eighteenth Amendment by millions of earnest, consecrated people will be

continued in effective support of practical measures for the promotion of genuine temperance. To that cause my own efforts will ever be devoted.

His letter repudiating Prohibition continued:

In my judgment it will be so difficult for our people as a whole to agree in advance on what the substitute should be, and so unlikely that any method will fit the entire nation, that repeal will be far less possible if coupled with an alternate measure ...[17]

Fosdick and Scott suggested that state, as well as national prohibition, was generally unwise. They stated:

One can scarcely study the history of liquor legislation leading up to the adoption of the Prohibition Amendment of 1920 without coming to the conclusion that too often we have attempted to impose on law a burden which law by itself is not equipped to carry. ... We have labored under a belief that law can be used as a shortcut to a desired end and that the agencies through which moral objectives are normally sought—for example, the home, the school, the Church—could be subordinated to a speedier process.[18]

They looked forward to a more realistic future.

With the passing of the national prohibition experiment there seems to be developing a recognition of the fact that law is not a royal road to a moral goal. We do not wish to underestimate the part that legislation can play as a social function. It can be a wise blend of accepted principle and courageous experiment, a judicious balance between the tradition and experience of the past and the adventure and promise of the future. But always it must be the articulate organ of the desires of living men.[19]

Law should not be seen as a nostrum; there was no "cure-all."[20]

The very title of the Rockefeller finance report, *Toward Liquor Control*, suggested the new stance: the approach was tentative. To be scientific was to be incremental in strategy as well as unemotional in outlook.[21] Although Fosdick and Scott dismissed regulation prior to Prohibition as a hodgepodge, they intentionally did not offer a fully worked out system to replace it. The approach was intended to be elaborated as public opinion permitted and circumstances suggested. *Toward Liquor Control* had all the earmarks and apparatus of a paradigmatic Progressive study. It began with a historical survey that criticized past efforts as unsystematic, a rule of thumb rather than a scientific approach. The pre-Prohibition debate was dismissed as being overly emotional. Dispassionate, scientific, nonideological study and policy formation was the goal. Fosdick and Scott and their staff then engaged in a broad comparative survey of Canadian and European practices.

This study also reflected the weakness of the Progressive approach. All of the comparative data bolstered the size of the study, but were little used. It was noted by others that the high tax practices of England and Denmark were praised as effective in these countries, but then not recommended.[22] American conditions were different. Our traditions of independence made consumer licensing problematic.[23] The need to undersell bootleggers made high taxes unwise, at least in the short run. All this may have been sensible, but the comparative data, it was observed, were somewhat unconnected to these conclusions. Such an approach may have been politically helpful, in any event, confirming that regulation was opposed everywhere and reassuring that others regulated more stringently.[24]

Fosdick and Scott justified the widespread insistence that tied houses should be prohibited because the vertical integration pursued by brewers before Prohibition and racketeers during it threatened effective control. They noted approvingly that almost every "beer and general liquor law" already enacted at the time they were writing included tied-house prohibitions.[25] "Tied houses," that is establishments under contract to sell exclusively the product of one manufacturer, were, in many cases, responsible for the bad name of the saloon. The "tied-house" system had all the vices of absentee ownership. "The manufacturer knew nothing and cared nothing about the community. All he wanted was increased sales. He saw none of the abuses, and, as a nonresident, he was beyond local social influence."[26] In effect, they proposed to protect community standards by limiting the power of out-of-state suppliers. In a sense, this was analogous to what the Webb-Kenyon Act and the 21st Amendment had done: giving states power over imports to prevent out-of-state shipments from rendering state regulation inefficacious. A national solution creating one uniform market did not work. Different states had different customs and values. Each state system was, however, vulnerable to contamination, distortion, and destruction from out-of-state pressures. Direct shipments of alcoholic beverages were one example. State systems were also vulnerable to pressures on in-state retailers from out-of-state suppliers to oversell. Another related concern was the pressure that could be exercised directly on consumers by out-of-state suppliers through the power of advertising, even as it was recognized that advertising in national magazines, for instance, could not be regulated by the states.[27]

Fosdick and Scott's book was generally reviewed favorably. Sometimes the structure of their approach was questioned: they considered law less important than public opinion, yet still focused almost entirely on law.[28] Sometimes it was noted that their comparative study did not really lead to any particular prescriptive or proscriptive insights. Their recommendation that profit making be constrained met general approval. Most states, however, chose not to impose a state monopoly system for the sale of hard spirits which Fosdick and Scott had recommended. Instead, they opted for license systems, a choice that Fosdick and Scott had conceded would commonly be made.

The recommendations of the Fosdick and Scott book were not the product of comparative research. They also were not really new, nor did the authors claim them to be.[29] They were a well-packaged and well-written version of ideas that were widely discussed and often had been for some time. The danger of nullification of Prohibition laws had long been observed by critics of state prohibition efforts. Fosdick and Scott were aware of this. When warning against efforts to legislate in advance of public opinion, they quoted James C. Carter who long before national Prohibition had written:

> Nothing is more attractive to the benevolent vanity of men than the notion that they can effect great improvement in society by the simple process of forbidding all wrong conduct, or conduct that they think is wrong, by law, and of enjoining all good conduct by the same means.[30]

Carter, along with Charles Eliot, president of Harvard, and Seth Low, mayor of New York City, were the directors of The Committee of Fifty Report on *The Liquor Problem in its Legislative Aspects*,[31] a study of legislation in eight states. In their introduction to the Report, they emphasized the significance of what they called public sentiment and what *Toward Liquor Control* later called public opinion:

> The most important question with regard to any form of liquor legislation is this: Is it adapted to secure the enforcement of the restrictions of the sale of intoxicants which experiences have shown to be desirable, assuming that those restrictions can be enforced which commend themselves to an enlightened and effective public sentiment.[32]

What Fosdick and Scott recommended also was consistent with what Fosdick and John D. Rockefeller, Jr., had thought well before the book was published. As an undergraduate at Brown University, John D. Rockefeller, Jr., studied "Practical Ethics" taught by Benjamin Andrews, the University President. In his biography of Rockefeller, Fosdick writes that Rockefeller's notes reflect his study of "methods for combating the liquor problem—the building of social centers, for example, to replace the saloon environment, the improvement of home life, and the possible elimination of the profit motive in the increase of liquor sales."[33] Fosdick had reached a similar conclusion when, in 1916, he studied military bases at the Mexican border for the War Department. "The only attractions in town were a few disreputable saloons and a red light district. Those institutions had the field all to themselves; there was nothing to compete with then."[34]

Fosdick himself was never in favor of Prohibition. After passage, but before its implementation, he urged that local police not be used in its enforcement. He warned: "It will mean the inevitable corruption and demoralization of our police and they have enough temptation as it is." He conceded a "new corps" of state or national enforcement officers would also inevitably be corrupted, "but their demoralization will not jeopardize any other duty which they are handling, whereas the chief business of our police is to protect the lives and property of the citizens."[35] His travels about the country during Prohibition confirmed his initial fears.

> Of all the cities I visited, there was scarcely one which did not bear the marks of demoralization arising from attempts to enforce laws which instead of representing the will of the community represented hardly anybody's will.[36]

Long before Repeal Fosdick himself had been skeptical about the overemphasis on law in the pursuit of temperance. In 1922, he warned Rockefeller not to commit too much money to the New York Anti-Saloon League, headed by William H. Anderson. He objected to Anderson's "continued insistence upon more law rather than more public opinion ... personally, I believe we have laws enough on the question of Prohibition. What we need now is more public opinion to back up the laws that we have."[37] In 1926, Fosdick criticized the Anti-Saloon League even more bluntly when advising Rockefeller.

> My own considered belief is that the Anti-Saloon League has largely outlived its usefulness and that there is a chance at the present time that it is doing more harm than good. Its refusal to face the facts of the present unhappy situation, its misleading statements and doctored statistics, seem to me to point the end of the Anti-Saloon League as a useful institution.[38]

Other commentators, more briefly, made similar recommendations. Most advocated public dispensaries for the sale of spirits; all believed that the profit motive needed taming. In January 1934, a Committee on Liquor Control Legislation of the National Municipal League proposed guidelines for post-Repeal laws. The Committee's recommendations resembled those of Fosdick and Scott, whose work it praised.[39] This was not surprising, because many of its members were part of the New York-based team of Rockefeller financed social researchers who had been affiliated with Rockefeller's Bureau of Social Hygiene and had been acknowledged as consultants or researchers by Fosdick and Scott.[40]

The Committee proposal began by listing three purposes of liquor control that it maintained were almost unanimously shared. These were what others called promoting temperance and what this committee described as eliminating "as far as possible"…"the abuses resulting from the intemperate use of alcoholic beverages." The Committee, like others, did not feel it necessary to specify these abuses more precisely. The second aim of regulation identified by the Committee was "to eliminate bootlegging, the speakeasy, corruption and all related forms of lawlessness," that is, what appeared and remains in many state statutes as fostering obedience to and respect for law. The third aim was one that was also widely shared, but, unlike the other two, was not amenable to clear articulation in the new state statutes that were emerging. This was "to relegate the liquor problem to its proper place so that it will not overshadow and dominate all other social and political issues." It then noted: "These objectives are interrelated and often in conflict."[41] Over aggressive efforts to promote temperance could backfire, as they did during Prohibition.

The Municipal League sought to reach these ends by establishing "liquor controls under *administrative* rules and supervision instead of under *detailed laws* subject to continued legislative change," by discouraging "continuous local option agitation by prohibiting too frequent local option elections," by regulating or prohibiting liquor advertising, and by adopting "a solution of the liquor control problem that by eliminating private profit largely takes liquor out of politics and politics out of liquor."[42] The recommendation also warned against overreliance on law for control of alcoholic beverage abuse: "Though legal provisions and administrative rules and regulations are of great importance, the major problem is not legislation but national habits. The failure, therefore, rests with education in its broadest sense."[43] Education, however, must be given time to work. Regulation was necessary.[44]

The architects of Repeal expressed a disapproval of both pre-Prohibition alcoholic beverages abuse and Prohibition lawlessness.[45] They aimed to avoid the seesaw oscillations in alcoholic beverage regulation which they believed had occurred in the past. They saw Repeal as the achievement of a normally unaroused and inarticulate majority, who were seeking effective and enforceable regulations.

John D. Rockefeller Jr. himself was in a sense a particularly austere[46] example of this American center. He supported Prohibition to end saloon abuses and to help create a world of sober and self-controlled individuals. He turned against Prohibition when it appeared to be creating more problems than it solved. While extreme wets accused the drys of having maneuvered Prohibition into existence, and extreme drys made the same allegation about Repeal, another discourse was developed, which criticized both. This discourse accepted both the legitimacy of Prohibition and of Repeal: each was an accurate reflection in its time of the wisdom of the majority of the population. According to this view, the majority of Americans were opposed to the abuses of the saloon, which included the stimulation of intemperate consumption and political corruption. The majority for Prohibition was composed of confirmed drys and those who hated the saloon for the abuses it was believed to encourage. Repeal came with the support of confirmed wets and those saloon haters who hated lawlessness as well.[47]

Those opposed to Prohibition had long-criticized Prohibitionists for having highjacked the word *temperance*, transforming it from self-control and moderation to enforced abstinence. The architects of Repeal sought to reclaim the word, by supporting Repeal as a path to true temperance. President Roosevelt's Repeal message was intended to appeal to such views. He counseled self-restraint, asking Americans not to support bootleggers, and requested that the saloon never be reestablished.[48]

The debate over the reemergence of saloons was not simply a terminologic game. The rejection of the saloon reflected an effort to find achievement in Prohibition. This was part of the effort to describe Repeal as being the defeat of confirmed drys, but not the achievement of confirmed wets. Prohibition had failed, but not completely. Most people, it was repeatedly insisted, did not want to revert to pre-Prohibition conditions, rejecting both the saloon and the speakeasy. Saloons were identified with and criticized for permitting drinking without eating, swinging doors, making the interior simultaneously difficult to police and enticing, and the practice of treating—a gesture of sociability and camaraderie that was allegedly manipulated by wily saloon keepers into excessive consumption.[49] The problem with the largely unregulated saloon, often a tied house, was that it was a site, indeed, had before Prohibition been the primary site, where alcoholic beverages were distributed and sold through the profit motive.[50] Private profit, at least when untempered by internal constraints of conscience and self-respect, or external ones of social respectability and legal coercion, was a desire limitless in scope.[51] The profit motive, it was generally agreed, had to be at least strictly limited.[52] The failure of Prohibition had demonstrated that the appetite for liquor could not be completely removed, but only controlled.

The plan for Repeal at its most ambitious assumed that the appetite for profit also should be controlled but not eliminated. Neither the monopoly states nor the license states made an effort entirely to eradicate the pursuit of profit nor had any of the commentators advocated doing so entirely. They just attempted to constrain it.[53] This was yet another example of how the Repeal regime was a compromise.[54] It was recognized that no solution was perfect. If any element of private profit was permitted to survive, there was a risk that stimulation of sale would result in over-consumption and abuse. The goal was in effect the moderate pursuit of profit to supply alcoholic beverages to those who would moderately consume them. This was all to be implemented by a regime of moderate legislation, which did not provoke defiance by putting an undue burden on drinkers and did not tarnish the reputations of those who provided alcoholic beverages by regulating them too extensively, thereby suggesting that the business was not a respectable one.[55]

Moderation was to be achieved through compromise and adjustment, through the constraints of law and the development of self-control. With regard to consumers, the aim was to reduce opportunities for abuse, by prohibiting, for instance, sales to the inebriated or the underaged, and aggressive sales techniques that "stimulated" an abnormal demand. Law was to restrain aggressive salesmanship sales techniques, including advertising to the extent possible, to give education the opportunity to slowly encourage self-control as it taught the risks of overindulgence.[56] Yet the law was never to be so strict as to invite defiance and stimulate illicit distribution and sale. Emmanuel Celler and Lewis Rosenstiel, a Congressman and a spirits manufacturer, for instance, reminded regulators "that undue relaxation of control will produce intolerable social evils, and on the other hand, that regulations and restraints which go too far beyond public opinion are simply not administered …"[57]

The aim, to reduce the likelihood that sellers would act in a socially undesirable manner, was pursued in multiple ways. Licensing restrictions were to eliminate from distribution and sales, to the extent possible, proven law-breakers and those likely to attempt to evade regulation. Law shielded respectable sellers from pressures to violate the laws by shoring up their independence, as with tied-house restrictions. The hope was that they would be more concerned to satisfy regulators than their suppliers. Law also was to protect sellers from unfair competition, which might lead sellers to violate the letter or the spirit of the law.[58] Stable and orderly distribution and sale would reduce this risk. Regulators deplored what they considered to have been the profligate granting of licenses just after Repeal and the entrance into the business of those described as seeking quick money rather than a steady business.[59]

The wide discretion granted to administrators, which minimized the need for detailed rules, in effect provided a mechanism for the education of sellers who needed to pay attention to the cautions and concerns of regulators. National Conference of State Liquor Administration meetings provided a forum for such cautionary instructions. To prevent pressure for more stringent regulation, the alcoholic beverage industry had to be persuaded to refrain from high-pressure merchandising.[60] Exhortation was of course not sufficient. Regulators noted that suppliers and wholesalers almost immediately began endangering the independence of retailers by providing lavish credit. More detailed tied-house regulation was the response.[61] Reliance on "the law of supply and demand" as a mechanism to prevent an excessive number of licenses was rejected. Regulation was necessary because "even a proprietor who would not otherwise resort to illegal practices will, when competition is severe, indulge in whatever business methods—whether legitimate or illegitimate—will secure a reasonable income."[62] Regulation was necessary to minimize the adverse social consequence of a disorderly market.

Regulation and law making was also supposed to be exercised in moderation. This, of course, meant that law should not constrain demand in ways the public would not accept. Sellers also were not to be unduly regulated. Selling alcoholic beverages was no longer illegitimate, as it was characterized by drys before Prohibition and by the law during Prohibition. Yet the sale of alcoholic beverages demanded regulation. Regulation was to have elements of both trust and verification.[63]

The architects of Repeal also exhorted lawmakers to exercise restraint and moderation in their tax policies, in the pursuit of profit by public rather than private institutions. Fosdick and Scott had advocated taxation for control rather than for revenue and this advice was often repeated.[64] The president of the NCSLA in 1937, Michael Costello, the chief regulator for Rhode Island, told the attending members: "There is no liquor administration within the sound of my voice who feels today that the biggest part of his job is the collecting of money. Regulation, control, education—those are our responsibilities—those are our compelling tasks and our very sacred duties."[65] In a manner reminiscent of a preacher, he continued: "Let us approach these various problems in the right spirit. Let us cast aside that tax gathering mindedness in material things; let us rather have our own heart imbued with the godly spirit of brotherly love."[66] Increased tax revenues had been an important argument for Repeal. It was the moderation, and not the rejection, of revenue taxes that was being counseled.

As a topic of public debate and expert investigation, trade practice regulation did not continue for long after Repeal [as a topic of public debate and expert investigation]. Attention was paid more to the structure of alcoholic beverage commissions rather than to the policies they advocated or enforced. This reflected a classic "good government" concern: that regulators be protected from the corruption of politics.[67] More significantly, foundations and scholars focused not on the sale of alcoholic beverages, but on alcoholism. This was a choice encouraged by funding availability.[68] Drys would not support any approach which implied the legitimacy of alcoholic beverage sales and consumption. Those who advocated Repeal as a step toward true temperance proved unwilling to fund research or educational efforts to measure or to effect public opinion. Public opinion, which all agreed was the measuring predicate for true temperance, was to a large degree, left uneducated and even unexamined. Everett Crosby's Moderation League, an organization advocating moderation, died for lack of funds.[69] Mrs. John Sheppard, the former New York state head of the Women's Organization for National Prohibition Reform and an original member of the New York State Liquor Board, personally paid for survey research into young people's practices and beliefs with regard to drinking.[70] But such generosity was unusual. The Moderation League had refused financial support from the alcoholic beverage industry, not wanting to antagonize drys, in particular, John D. Rockefeller, Jr. Industry, on the other hand, was happy to support research into alcoholism, a subject which ignored trade regulation, sellers, and most buyers, focusing on those buyers whose illness led to overconsumption. Unsurprisingly, researchers followed the funding.

An occasional appeal was made for a more detailed study "of the management of the traffic."[71] However, most evaluations of the effectiveness of Repeal policies were brief. Unreconstructed drys called Repeal a failure, highlighting drinking and selling abuses, which, of course, had not been eliminated.[72] The Repealist appraisals were, to the contrary, favorable, while conceding the need for better educational efforts and continued vigilance against the reappearance of vertical integration, overaggressive marketing, and political corruption.[73] There was still concern that drys would exploit abuses in an effort to reestablish Prohibition.[74] Their failure to do so at the state level encouraged Repealists.[75] The New York State Liquor Authority, for instance, took comfort in the declining rate of dry local option victories.

State policy remained constant: meeting the demand for alcoholic beverages without permitting abuses that might stimulate pressures to overregulate. "The purpose of public control of alcoholic beverages is to make them available without stimulating excessive consumption or encouraging undesirable distribution practice."[76]

Repealists feared a continuation of the wet-dry cycle, alternation between abuses from underregulation and from overregulation, that they thought characterized American history up to that time.[77] When they wrote of solving the liquor problem, they meant minimizing the intensity of the oscillations, substituting undramatic adjustments, preferably undertaken through administrative discretion, for dramatic flip-flops in statutory policy.

Regulators pointed with satisfaction to the decline of contentious public debate, but deplored what they saw as public apathy over alcoholic beverage regulation.[78] Public quiescence, evidence of the policy's success, increased the risk of reemergence of abuses. Yet alcoholic beverage regulation had been moved to the back burner of American politics, to be treated as a chronic rather than an acute problem, to be managed rather than conclusively solved.[79]

References

1. Kyvig, David E. "Sober Thoughts: Myths and Realities of National Prohibition after Fifty Years." In: *Law, Alcohol, and Order: Perspectives on National Prohibition,* edited by David E. Kyvig, 1985.
2. Dayton E. Heckman. "Contemporary State Statutes for Liquor Control." *American Policy Scientific Review* 28 (1934): 628.
3. Lender, Mark Edward. "The Historian and Repeal: A Survey of the Literature and Research Opportunities." In Kyvig, *supra,* at 177.
4. Burnham, J. C. "New Perspectives on the Prohibition "Experiment" of the 1920's." *Journal of Social History* (1968) 51–68; Clark, Norman H. *Deliver Us From Evil: An Interpretation of American Prohibition* (1976); Pegram, Thomas R. *Battling Demon Rum* (1998): 136–165.
5. Merz, Charles. *The Dry Decade* (1930): 295.
6. Lawrence, David. "Liquor a la Code," 206 *The Saturday Evening Post* 8, 9 (Nov. 11, 1933); McGeary, M. Nelson. *Pennsylvania And The Liquor Business: A Study of the Pennsylvania Liquor Control Board* (1948): 30.
7. At least until the passage of the Webb-Kenyon Act.
8. Brown, Everett Somerville. *Ratification of the Twenty-First Amendment and the Constitution of the United States; State Convention Records and Laws* (1938): 66.
9. Johnsen, Julia E. "Introduction." In *Selected Articles on The Problem of Liquor Control,* edited by Johnsen. (1934): 12–3.
10. "Problem of State Liquor Control." *Colgate University versus Princeton University,* chapter X. *University Debaters' Annual: Constructive and Rebuttal Speeches, Delivered at American Colleges and Universities, During The College Year, 1933–1934,* edited by Edith M. Phelps, 1934.
11. *Id.,* a selection of such proposals is excerpted in Johnsen, *Id.,* Part III and more are cited in the bibliography.
12. *Id.,* at 251.

13. Fosdick, Raymond B. and Albert L. Scott. *Toward Liquor Control: With a Forward by John D. Rockefeller, Jr.* (1933); Fosdick, Raymond B. *John D. Rockefeller, Jr.: A Portrait* (1956): 259.

14. Fosdick, Raymond B. *Chronicles of a Generation: An Autobiography* (1958): 124–5.

15. *Id.*, at 129.

16. Rockefeller, in Fosdick and Scott, *Id.* at IX.

17. Fosdick, Raymond B. *John D. Rockefeller, Jr., supra*, at 257. This letter appeared in the *New York Times*, June 7, 1932: 12.

18. Fosdick and Scott, *supra*, at 5–6.

19. *Id.*, at 7.

20. *Id.*, at 5.

21. Johnsen, Julia E. "Introduction." In Johnsen ed., *supra*, at 11–2.

22. Fosdick and Scott, *supra*, at 37; Garrison W. E. "Fitting the Law to the Lawless." *The Christian Century* 50 (Nov. 29, 1933): 1505–6.

23. Fosdick and Scott, *supra*, at 39–40.

24. *Id.*, at 80; *Proceedings of the NCSLA: Fourth Annual Convention* (1937): 145–8; *Proceedings of the NCSLA: Fifth Annual Convention* (1938): 75, (Mahoney, William. Minnesota Liquor Control Commissioner); and at Loesch, Frank J. "Regulated, Licensed Retailer Plan." Rotarian 44 (Jan. 1934): 14–5, in Johnsen, *supra* at 380, 382; Committee on Liquor Control Legislation of the National Municipal League. "Principles Governing Liquor Control Legislation." *National Municipal Review* 23 (Jan. 1934): 48.

25. Fosdick and Scott, *supra*, at 44, footnote 2.

26. *Id.*, at 43.

27. Fosdick and Scott, *supra*, at 80.

28. Villard, Oswald Garrison. "Issues and Men: John D. Rockefeller, Jr., Does a Fine Job." *The Nation* 529 (Nov. 8, 1933) 137; "The Rockefeller Report." *The Commonwealth* 18 (Oct. 27, 1933): 603–9; "The Next Step After Repeal." Letter from Stoddard Lane. *Religious Education* 29 (January 1934): 19; more critical is W. E. Garrison, *Id.*, at 1505–6; but see the response by W. E. Lovett, "The Rockefeller Liquor Report," *Id.*, at 1645 (Dec. 27, 1933); see the address of Professor Marshall Dimock before a Chicago citizens group, in Public Management 373–374 (Dec. 1933).

29. Luther Gulick, who was then a professor at Columbia and Director of the Institute of Public Administration and involved in the writing of the Fosdick and Scott book, later wrote that the committee had arrived at its conclusion before commencing the study. Letter of Luther Gulick to Laurance Rockefeller, May 2, 1977, Rockefeller Archive Center.

30. Fosdick and Scott, *supra*, at 6.

31. Wines, Frederic H. and John Koren. *The Liquor Problem in its Legislative Aspects: An Investigation Made under the Direction of Charles W. Eliot, Seth Low, and James C. Carter, Sub-Committee of the Committee of Fifty to Investigate the Liquor Problem* (1897). See Levine H. G., and C. Reinarman. "From Prohibition to Regulation: Lessons from Alcohol Policy for Drug Policy." *The Milbank Quarterly* 69 (1991): 475–6.

32. *Id.*, at 11.

33. Fosdick, *Rockefeller, supra*, at 248.

34. Fosdick, *Chronicles, supra*, at 140.

35. *Id.*, at 235.

36. *Id.*, at 233–4.

37. Fosdick, *Rockefeller, supra*, at 252.

38. *Id.*, at 253. Fosdick pointed instead to Rockefeller's recent support of the Social Science Research Council "for a scientific study of the operation and result of the Eighteenth Amendment." In true Progressive fashion, he insisted: "What we need at the present time is not propaganda, but facts."

39. The Committee on Liquor Control Legislation of the National Municipal League. *National Municipal Review* 23 (Jan. 1934): 47.

40. Luther Gulick asserted that he had been the one who initiated the National Municipal League proposal because he believed that, while Fosdick was correct in not offering one, a model statute should be provided. Letter of Gulick to Laurance Rockefeller, *supra.*

41. The Committee on Liquor Control Legislation of the National Municipal League, *supra*, at 48.

42. *Id.*, at 49–50.

43. *Id.*, at 51. In 1934, the National Conference of State Liquor Administrators (NCSLA), at its inaugural meeting similarly stated: "The prime objective of Repeal was to promote temperance, to create respect for law and order, to prevent the illicit consumption of liquor and to exact payment of reasonable federal and state taxes ...." *Proceedings of the NCSLA* (1934): 103.

44. *Proceedings of the NCSLA: Fourth Annual Convention,* (1937): 152. (Edith McClure Patterson, a member of the Ohio Liquor Control Board); Marshall E. Dimock, "Liquor Control: A Plan for Illinois," a publication of The Public Affairs Committee of the Union League Club (Dec. 5, 1933), in Johnsen, *supra*, at 355. Governor Lehman of New York in January 1933 addressed the state advisory commission, telling them: "It will be your task to formulate a method of regulation which will do away with the evils of Prohibition and at the same time prevent a lapse into the scandalous conditions of the days before," in Buel W. Patch. "Preparations for Prohibition Repeal." *Editorial Research Report* (1933): 83–4.

45. *Proceedings of the NCSLA: Fourth Annual Convention.* (F. Clyde Keefe, Commissioner, New Hampshire State Liquor Commission). (1937): 183.

46. *Proceedings of the NCSLA: Second Annual Meeting* (1935): 96. (Harris E. Willingham, Associate Administrator, Federal Alcohol Administration, comments that "in the case of the Rockefeller Report, because its sponsor had been active supporter of one of the national Dry organizations for many years, its conclusions were labelled by many as being too drastic and representing the views of an ardent dry....")

47. Rogers, Lindsay. "After Prohibition – What?" *New Republic* 73 (Dec. 1932): 88; Gifford Pinchot. "State Store Plan." 44 *Rotarian* (Jan. 1934): 12–3, excerpted in Johnsen, *Id.*, at 366, 371; address of Becker, E. J., Supervisor, Department of Liquor Control, Jefferson City, Missouri, in *Proceedings of the National Conference of State Liquor Administrators* (January 1935) at 38; *Proceedings of the NCSLA: Fifth Annual Convention* (1938): 84–5 (Arthur S. Smith, Chairman of the Illinois Liquor Control Commission), and at 98, (Ambrose Fuller, consultant to the American Municipal Association, quoting *After Repeal, supra*, at 228). "The state control plan must have the respect and support of reasonable wets and reasonable drys." *Message of Clarence D. Martin, Governor of Washington, to the Legislature.* (Extraordinary Session, 1933–1934): 19.

48. In Johnsen, *supra,* at 172–3.

49. Critics claimed that the bartender would herd drinkers into large groups for which the obligations of reciprocity would lead to over-consumption.

50. Smiley, J. E. "What Is a Saloon?" 49 *Christian Century* (Oct. 26, 1934): 1304; Loesch in Johnsen, *supra,* at 380. In 1931 The National Commission on Law Observance and Enforcement, popularly known as the Wickersham Commission, delivered its report to President Hoover. In its introduction, it observed: "Probably the institution which most strongly aroused public sentiment against liquor traffic was the licensed saloon. The number of saloons was increasing in many states. In general, they were either owned or controlled by brewers or wholesale liquor dealers. The saloon keepers were under constant pressure to increase the sale of liquors. It was a business necessity for a saloon keeper to stimulate the sale of all the kinds of liquor he dealt in." "Report on the Enforcement of the Prohibition Laws of the United States." House Doc. No. 722, January 7, 1931, at 6. The Report's introduction concluded: "It is significant that almost all of the bodies at the present time seeking the repeal of the Eighteenth Amendment concede that under no circumstances should the licensed saloon be restored. Admittedly, the great achievement of the Eighteenth Amendment has been the abolition of the saloon." *Id.*, at 7.

51. Duffus, R. L. "Ten Questions Left Unsettled by Repeal." *New York Times*, Dec. 10, 1933, at sec. 9, p. 1 (quoting Senator Seabury Mastick); Nutter, George R. "Possible Plan for Liquor Control presented to the Special Commission on State Liquor Control Laws." *Massachusetts Law Quarterly* 18 (Feb. 1933): 31, 36, and 38; Patch, Buel W. "Liquor Control after Repeal." *Editorial Research Reports* (Oct. 1933): 231, 236; Kennedy, Albert J. "The Saloon in Retrospect and Prospect." *Survey Graphic* 22 (April 1933): 203, 205; Celler, Emmanuel, and Lewis Rosenstiel. "A County License Plan That Should Promote True Temperance." *Hotel Management* 23 (Jan. 1933): 20–1; Loesch, Frank J. "Regulated, Licensed Retailer Plan." in Johnsen, *supra*, at 380, 384; *Proceedings of the NCSLA* (1934), *supra*, at 47 (Wm. P. Hayes, Chairman of the Massachusetts ABC); but see a lament for the old male-only saloon, *Proceedings of the NCSLA: Fifth Annual Convention* (1938): 120 (Michael Costello, Chief, Rhode Island Division of Intoxicating Beverages).

52. Dimock, Marshall E. "Liquor Control: A Plan for Illinois," in Johnsen, *supra*, at 355, 357; *Proceedings of the NCSLA: Fourth Annual Convention* (1937), at 149 (Wm. Mahoney, Commissioner, Minnesota Liquor Control Commission); *Proceedings of the NCSLA: Fifth Annual Convention* (1938): 75 (Wm. Mahoney).

53. In both the Colgate-Princeton debate, *supra*, and the outlined debate, "Resolved" That the State Alcohol Control Authority plan be adopted by the various states to regulate the liquor traffic," in *Johnsen, supra* at 313–4, the negative side noted that manufacturers would remain private and would continue to attempt to stimulate sale of alcoholic beverages.

54. Clark, Norman H. *The Dry Years: Prohibition and Social Change in Washington* (1965): 243. For example, Proceedings of the NCSLA (1934): 46–7 (Wm. P. Hayes, Chairman of the Massachusetts ABC): 47 (Edward P. Mulrooney, Chairman, New York State Liquor Authority): 123 (Martin H. Foss, assistant corp. council of Chicago).

55. Mrs. John Sheppard of New York made a similar point when addressing the NCSLA in 1935: "All through history the liquor business has been hampered and harassed and hedged about with restrictions. There have been times, of course, of very lenient laws, very liberal laws, but because of abuses which have come from under those laws, we have had the following restrictions and stringent regulations which have been very unfortunate for everybody. The result has been that the liquor business has always been uncertain and unstable. Many sound, responsible business people have hesitated to enter into it, to engage in it. There has been a general feeling that as much money must be made as possible, just as quickly as possible, because there was no assurance that the business would be allowed to continue." *Proceedings of the National Conference of State Liquor Administrators*: Second Annual Meeting (November 14–15, 1935): 40–1. The previous year, she had complained to the *New York Times*: "In some of the provisions of our laws we are treating the liquor business as a reputable business, while in other provisions in the same law we are stamping it as disreputable," *NYT*, 6/13/34, sect. 6. On the three moderations, see *Proceedings of the NCSLA: Fourth Annual Convention* (1937) 223 (Arthur Palmer, former director, Wisconsin Beverage Tax Division); D. Frederick Burnett, commissioner, Dept. of Alcoholic Beverage Control, a radio address, "You and Your Government," in 2 *Repeal Review* No.1 (Jan.–March 1937): 15. ("Laws should not be put on the books unless they are meant to be obeyed, are capable of enforcement, and are going to be enforced."); and Naylor Rex Maurice. "Control and Reduction of the Liquor Traffic." *Yale Review* (Dec. 1931): 297–9, quoted in Johnsen, *supra*, at 180–1. On the danger of excessive regulation, see *Proceedings of the NCSLA* (1934) 37, (Walter Conway, South Dakota Attorney General); *Proceedings of the NCSLA* (Jan. 1935); and at 38 (E. J. Becker, Supervisor, Missouri Dept. of Liquor Control); *Proceeding of the NCSLA: Second Annual Meeting* (Nov. 1935): 40 (Mrs. John Sheppard, warning that "sound and respectable" people would hesitate to enter a business made "uncertain and unstable" by oscillations between too strict and too lenient treatment); *Proceedings of the NCSLA: Fourth Annual Convention* (1937): 178 (W. J. Lindberg, of the Washington Liquor Control Board); State of New York, *Report of the State Liquor Authority*: January 1, 1940, to December 31, 1940 (1941): 12: "It is not the intention of the state to dominate the industry by regulating its interval business affairs, except when its conduct affects the welfare of the people of this state … Individual initiative has not been stifled, nor is it the purpose of the law to hamper normal business within the bounds of public welfare." On the importance of making the selling of alcoholic beverages respectable, see *Proceedings of the NCSLA* (1934): 69 (A.J. Palmer, Director, Wisconsin Beverage Tax Division); Proceedings of the NCSLA (Jan. 1935):

46 (Edward Mulrooney, chairman, New York State Liquor Board; *Proceedings of the NCSLA: Fourth Annual Convention* (1937) 154. (Edith McClure Patterson, member, Ohio Department of Liquor Control). This point had been made by Louis Brandeis in 1891. He criticized the "enactment of harassing legislation, which should prevent any man, who respects himself, from engaging in the business, and which tends to deprive those already in it of what self-respect they may have." Brandeis, Louis. *The Anti-bar law; the Twenty-five feet law; argument before the Joint Committee on Liquor Law of the Massachusetts Legislature.* Boston (Feb. 1891): 7.

56. *Proceedings of the NCSLA: Fourth Annual Convention* (1937) 98 (Ambrose Fuller, speaking of Minnesota: "The Commission is also charged with the duty of restricting advertising so that it might counteract temperance education.")

57. Celler and Rosenstiel, *supra*, at 21. Fosdick and Scott, *supra*, at 99 had defined the regulatory goal as "to leave no legislative need for the bootlegger to satisfy; and at the same time, to avoid stimulating the demand for liquor."

58. *Proceedings of the NCSLA: Second Annual Meeting* (1935): 83 (Mark Graves, a New York State tax administrator).

59. *Proceedings of the NCSLA: Fourth Annual Convention* (1937): 25 (Matthew G. Patterson, executive director of the National Retail Liquor Package Stores Association), deploring "the first hectic guide money-making period directly following Repeal" *Proceedings of the NCSLA: Sixth Annual Convention* (1939): 77 (J. Norman Peterson, Minnesota Liquor Control Commissioner). Repeal Associates, a successor or organization to the Association Against the Prohibition Amendment (AAPA) in part blamed the continuing agitation of drys for pressuring sellers into seeking profits. *Proceedings of the NCSLA: Second Annual Meeting* (1935): 103 (Capt. W. H. Stayton, former head of the AAPA, speaking on behalf of Repeal Associates.

60. *Proceedings of the NCSLA: Fifth Annual Convention* (1938), at 99 (Ambrose Fuller); at 124 (Michael Costello); at 198 (Arthur Smith).

61. *Proceedings of the NCSLA* (1934) at 37, (Walter Conway); at 58, (Frank A. Picard, chairman, Illinois Liquor Control Commission); at 111 and 113 (R.W. Jackman, attorney in the Wisconsin Beverage Tax Division); *Proceedings of the NCSLA: Fifth Annual Convention* (1938): 87–8 (Arthur S. Smith, chairman, Illinois Liquor Control Commission); at 122 (Michael F. Costello, chief, Rhode Island Division of Intoxicating Beverages); State of New York, *Report of the State Liquor Authority: January 1, 1940 to December 31, 1940* (1941), at 14–5, explaining that attention was only focussed on problems with the retailer "because he is the contact point with the consumer. On the contrary, the distillers involved were the ones who were mainly responsible for the creation and continuance of this unsettled market by their desire to capture more than what actually was their normal market, and by their lack of a stable, sound and business-like merchandising policy." Clark, Norman. *The Dry Years, supra,* at 244–5.

62. Harrison, Leonard V. and Elizabeth Laine. *After Repeal: A Study of Liquor Control Administration* (1936): 96. The authors had been assistants to Fosdick and Scott. This book, as with *Toward Liquor Control* was financed by John D. Rockefeller, Jr.; Luther Gulick, "Forward," *Id.*, at xix.

63. See note 53.

64. Fosdick and Scott, *supra*, at 107–30. *Proceedings of the NCSLA* (1935) 100 (Neil H. Jacobs, supervisor, Legal and Research Division, Illinois Dept. of Finance); *Proceedings of the NCSLA: Third Annual Convention* (1936): 51–2 (Report of the Committee on Taxation); at 134 (Elizabeth Laine condemning "greed for revenue"); *Proceedings of the NCSLA: Fourth Annual Convention* (1937): 37 (Report of the Committee on Taxation).

65. *Proceedings of the National Conference of State Liquor Administrators: Fourth Annual Convention* (1937) 12.

66. *Id.*, at 15. The next year, the message came directly, if less flamboyantly, from a member of the cloth. In his invocation to open the 1938 NCSLA meetings, the minister asked: "May our judgment not be swayed by the demands of special groups, but even be steadied by the concern for the welfare of humanity. May we think effectively not in terms of profits or even of taxes, but in terms of human life, American homes, and the deeper needs of her people." [Rev. T. F. Rutledge Beale, in *Proceedings of the NCSLA: Fifth Annual Convention* (1938): 1].

67. *After Repeal, supra*, especially chapters 3–4; *Heckman, supra*; Culver, Dorothy C. and Jack E. Thomas. "State Liquor Control Administration: No Two State Administer Liquor Control Laws Alike in All Respects." *State Government* 89 (May 1940).

68. Roizen, Ron. The American Discovery of Alcoholism, 1933–1939 (Ph.D. dissertation, Sociology, University of Calif., Berkeley (1991); Lender, Mark Edward. "The Historian and Repeal: A Survey of the Literature and Research Opportunities." in Kyvig, ed., *supra* at 190–4; Keller, Mark. "Alcohol Problems and Policies in Historical Perspective," in *Id.*, at 164–8.

69. Roizen, Ron. "Redefining Alcohol in post-Repeal America: Lessons from the Short Life of Everett Colby's Council for Moderation, 1934–1936." *Contemporary Drug Problems* 18 (Summer 1991): 237–72; Harrison, Leonard, and Elizabeth Laine, authors of *After Repeal*, were among the four original incorporators of the League.

70. Paul Studenski, *Liquor Consumption among the American Youth*. Report of the Social Study Committee of the National Conference of State Liquor Administrators, Mrs. John S. Sheppard, Chairman (1936). Mrs. Sheppard described the study by Dr. Studenski, a professor of economics at N.Y.U., in *Proceedings of the NCSLA: Fourth Annual Convention* (1937): 64–106. She noted that the Committee was unable to interest foundations in the project, so she financed it herself. Mrs. Sheppard recommended that each liquor control board should have a research department "which is to find whether there is increase or decrease in drinking, especially among the young, what effect the use of alcohol is having in crime, on education, on health, on motor traffic, and kindred subjects throughout the state." *Id.*, at 109. Professor Studenski had already published a pamphlet, *Taxation of Liquor: A Study of Liquor Taxes and License Fees or Liquor Prices and Illicit Trade*, undertaken and published by the Citizens' Committee For Sane Liquor Laws (March 20, 1934).

71. Michigan Liquor Study Committee. *Liquor Control – or – Chaos* (Oct. 1940): iv. The Committee was a self-constituted group, all of whom "were in some way active in the Repeal drive." *Id.*, at iii.

72. Holmes, John Haynes. "One Year of Repeal." *The Christian Century* (November 7, 1934): 1403–9; Holmes, John Haynes. "Second Year of Repeal." *The Christian Century* (November 4, 1935): 1546–9; Holmes, John Haynes. "The Third Year of Repeal." *The Christian Century* (November 25, 1936): 1555–8. Cutten, George Barton. "Meet a Prohibitionist: Liquor Advocates Have Failed in Every Court," an address delivered Sept. 20, 1939, in *Vital Speeches of the Day* 5: 758–62.

73. Michigan Liquor Study Committee, *supra,* at iv–xi; Mrs. John S. Sheppard. "Clinching Repeal: A Big Task Remains," *New York Times* (Dec. 6, 1936), Sunday Mag. at 5. Mrs. John S. Sheppard. "After Five Years, What Has Repeal Achieved?" *New York Times,* Dec. 4, 1938, at SM5; Paul Studenski. "Liquor Regulation: Success or Failure?" 32 *National Municipal Review* 32 (1943): 180–9.

74. For expressions of concern over the possible return of Prohibition, see *Proceedings of the NCSLA: Second Annual Meeting* (1935): 81 (Mark Graves, a New York State tax official); *Proceedings of the NCSLA: Third Annual Convention* (1936): 24 (Professor George E. Brooks); and at 183 (Paul A. Dever, Attorney General of Massachusetts); *Proceedings of the NCSLA: Fourth Annual Convention* (1937), at 34 (Michigan Governor Frank Murphy). See 2 *Repeal Review* 4 (Oct.–Dec. 1937): 8. Repeal Associates was equally concerned with preventing industry abuses, which "furnishes ammunition to the drys, and such progress as they have made they owe largely to the stupid assistance of the booze trade. There is much evidence to support the view that the trade hanged itself twenty years ago, and there is no evidence whatsoever that it cannot hang itself again." *Repeal Review* 1 (Jan.–Mar. 1938): 28.

75. State of New York, Report of the State Liquor Authority: January 1, 1936, to December 31, 1936 (1937): 5–6.

76. Liquor Control – or – Chaos, *supra* at 1.

77. *Proceedings of the NCSLA: Third Annual Convention* (1936), at 177–8 (Mrs. John Sheppard, member of the New York State Liquor Authority; *Proceedings of the NCSLA: Fifth Annual Convention* (1938) 96 (Ambrose Fuller); see John Holley Clark, Jr. "The Prohibition Cycle." *The North American Review* 235 (May 1933): 413–9.

78. As early as April 8, 1934, Mrs. Sheppard expressed concern about public indifference to liquor control. *New York Times.* State of New York, Report of the State Liquor Authority: January 11–December 31, 1936 (1937): 5. To overcome public apathy, New Jersey Commissioner Frederick Burnett concluded his radio address by reminding his listeners "that this business of alcoholic beverage control is your own business; that it involves your taxes; your children; your homes," in 2 *Repeal Review, supra,* at 17.

79. In his radio address, *Id.,* at 16, Burnett stated: "It must be recognized that liquor is a commodity inherently dangerous. But that conclusion is not a terminus but merely the beginning point." He then analogized alcoholic beverage abuse to Mississippi and Ohio River floods: "The remedy is to build dikes and levees so high, so reinforced, so planned as to control the natural flow of the stream by regulating it as distinguished from the attempt to destroy it altogether, to make it flow through defined channels…."

Chapter 7

Sociological/Cultural Influences of Drinking

Jonathan P. West
Department of Political Science, University of Miami
Colleen M. West
Miami Department of Veterans Affairs Medical Center

Contents

The use and abuse of alcohol is widespread in the United States. The costs of alcohol abuse and dependence are significant in dollars, impairment, and death. For example, 100,000 deaths per year in the United States have been attributed to use of alcohol (Nelson et al., 2004). A rich literature has examined the influence of alcohol, the etiology of addiction, and the impact of alcoholism. The sociologic and cultural influences of drinking are important because they help to explain the differences in alcohol use among special populations, the societal problems that result from excessive drinking, and the policy or program strategies that might help to control or mitigate these problems. This chapter seeks to explore such issues. Specifically, after a brief examination of competing explanations for the origins of addiction, we examine issues surrounding levels of consumption, variation in alcohol use among demographic groups, problematic behaviors associated with overconsumption, and some social control and social norm strategies for addressing alcohol-related problems.

Three types of theories help to explain the etiology of addiction: physiological and genetic theories, psychological and family/peer theories, and sociological theories. The physiological or disease model stresses the inherited biological susceptibility that makes certain people more prone to addiction than others. A series of studies involving twins, adoptions, sons of addicted fathers, and animals has provided some evidence that there is a genetic basis for risk of alcoholism. Other theorists look beyond the biological genetic factors to psychological and socialization theories that consider the context of learned or conditioned behaviors. Social learning theory, behavior modeling, and operant conditioning stress the role of environmental variables, including family and peers, in influencing addictive behaviors. Psychoanalytic theory points to "self-regulatory impairments" stemming from experiences in infancy as a possible reason for substance abuse, whereas family systems theorists examine family roles and rules for explanations. Sociological theories suggest that broad social influences other than biochemical or psychological variables (e.g., job dissatisfaction, demographics, subcultures) affect the risk of alcoholism (Margolis and Zweben 1998). These psycho-socio-cultural influences of drinking, both as causes and consequences, are the principal focus of this chapter together with consideration of legal or policy issues.

Although these theories focus on the etiology of addiction, it is important to note that many people either do not drink or do so moderately without becoming addicted. Alcohol use can be examined by considering three levels of consumption: abstention/light consumption, moderate consumption, and excessive consumption. Although scholars differ somewhat in their use of measures, which are admittedly imprecise, the first category refers to those who do not drink (e.g., lifetime abstainers, ex-drinkers) or those who drink a small amount. One national survey classifies "abstainer" as someone who consumes less than one drink of liquor, wine, or beer in the prior year, whereas another uses this classification for those consuming 12 or fewer drinks in that period (see Dufour 1999).

Moderate consumption has been defined as 4 to 14 drinks per week (i.e., 0.22 to 1.00 fluid ounces per day; Dawson et al., 1995). However, Dufour (1999) has summarized some of the thorny issues involved in measuring "moderate" consumption. National dietary guidelines for safe limits of consumption recommend that healthy men consume no more than two drinks daily and one drink daily for women (USDA and DHHS 2000)—an amount consistent with moderate consumption. Nevertheless, the actual beverage amounts of a "standard drink" could have different effects depending on whether the drink was beer, wine, or hard liquor, the characteristics of those drinking (e.g., pregnant women, those underage or on medication), the context (e.g., binge drinking), and so forth.

Excessive consumption usually involves more than two drinks per day (1.00 fluid ounce or more). Heavy use, according to the Department of Health and Human Services (2002), is five or more drinks on the same occasion on at least five different days in the past month. Drinking in excess of five drinks per day is linked to serious negative impacts, both acute and chronic (Midanik et al., 1996). Greenfield and Rogers (1999) report that the heaviest drinking adults (top 2.5 percent) account for more than one quarter (27 percent) of alcohol consumption in the United States. Foster and her colleagues (2003) conservatively estimate that adult heavy drinking accounts for a slightly higher percentage of alcohol consumed (30.4 percent) and a similar percentage of all money spent (29.6 percent) on alcohol in 1999. Addiction, health, and accident problems are much more evident among heavy drinkers.

Classification as "alcohol dependent," according to the DSM-111-R, occurs when someone experiences one or more symptoms on at least three of nine criteria in the prior year:

- Tolerance
- Characteristic withdrawal state
- Drinking to relieve or avoid withdrawal
- Persistent desire or unsuccessful efforts to stop or cut down on drinking
- Drinking larger amounts or for longer periods than intended
- Spending a great deal of time obtaining alcohol, drinking, or recovering from the effects of alcohol
- Frequent intoxication or withdrawal when expected to fulfill major role obligations
- Important social, occupational, or recreational activities given up or reduced in favor of drinking
- Continuing to drink despite a persistent or recurrent social, psychological, or physical problem caused or exacerbated by drinking (Archer et al., 1995).

Special Populations

With these definitions and distinctions in mind, let's examine the drinking experience of some special populations, including adolescents and young adults, the elderly, women, and selected racial, ethnic, and religious groups. Here we rely heavily on results from the 2002 National Survey on Drug Use and Health conducted by the Department of Health and Human Services. This survey reports that more than 18 million people are classified as alcohol dependent or alcohol abusers, representing 7.7 percent of those 12 or older, and the figure is even higher among those who used alcohol in the past year (11.6 percent) (HHS 2002a).

Regional/Population Density Differences

National survey data show that alcohol use for those 12 or older was highest in New England (57.2 percent) and lowest in the East South Central regions (36.7 percent).

The use and heavy use of alcohol varied by population density as well: large metropolitan areas (54.0 percent use, 6.3 percent heavy use); small metropolitan areas (51.3 percent and 7.9 percent, respectively); and non-metropolitan areas (42.9 percent and 6.1 percent, respectively). Binge drinking rates for underage youth (12 to 17 years) were marginally higher in non-metropolitan areas (12.6 percent) than in large (10.1 percent) or small (10.3 percent) metropolitan areas (HHS 2002a).

Nelson and his colleagues (2004) estimated adult binge drinking prevalence in 120 U.S. metropolitan areas in 48 states and the District of Columbia. They found considerable variation across metropolitan areas ranging from 23.9 percent in San Antonio, Texas, to 4.1 percent in Chattanooga, Tennessee. Metropolitan areas in Texas, Nevada, and the upper Midwest had the highest estimates.

Adolescents and Young Adults

Analysis by Foster et al. (2003) reveals three important findings regarding underage drinking: First, approximately half of all 12- to 20-year-olds drink. Second, one fifth (19.7 percent) of the alcohol consumed in the United States in 1999 was by underage drinkers. Third, this age group accounted for about one fifth (19.4 percent, $22.5 billion) of consumer spending that year for beer, wine, and distilled spirits. Why do young people drink alcohol? According to a survey of twelfth graders (O'Malley et al., 1998) the main reason is "to have a good time with friends." Other reasons include curiosity, the desire to feel good or get high, to relax or relieve tension, or because it tastes good. Adolescent drinking is also linked to alcohol use by parents, siblings, and peers (Rittenhouse and Miller 1984; Brook et al., 1986; Botvin et al., 1998; Bobo et al., 2000).

National survey data reveal that underage alcohol use and binge use increased with increasing age:

- 2.0 percent at age 12; binge use 0.8 percent
- 6.5 percent at age 13; binge use 2.8 percent
- 13.4 percent at age 14; binge use 7.0 percent
- 19.9 percent at age 15; binge use 11.6 percent
- 29.0 percent at age 16; binge use 17.9 percent
- 36.2 percent at age 17; binge use 25.0 percent

This trend continued to 70.9 percent (use) and 50.2 percent (binge) at age 21 years (HHS 2002a). Furthermore, more than one fourth of the age group 12 to 20 (28.8 percent or 10.7 million persons) reported drinking alcohol in the prior thirty days. Nearly one fourth of those in this age group (7.2 million, 19.3 percent) were binge drinkers and a smaller percentage (6.2 percent, 2.3 million) were heavy drinkers. Males more frequently than females ages 12 to 20 reported binge drinking (21.8 percent vs. 16.7 percent) (HHS 2002a). There was some variation among geographic divisions in underage alcohol use rates (e.g., Pacific 24.2 percent; East South Central 26.4 percent; New England 33.9 percent); however, use rates for this group varied little by population density (e.g., large metropolitan areas 27.2 percent, small metropolitan areas 30.7 percent; non-metropolitan rural areas 26.0 percent) (HHS 2002a).

Elderly and Women

Government estimates are that 2.5 million older adults in the United States experience alcohol-related problems (HHS 2001a). Recommendations from the National Institute of Alcohol and Alcoholism (NIAAA 1995) are that people 65 years of age or older should consume no more than one drink a day. The definition of one drink is 12 ounces of beer, 5 ounces of wine, or 1.5 ounces of distilled spirits. A national survey in 2002 found that heavy drinking was reported by:

- 3.8 percent of people 55 to 59 years of age
- 4.7 percent of people from 60 to 64
- 1.4 percent of adults 65 and older (HHS 2002a)

This survey also found that 6.35 million people 55 and older had been binge drinking (five drinks or more on a single occasion) in the previous thirty days.

The Substance Abuse and Mental Health Services Administration of the Department of Health and Human Services brochure on alcohol and aging identifies warning signs of alcohol abuse:

- memory trouble after drinking or taking medications
- problems with coordination
- altered sleeping or eating habits
- failure to bathe
- mood swings (irritability, depression, sadness)
- failure to maintain contact with family and friends
- difficulty completing sentences
- inexplicable bruises or chronic pain
- disinterest in customary activities
- lack of self assurance
- problems concentrating (HHS 2001b)

Seniors may be more vulnerable to alcohol misuse because of considerable free time; losses associated with physical capabilities or divorce; the absence of monitoring by work associates; or the need for drinking to cope with stress. Furthermore, the adverse effects of alcohol on the elderly may be exacerbated by medications or the physical aging of the body (including decreased body water, diminished tolerance to alcohol, and changes in metabolic processes) (Morris 2004a, 2004b). Drinking can trigger serious health problems, especially for the elderly, including:

- heightened risk for hypertension and cardiovascular disease
- increased vulnerability to stroke
- impaired immune system
- cirrhosis and other liver diseases
- lessened bone density
- malnutrition
- gastrointestinal bleeding (HHS 2000b)

Women's use and response to alcohol differs from men. In response to a 2002 national survey question about alcohol drinking in the past month, men were more likely than women to report drinking: the percentage for those age 12 or older was 57.4 percent for men and 44.9 percent for women (excluding youths ages 12 to 17). No gender difference was found among the 12 to 17 year-old age group. When considering pregnant women ages 15 to 44, alcohol use (9.1 percent) and binge drinking (2.1 percent) occurred in the thirty days before the survey.

Although 9 percent of men are heavy drinkers, the proportion of women is 2 percent (SAMHSA 1998). Thus it is not surprising that there is a significantly lower prevalence of alcohol-related problems among women. Nonetheless, a critical review of the literature by Mumenthaler and his colleagues (1999) reveals that women experience greater cognitive impairment than men after drinking the same amount of alcohol, and they are more vulnerable to such long-term health effects of drinking as alcoholic liver disease. Also, women are found to experience faster alcohol disappearance rates than men (i.e., per hour elimination of more alcohol per volume of blood).

Race and Ethnic Groups

Race and ethnicity differences are notable regarding alcohol use and binge drinking as well. National survey data from 2002 reveal the following use and binge use patterns across racial and ethnic groups:

- 55.0 percent whites; binge use 23.4 percent
- 44.7 percent American Indians/Alaska Natives; binge use 27.9 percent
- 42.8 percent Hispanics; binge use 24.8 percent
- 39.9 percent Blacks; binge use 21.0 percent
- 37.1 percent Asians; binge use 12.4 percent

When underage drinking is examined by racial/ethnic groups, data shows fewer Asians and blacks age 12 to 17 reported alcohol use in the past (7.4 percent and 10.9 percent, respectively); with rates higher than 15 percent for other racial/ethnic groups (HHS 2002a).

Religious and Cultural Groups

Sociocultural norms, such as religious beliefs, likely affect drinking patterns. For example, a number of religious groups, such as Mormons, Seventh Day Adventists, Nazarenes, and Southern Baptists, have strong prohibitions against alcohol use (Nelson et al., 2004). These mores may partially explain low consumption rates and binge drinking in Utah and portions of the South. Similarly, research by Chaloupka and Wechsler (1996) finds that students who value the importance of participation in campus religious activities are less likely to drink or binge drink than those who do not value such activities as important.

Patock-Peckham and her colleagues (1998) studied college students with no religious affiliation together with those of either Catholic or Protestant affiliation. Levels of drinking frequency and quantity as well as getting drunk and drinking for celebratory reasons were higher for those without religious affiliation than for those with Catholic or Protestant affiliation. The authors distinguished between religious affiliation and intrinsic religiosity (ego involvement with religious tenets), finding that religiosity played a more important negative role over drinking behavior for Catholics than for Protestants.

Engs and her colleagues (1990) compare U.S. and Canadian students and find that American Catholic and Protestant students drink more and experience alcohol abuse problems more frequently than Canadian students with the same religious affiliation. In considering whether religion or culture are more significant influences

on drinking behavior, these authors conclude from their student sample that "...
religious norms have greater influence in cohesive religious groups and culture has
greater influence in less cohesive religious groups..." (p. 1482).

Mizruchi and Perrucci (1970) used a U.S. sociocultural approach to develop a three-
fold typology: proscriptive (Mormons and Methodists where drinking is religiously
forbidden), prescriptive (Jews and Italians where drinking is expected, but drunkenness prohibited), and permissive (unspecified norms). Room and Makela (2000) review
numerous typologies of the cultural position of drinking in the social science literature
and then develop their own four ideal types: abstinent societies (some Islamic societies),
constrained ritual drinking (Orthodox Jews), banalized drinking (southern European
wine cultures), and fiesta drunkenness (carnival in Rio de Janeiro).

Consequences of Consumption

Having examined the drinking patterns of particular groups, the focus shifts to
the consequences of alcohol use focusing on high risk behaviors and some resulting
social problems. Here a brief overview is provided of alcohol-related consequences
such as driving while intoxicated, risk-taking behaviors, suicide and injuries, violence, and other forms of substance abuse. This is a selective set of consequences
that excludes other significant social problems such as school/work/family difficulties, psychopathologies, morbidity/mortality, and productivity/health costs.

Driving Under the Influence

Driving under the influence of alcohol is a growing problem in the United States.
National survey data indicate that among Americans 12 or older, 14.2 percent (33.5
million persons) admit to driving under the influence once or more in the year
preceding the interview. Women were half as likely as men (9.9 percent vs. 18.8
percent) to drive under the influence of alcohol. Among those 18 to 25 years, more
than one fourth reported driving under the influence one or more times in the past
year (HHS 2002a).

Risk-Taking

Studies of alcohol-related risk taking among teenagers have found that those at
highest risk have:

- lower needs for academic achievement
- families with poorer parenting competencies
- greater needs for sensation seeking
- more interactions with deviant peer groups (Burns et al., 1993)

Research by Severson and associates (1993) of adolescents' risk perceptions finds that those more often pursuing high-risk activities such as alcohol use:

- are more knowledgeable about risks
- are less fearful of risks
- are less able to avoid risky activities
- perceive greater control over risk
- perceive greater peer participation in such activities

Suicide and Injuries

Sociologic and psychologic studies have examined the relationship between alcohol use and suicide. Sociologic research stresses explanations linking drinking and suicide, focusing on weakened social integration, impaired social relations, problems meeting social role expectations, loss of significant others, and social isolation (Cahalan and Room 1974; Kendall 1983; Norstrom 1988; Skog 1991; Stack and Wasserman 1993). Psychologic explanations consider the connection of alcoholism, depression, and suicide, stressing that impulsive behavior associated with alcohol use can increase the risk of suicide (Wasserman 1989; Skog 1991; Lester 1992a; 1992b; Stack and Wasserman 2001). Also, excessive alcohol use can be associated with loss of self esteem and enhanced possibility of lethal overdose of certain drugs (Lester 1992a, 1992b).

Some results linking alcohol and suicide are mixed. For example, an examination of U.S. suicide rates by Gruenwald et al. (1995) found such deaths were not related to beer or wine consumption, but they were linked to consumption of hard liquor. Research by Smart and Mann (1990) in Canada found that in some periods (1963–1974), there was a significant association between suicide rates and alcohol consumption, but in other time periods (1975–1983), there was no relationship. This finding they attribute to increasing alcohol consumption in the first period versus stable or decreasing consumption in the second period.

Several studies have documented that heavy drinkers and alcoholics have high injury rates, often resulting in death (e.g., drownings, ski injuries, pedestrian fatalities). For example, Mann and his colleagues (2001) examined survey-based injury data from Ontario, Canada, between 1977 and 1996 and found that injury deaths were significantly associated with the percentage of daily drinkers and per capita consumption of alcohol.

Violence

The significant association between the availability and use of alcohol and violence of various kinds is well established (Spunt et al., 1994; Friedrich et al., 1995; Alaniz et al., 1998, 1999). For example, Parker and Auerhaun (1998, p. 303) examine

literature explaining the relationship between alcohol availability and youth violence as a partial byproduct of the spatial distribution of alcohol outlets and the
social context (setting, circumstances, permissive atmosphere) where youths consume alcohol. Such factors may "disinhibit" normal behaviors and diminish external social controls on violence (Sherman et al., 1989; Roncek and Maier 1991;
Alaniz et al., 1998). Furthermore, use of cultural symbols in advertisements targeting minority communities have been examined by Alaniz et al. (1999) and Alaniz
and Wilkes (1995) to confirm the link between density of alcohol outlets and youth
violence.

Alcohol is a significant factor in other incidents of domestic violence as well.
For example, alcohol is involved in approximately 40 percent of child maltreatment
cases (Children of Alcoholics Foundation 1996). In many cases alcohol has been
used prior to instances of child abuse (Gil 1973; Behling 1979; Famularo et al.,
1986) as well as criminal assaults and rapes (Collins 1981). This association between
alcohol use and violence is not only attributable to social and cultural determinants,
but also to pharmacologic, endocrinologic, neurobiologic, and environmental factors. Although the relationship between alcohol use and violence is complex, alcohol
use may be offered as a justification for violent behavior (Gelles and Cornell 1990).

Tobacco and Drug Use

There is an association between alcohol use and both illicit drug and tobacco use.
Among those alcohol users aged 12 or older, the use of illicit drugs in the prior
month was as follows:

- Heavy drinkers, 32.6 percent used illicit drugs
- Binge drinkers, 16.6 percent used illicit drugs
- Past month alcohol use but not binge drinking, 5.8 percent used illicit
  drugs
- No alcohol use, 3.6 percent used illicit drugs

Among heavy drinking youth, this pattern is even more pronounced with 67 percent
using illicit drugs compared with 5.6 percent among nondrinkers (HHS 2002a).

Alcohol use is linked to tobacco use as well. This is evident when drinking patterns are examined for those who smoke currently and those who do not currently
smoke:

- Binge alcohol use, 43.1 percent current smokers vs. 15.8 percent nonsmokers
- Heavy alcohol use, 15.9 percent vs. 3.5 percent (HHS 2002a).

Risky behaviors such as those discussed have potentially serious social consequences.
Alcohol dependence and abuse is also linked with problems in the home, school, and

workplace as well as impairing mental and physical health and adding costs to health care and workforce productivity. Given these concerns, what can be done from a legal, policy, or program perspective to control, prevent, or treat alcohol-related problems? Certain social control strategies have been used with varying levels of success, including sale/use restrictions, blood alcohol tests, drivers license withdrawal, and modifications of the drinking age. These will be briefly discussed together with certain preventive policies such as pricing/taxing policies, warnings, advertising limits, and convenience or access restrictions. Here the gap between those who needed and received alcohol-related treatment is considered. Finally, social norms and the prevention of alcohol abuse are examined with specific attention to university settings.

Strategic Responses

Legal/Social Controls

Federal and state governments have enacted traffic safety laws to reduce motor vehicle fatalities. The Federal Uniform Drinking Age Act of 1984 led states to set the minimum legal drinking age at 21 years and Public Law 100-690 required warning labels on alcohol containers regarding drinking and driving and drinking while pregnant. A national study for the period between 1978 and 1985 found that blood alcohol concentration (BAC) laws and administrative per se laws (facilitating license withdrawal from suspected drunk drivers) reduced fatal automobile crashes by an average of 2.4 percent and 4.6 percent, respectively. For example, Oklahoma enacted such drinking and driving laws in the early 1980s. Subsequently, there were one third fewer automobile fatalities and fatal crashes. Although this reduction was primarily attributed to lower per capita alcohol use and higher unemployment, a combination of BAC and administrative per se laws were found to reduce the state's traffic fatalities and fatal crashes by 9 percent in the four years after passage. These factors were more important in accounting for the reduction than raising of the state's minimum drinking age law (Muller 1989).

Regulatory strategies such as those considered above are often insufficient to adequately address the adverse effects of alcohol dependence and abuse. Preventive strategies are needed as well. These are discussed in the following section.

Pricing/Taxing Policies

Several studies have examined the influence of alcohol pricing policies on the consumption patterns of adolescents and adults. In general, these studies indicate that adolescents are more sensitive to price increases than are adults. For example, Grossman et al. (1993) found that for young people a combination of tight budgets and less importance attributed to future costs or consequences of drinking helps to explain why they differ from adults in their reaction to alcohol pricing. Chaloupka and Wechsler (1996) focused on college students' reactions to alcohol pricing and drunk-driving laws as deterrents to drinking and binge drinking. They found that, compared with other groups, college students were less responsive to the price of alcohol, but that the severity of penalties for drunk driving reduced drinking and binge drinking. Research by Grossman et al. (1995) and by Chaloupka and associates (1993) conclude that increased tax on alcohol would reduce adolescent alcohol consumption as well as drinking-related injuries and death. Other research on the influence of pricing finds that increasing beer tax can lead to a reduction of domestic violence against children (Markowitz and Grossman 1998).

Warnings

Alcohol warning labels are a potential deterrent to alcohol use and abuse. However, there is little evidence demonstrating that alcohol-related attitudes or behaviors have changed after the addition of container warnings (Andrews 1995; MacKinnon 1995). There is a body of research suggesting that gender, socioeconomic status, religion, and race/ethnicity may influence the receptivity and efficacy of warnings. In general, there is some evidence that women are more likely than men to seek out, read, and heed product warnings and to view alcohol as harmful (Godfrey et al., 1983; LaRue and Cohen 1987; Laughery and Brelsford 1991; Nohre et al., 1999), whereas men are more conscious that alcohol warnings exist and more accurate in recalling the warning than women (Graves 1983; Kaskutas and Greenfield 1992, 1997). Lower socioeconomic status (SES) adults are found to more frequently think alcohol is harmful and to believe warnings that are on alcohol containers than higher SES adults, but they are less frequently correct in recalling specific risks associated with alcohol abuse (Mazis et al., 1991). Practicing Mormons, conscious of their church's admonishment against alcohol use and Utah's restrictive alcohol control laws, less frequently view the alcohol warning label than non-Mormons (Mayer et al., 1991). Some researchers detect no differences among African Americans, Hispanics, and whites (Mazis et al., 1996; Kaskutas and Greenfield 1997), whereas MacKinnon (1995) find nonwhites have greater awareness of the warning label law but no greater exposure. The latter study of high school seniors also finds other "receiver characteristics" to be associated with warning label measures in addition to those already mentioned, including student grades, heavy drinking experience, student friendship with alcohol users, drinking from the alcohol container, attendance at religious services, and television watching, among others.

Advertising Limits

Targeted marketing of alcohol to underage drinkers has been a recurring issue. Research by Grube and Wallack (1994) showed that exposure to beer advertisements among fifth- and sixth-grade students was significantly linked to their intentions to drink in adulthood. Three additional examples developed by Beauchamp and his colleagues (2004) highlight the marketing aspect of the problem: Cisco wine, Hooper's Hooch, and Absolut vodka. In the Cisco wine case, a drink classified as a fortified desert wine, but with a 20 percent alcohol level, was packaged in a "cooler style" appearance, sold in single bottles at convenience stores, priced affordably, and marketed with a slogan "Cisco takes you by surprise." When the U.S. Surgeon General referred to the drink as "dangerous" and a "wine fooler" and other public interest groups complained, some stores discontinued sales. Despite modification of the label and discontinuation of the marketing slogan, underage drinkers continued to use it as a cheap way to get high. Eventually, the bottle and the label were further modified to the satisfaction of the Surgeon General, the Bureau of Alcohol, Tobacco, and Firearms (BATF), and the Federal Trade Commission (FTC). Hooper's Hooch and other drinks known as "alcopops" are fruit drinks with alcohol content between 5 and 7 percent. Some firms were accursed of target marketing these drinks to youths. Objections by the Center for Science in the Public Interest, the BATF and FTC alleged a connection between underage drinking and advertising. Finally, Absolut vodka advertisements and Web site (despite restricted access) gained popularity with adolescents, which some journalists thought might influence youthful drinkers. These examples illustrate the controversy surrounding niche marketing of alcohol products to underage drinkers.

Convenience/Access

There is a positive association between the increased availability of alcohol and its use and abuse. This has prompted some to advocate tight restrictions on the sale of alcohol, but others believe such restrictions are ineffective (Morgan 1992). There is some evidence to suggest that making alcohol less accessible may lead to a reduction in severe violence (Markowitz and Grossman 1998).

When regulation and prevention fail, or inadequately address the problem, the focus shifts to treatment alternatives. These might include support groups, medication, family interventions, and cognitive-behavior therapy. Each of these holds some promise for ameliorating the problems facing specific alcohol abusers. However, the proportion of people needing treatment for an alcohol problem vastly exceeds the number receiving treatment. It is estimated that 18.6 million people (7.9 percent of the total population) need treatment, whereas only 1.5 million (8.3 percent of the needy) receive it. Among those needing but not receiving treatment, most failed to acknowledge the need for treatment of an alcohol problem. Of the group acknowledging the need, 35 percent tried but were unsuccessful in obtaining treatment and 65 percent failed to seek treatment. For those receiving treatment, the highest proportion (46.3 percent) used their own savings to pay for it, a smaller proportion used private insurance (31.7 percent), and about equal proportions relied on Medicaid (21.4 percent) or another form of public assistance (21.5 percent) (HHS 2002a).

Social Norms

A large and growing body of research focuses on social norms and drinking, especially among college students. Social norms research examines the actual or perceived behavior of those in one's social network and whether those in the network approve the behavior (Simon 2003). Using this approach, alcohol-related research finds that young adults and college students often overestimate the number of their peers who consume alcohol, the amount consumed, and the number who drink excessively (Perkins and Berkowitz 1991; Agostinelli and Miller 1994; Perkins 1994, 2002; Perkins et al., 1999). Furthermore, peer norms are deemed more significant than other reference groups or factors in explaining alcohol consumption, including parents, faculty, and resident advisors as well as other sociodemographic and contextual variables. Peer norms are important because if there is a large gap between actual and perceived student drinking norms, the exaggerated beliefs of peer drinking norms may facilitate alcohol misuse as students seek to conform to perceived norms. The premise of many prevention programs is that correcting students' misperceptions regarding classmates' alcohol consumption would alter their perception of the social norm and thus lead to reduced campus drinking. This section reviews selected studies of social norms, some related programmatic alternatives to reduce campus drinking, and a few of the lessons learned from such efforts.

Rimal and Real (2003) make the distinction between two types of perceived norms: descriptive and normative. Descriptive norms refer to peoples' beliefs about how prevalent a particular behavior (drinking) is among their cohort group. Such perceptions may be accurate or inaccurate. Injunctive norms refer to the degree to which people perceive pressure to conform to particular behaviors (consuming alcohol). These pressures may take various forms, including exclusion from the group. The authors assume that congruence between these two types of norms (beliefs that most students drink and pressures exist to comply) strongly influences behavior. Based on a survey of college students, Rimal and Real found that the two types of norms had differential effects on behavior: descriptive norms failed to achieve significance when other factors were included in the model, but perceived benefits to oneself were significantly linked to consumption. Their findings suggest that health campaigns designed to reduce consumption should not only correct misperceptions about the extent of drinking, but also alter students' perceptions regarding the benefits from consumption. This could be done through antialcohol campaigns challenging the perceived benefits associated with alcohol consumption or, alternatively, conveying the benefits of moderate or no drinking while stressing the costs associated with heavy drinking.

Sociocultural explanations for alcohol use are especially apt for heavy drinkers. Research by Wild (2002) found that heavy consumers of alcohol (five or more drinks at least once per week or more) were more likely than those who use less alcohol to believe their drinking habits were more typical of consumption patterns among friends, coworkers, and the general public and that others consumed more alcohol in various social settings than they did. They were also more likely to attribute alcohol problems to others and to have fewer qualms about the drinking habits of friends, coworkers, and the general public. This leads heavy drinkers to view their own drinking patterns as "normative, rather than unusual or deviant" (Prentice and Miller 1993; Wild 2002, p. 474).

How can student misperceptions of peer norms be reduced? One way is to communicate the actual student norms regarding drinking, thereby dispelling myths. This approach is deemed to be simple, efficient, and effective. Advertisements and articles in student newspapers, lectures, posters, radio spots, and so forth can be included in such an information campaign (Berkowitz and Perkins 1991; Steffian 1997; Barnett et al., 1996). Certain groups can be targeted for programming (e.g., fraternities and sororities, residence halls, heavy drinkers). Media campaigns focusing on the adverse consequences of heavy drinking have been launched in Boston ("Party Smart"), Ohio ("Dirk" campaign), and elsewhere; however, such information campaigns have had negligible impact on student drinking (DeJong 2002). Advocacy campaigns take a more aggressive stance by urging students to get involved to do something to reduce behaviors such as binge drinking. Web sites such as HadEnough.org stress the adverse consequences of heavy drinking. DeJong identifies several guidelines and lessons based on the successes and failures of past mass communication campaigns:

- Launch a strategic planning process
- Select a strategic objective
- Select the target audience
- Develop a staged approach
- Define the key promise
- Avoid fear appeals
- Select the right message source
- Select a mix of media channels
- Maximize media exposure
- Conduct formative research
- Conduct process and outcome evaluations (p. 186–189)

Within the public health community, there is a recognition that it may be counterproductive to pursue preventive approaches which depend on calling attention to the severity of alcohol use (e.g., binge drinking) and that a more useful strategy is to base campaigns on perceptual norms. This is predicated on the belief that if the "perceived prevalence of drinking can be reduced, then actual consumption will decline as well" (Haines 1996; Perkins et al., 1999; Steffian 1997; Rimal and Real 2003, p. 196).

Conclusion

There is a rich literature on alcohol—its use, abuse, and the consequences of consumption. This chapter provides an overview of some of the sociocultural dimensions of this issue, but barely scratches the surface of this complex topic. It highlights the alcohol consumption patterns of diverse special populations, selected consequences of excessive consumption, and some social control strategies to deal with the resulting social problems. Much of the literature has focused on the underage drinker and the heavy drinker, emphasizing the social context for drinking and the social consequences of consumption. Legal strategies have had some impact on ameliorating the adverse consequences of underage and heavy drinking, but other preventive and treatment strategies are needed together with public education, controlled access, appropriate advertising, and pricing policies to adequately address the problem. This is especially important given the gap between treatment needed and treatment received. Public policy initiatives such as increased public funding of treatment programs and additional publication of resource guides for community leaders are needed as well. Prevention programs centered on social norms offer another strategy for addressing issues surrounding alcohol consumption. Public health initiatives focused on information dissemination, marketing, and advocacy campaigns have shown promising results in selected settings. Regardless of the strategic approach employed, sensitivity to cultural differences and contextual factors will aid in tailoring interventions and policies to properly address the needs of diverse demographic and cultural groups.

References

Agostinelli, G., and W. Miller. "Drinking and Thinking: How Does Personal Drinking Affect Judgments of Prevalence and Risk?" *Journal of Drug Education* 55 (1994): 327–37.

Alaniz, M., R. Parker, A. Gallegos, and R. Cartmill. "Immigrants and Violence: The Importance of Context." *Hispanic Journal of Behavioral Science* 20:2 (1998): 81–6.

Alaniz, M., R. Parker, A. Gallegos, and R. Cartmill. "Ethnic Targeting and the Objectification of Women: Alcohol Advertising and Violence Against Young Latinos." In *Currents in Criminology,* edited by Parker, R. 1999.

Alaniz, M., and C. Wilkes. "Reinterpreting Latino Culture in the Commodity Form: The Case of Alcohol Advertising in the Mexican American Community." *Hispanic Journal of Behavioral Science* 17:4 (1995): 430–51.

Andrews, J. "The Effectiveness of Alcohol Warning Labels: A Review and Extension." *American Behavioral Scientist* 83 (1995): 622–33.

Archer, L., B. Grant, and D. Dawson. "What If Americans Drank Less? The Potential Effect on the Prevalence of Alcohol Abuse and Dependence." *American Journal of Public Health* 85:1 (1995): 61–6.

Barnett, L., J. Far, A. Mauss, and J. Miller. "Changing Perceptions of Peer Norms as a Drinking Reduction Program for College Students." *Journal of Alcohol and Drug Education* 41:2 (1996): 39–62.

Beauchamp, T., J. Cuddihy, J. Greene, M. Hammer, and D. Spring. "Marketing Alcoholic Beverages and its Impact on Underage Drinkers." In *Case Studies in Business, Society and Ethics*, edited by T. Beauchamp. Upper Saddle River, NJ: Prentice Hall, 2004: 169–76.

Behling, D. "Alcohol Abuse Encountered in 51 Instances of Reported Child Abuse." *Clinical Pediatrics* 18 (1979): 87–91.

Bobo, J., and C. Husten. "Sociocultural Influences on Smoking and Drinking." *Alcohol Research & Health* 24:4 (2000): 225–40.

Botvin, G., R. Malgady, K. Griffin, L. Scheier, and J. Epstein. "Alcohol and Marijuana Use Among Rural Youth: Interaction of Social and Intrapersonal Influences." *Addictive Behaviors* 23:3 (1998): 379–87.

Brook, J., M. Whiteman, A. Gordon, C. Nomura, and D. Brook. "Onset of Adolescent Drinking: A Longitudinal Study of Intrapersonal and Interpersonal Antecedents." *Advances in Alcohol and Substance Abuse* 5:3 (1986): 91–110.

Burns, W., S. Hampson, H. Severson, and P. Slovik. "Alcohol-Related Risk Taking Among Teenagers: An Investigation of Contributing Factors and a Discussion of How Marketing Principles Can Help." *Advances in Consumer Research* 20 (1993): 183–7.

Cahalan, D., and R. Room. *Problem Drinking Among American Men.* New Brunswick, NJ: Rutgers Center of Alcohol Studies, 1974.

Chaloupka, F., H. Saffer, and M. Grossman. "Alcohol-Control Policies and Motor Vehicle Fatalities." *Journal of Legal Studies* 22:1 (1993): 161–86.

Chaloupka, F., and H. Wechsler. "Binge Drinking in College: The Impact of Price, Availability, and Alcohol Control Policies." *Contemporary Economic Policy* 14:4 (1996): 112–25.

Children of Alcoholics Foundation. *Helping Children Affected by Parental Addiction and Family Violence: Collaboration, Coordination, and Cooperation.* New York: CAF, 1996.

Collins, J. *Drinking and Crime: Perspectives on the Relationships Between Alcohol Consumption and Criminal Behavior.* New York: The Guilford Press, 1981.

Dawson, D., B. Grant, and P. Chou. "Gender Differences in Alcohol Intake." In *Stress, Gender, and Alcohol-Seeking Behavior*, edited by Hunt, W., and S. Zakhari, S. NIAAA Research Monograph No. 29. NIH Pub. No. 95-3893. Bethesda, MD: NIAAA: 1995: 1–21.

DeJong, W. "The Role of Mass Media Campaigns in Reducing High-Risk Drinking Among College Students." *Journal of Studies on Alcohol* 14 (2002): 182–92.

Dufour, M. "What is Moderate Drinking?" *Alcohol Research & Health* 23:1 (1999): 5–20.

Engs, R., D. Hanson, L. Gliksman, and C. Smythe. "Influence of Religion and Culture on Drinking Behaviours: A Test of Hypotheses Between Canada and the USA." *British Journal of Addiction* 85 (1990): 1475–82.

Famularo, R., K. Stone, R. Barnum, and R. Wharton. "Alcoholism and Severe Child Maltreatment." *American Journal of Orthopsychiatry* 56 (1986): 481–5.

Foster, S., R. Vaughan, W. Foster, and J. Califano. "Alcohol Consumption and Expenditures for Underage Drinking and Adult Excessive Drinking." *Journal of the American Medical Association* 289:8 (2003): 989–95.

Friedrich, M., M. Mackesy-Amiti, P. Goldstein, B. Spunt, and H. Brownstein. "Substance Involvement Among Juvenile Murderers: Comparison with Older Offenders Based on Interviews with Prison Inmates." *International Journal of Addictions* 30:22 (1995): 1363–82.

Gelles, R., and C. Cornell. *Intimate Violence in Families*. Newbury Park, CA: Sage Publications, 1990.

Gil, D. *Violence Against Children: Physical Child Abuse in the United States*. Cambridge, MA: Harvard University Press, 1973.

Godfrey, S., L. Allender, K. Laughery, and V. Smith. "Warning Messages: Will the Consumer Bother to Look?" Proceedings of the Human Factors Society. 27th annual meeting. Santa Monica, CA: HFS: 1983: 950–4.

Graves, K. "An Evaluation of the Alcohol Warning Label: A Comparison of the United States and Ontario, Canada in 1990 and 1991." *Journal of Pubic Policy and Marketing* 12 (1993): 19–29.

Greenfield, T., and J. Rogers. "Who Drinks Most of the Alcohol in the U.S.? The Policy Implications." *Journal of Student Alcohol* 60 (1999): 78–89.

Grossman, M., J. Sindelar, M. Mullahy, and R. Anderson. "Policy Watch: Alcohol and Cigarette Taxes." *Journal of Economic Perspectives* 7:4 (1993): 211–22.

Grossman, M., F. Chaloupka, H. Saffer, and A. Laixuthai. "Effects of Alcohol Price Policy on Youth: A Summary of Economic Research." In *Alcohol Problems Among Adolescents: Current Directions in Prevention Research*, edited by Boyd, G., J. Howard, and R. Zucker, R. Hillsdale, NJ: Lawrence Erlbaum Associates, 1995: 225–42.

Grube, J., and L. Wallack. "Television Beer Advertising and Drinking Knowledge, Beliefs, and Intentions Among Schoolchildren." *American Journal of Public Health* 84:2 (1994): 254–9.

Gruenwald, P., W. Ponicki, and P. Mitchell. "Suicide Rates and Alcohol Consumption and Problems in Ontario, 1975–1983. *Addiction* 90 (1995): 1063–75.

Haines, M. P. "Social Norms Approach to Preventing Binge Drinking at Colleges and Universities." Newton, MA: Higher Education Center for Alcohol and Other Drug Prevention, Department of Education, 1996.

Kaskutas, L., and T. Greenfield. "First Effects of Warning Labels on Alcoholic Beverage Containers." *Drug and Alcohol Dependence* 31 (1992): 1–14.

Kaskutas, L., and T. Greenfield. "The Role of Health Consciousness in Predicting Attention to Health Warning Messages." *American Journal of Public Health Promotion* 11 (1997): 186–193.

Kendall, R. "Alcohol and Suicide." *Substance and Alcohol Actions/Misuse* 4 (1983): 121–7.

LaRue, C., and H. Cohen. "Factors Affecting Consumers' Perceptions of Product Warnings: An Examination of the Differences Between Male and Female Consumers." Proceedings of the Human Factors Society. 31st annual meeting. Santa Monica, CA: HFS, 1987: 610–4.

Laughery, K., and J. Brelsford. "Receiver Characteristics in Safety Communications." Proceedings of the Human Factors Society. 35th annual meeting. Santa Monica, DA: HFS, 1991: 1068–72.

Lester, D. "Alcoholism and Drug Abuse." In *Assessment and Prediction of Suicide*, edited by Maris, R., A. Berman, J. Maltsberger, and R. Yufit. New York: Guilford, 1992a: 321–6.

Lester, D. *Why People Kill Themselves*. 3rd edition. Springfield, IL: Charles C. Thomas, 1992b.

MacKinnon, D. "Review of the Effects of the Alcohol Warning Label." In *Drug and Alcohol Abuse Reviews. Alcohol, Cocaine, and Accidents*, Vol. 7, pp. 131–161. Ed. Watson, R. Totowa, NJ: Humana Press, 1995.

Mann, R., H. Suurvali, and R. Smart. "The Relationship Between Alcohol Use and Mortality Rates from Injuries: A Comparison of Measures." *American Journal of Drug and Alcohol Abuse* 27:4 (2001): 737–48.

Margolis, R., and J. Zweben *Treating Patients with Alcohol and Other Drug Problems: An Integrated Approach*. Washington, D.C.: American Psychological Association, 1998.

Markowitz, S., and M. Grossman. "Alcohol Regulation and Domestic Violence Towards Children." *Contemporary Economic Policy* 16:3 (1998): 309–21.

Mayer, R., K. Smith, and D. Scammon. "Evaluating the Impact of Alcohol Warning Labels." *Advances in Consumer Research* 18 (1991): 706–14.

Mazis, M., L. Morris, and J. Swasy. "An Evaluation of the Alcohol Warning Label: Initial Survey Results." *Journal of Public Policy and Marketing* 10 (1991): 229–41.

Mazis, M., L. Morris, and J. Swasy. "Longitudinal Study of Awareness, Recall, and Acceptance of Alcohol Warning Labels." *Applied Behavioral Science Review* 4 (1996): 111–20.

Midanik, L., T. Tam, T. Greenfield, and R. Caetano. "Risk Functions for Alcohol-Related Problems in a 1988 National Sample." *Addiction* 91 (1996): 1427–37.

Mizruchi, E., and R. Perrucci. "Prescription, Proscription and Permissiveness: Aspects of Norms and Deviant Drinking Behavior." In *The Domesticated Drug: Drinking Among Collegians*, edited by Maddox, G. New Haven, CT: College & University Press, 1970: 234–53.

Morgan, J. "Prohibition Was and Is Bad for the Nation's Health." In *Substance Abuse: A Comprehensive Textbook*, edited by Lowinson, J., P. Ruiz, R. Millman, and J. Langrod, J. 2nd edition. Baltimore: Williams & Wilkins, 1992: 1012–8.

Morris, B. R. "Help for Older People with Alcohol Problems." *New York Times* D5. May 18, 2004a.

Morris, B. R. "When Retirement Leaves an Emptiness, Some Fill it with Alcohol." *New York Times* D5. May 18, 2004b.

Muller, A. "Business Recession, Alcohol Consumption, Drinking and Driving Laws: Impact on Oklahoma Motor Vehicle Fatalities and Fatal Crashes." *American Journal of Public Health* 79:10 (1989): 1366–70.

Mumenthaler, M., J. Taylor, R. O'Hara, and J. Yesavage. "Gender Differences in Moderate Drinking Effects." *Alcohol Research & Health* 23:1 (1999): 55–67.

National Institute on Alcohol Abuse and Alcoholism. *Physician's Guide to Helping Patients with Alcohol Problems*. Rockville, MD: NIAAA. NIH Pub. No. 95-3769, 1995.

Nelson, D., T. Naimi, R. Brewer, J. Bolen, and H. Wells. "Metropolitan Area Estimates of Binge Drinking in the United States." *American Journal of Public Health* 94:4 (2004): 663–72.

Nohre, L., D. MacKinnon, A. Stacy, and M. Pentz. "The Association Between Adolescents' Receiver Characteristics and Exposure to the Alcohol Warning Label." *Psychology & Marketing* 16:3 (1999): 245–59.

Norstrom, T. "Alcohol and Suicide in Scandanavia." *British Journal of Addiction* 83 (1988): 553–9.

O'Malley, P., D. Lloyd, and J. Bachman. "Alcohol Use Among Adolescents." *Alcohol Health & Research World* 22:2 (1998): 85–94.

Parker, R., and K. Auerhahn. "Alcohol, Drugs, and Violence." *Annual Review of Sociology* 24 (1998): 291–311.

Patock-Peckham, J., G. Hutchinson, J. Cheong, and C. Nagoshi. "Effect of Religion and Religiosity on Alcohol Use in a College Student Sample." *Drug and Alcohol Dependence* 49 (1998): 81–8.

Perkins, H. "The Contextual Effect of Secular Norms on Religiosity as Moderator of Student Alcohol and Other Drug Use." In *Research in the Social Scientific Study of Religion*, edited by Lynn, M., and D. Moberg. Greenwich, CT: JAI Press, 1994: 187–208.

Perkins, H. "Social Norms and the Prevention of Alcohol Misuse in Collegiate Contexts." *Journal of Studies on Alcohol* Supplement No. 14 (2002): 164–72.

Perkins, H., and A. Berkowitz. "Collegiate COAs and Alcohol Abuse: Problem Drinking in Relation to Assessments of Parent and Grandparent Alcoholism." *Journal of Counseling Development* 69 (1987): 237–40.

Perkins, H., P. Meilman, J. Leichliter, J. Cashin, and C. Presley. "Misperceptions of the Norms for the Frequency of Alcohol and Other Drug Use on College Campuses." *Journal of American College Health* 47 (1999): 253–8.

Prentice, D., and D. Miller. "Pluralistic Ignorance and Alcohol Use on Campus: Some Consequences of Misperceiving the Social Norm." *Journal of Personality and Social Psychology* 64 (1993): 243–56.

Rimal, R., and K. Real. "Understanding the Influence of Perceived Norms on Behavior." *Communication Theory* 13:2 (2003): 184–203.

Rittenhouse, J., and J. Miller. "Social Learning and Teenage Drug Use: An Analysis of Lustily Dyads." *Health Psychology* 3:4 (1984): 329–45.

Roncek, D., and P. Maier. "Bars, Blocks, Crimes Revisited: Linking the Theory of Routine Activities to the Empiricism of 'Hot Spots'." *Criminology* 29 (1991): 725–54.

Room, R., and K. Makela. "Typologies of the Cultural Position on Drinking." *Journal of Studies on Alcohol* (May 2000): 475–83.

Severson, H., P. Slovic, and S. Hampson. "Adolescents Perception of Risk: Understanding and Preventing High Risk Behavior." *Advances in Consumer Research* 20 (1993): 177–81.

Sherman, I., P. Gartin, and M. Buerger. "Hot Spots of Predatory Crime: Routine Activities and the Criminology of Place." *Criminology* Vol. 27 (1989): 27–56.

Simon, J. "Differential Prediction of Alcohol Use and Problems: The Role of Biopsychological and Social-Environmental Variables. *The American Journal of Drug and Alcohol Abuse* 29:4 (2003): 861–79.

Skog, O. "Alcohol and Suicide—Durkheim Revisited." *Acta Sociologica* 34 (1991): 193–206.

Smart, R., and R. Mann. "Changes in Suicide Rates After Reductions in Alcohol Consumption and Problems in Ontario, 1975–1983." *British Journal of Addiction* 85 (1990): 463–8.

Spunt, B., P. Goldstein, H. Brownstein, M. Fendrich, and S. Langley. "Alcohol and Homicide: Interviews with Prison Inmates." *Journal of Drug Issues* 24:1 (1994): 143–63.

Stack, S., and I. Wasserman. "Marital Status, Alcohol Consumption, and Suicide: An Analysis of National Data." *Journal of Marriage and the Family* 55 (1993): 1018–24.

Steffian, G. "Correction of Normative Misperceptions: An Alcohol Abuse Prevention Program." *Journal of Drug Education* 29 (1997): 115–38.

Substance Abuse and Mental Health Services Administration. *Preliminary Results from the 1997 National Household Survey on Drug Abuse.* NHSDA Series H-6. DHHS Pub. No. (SMA) 98-3251. Rockville, MD: SAMHSA, 1998.

United States Department of Agriculture. *Nutrition and Your Health: Dietary Guidelines for Americans.* Washington, D.C.: U.S. Department of Health and Human Services, 2000.

United States Department of Health and Human Services. *Aging, Medicine and Alcohol.* Washington, D.C.: HHS: Publication No. SMA 02-3619 or PHD 882, 2001b.

United States Department of Health and Human Services. *Alcohol Use Among Older Adults.* Washington, D.C.: HHS: Publication No. SMA 02-3621, 2001a.

United States Department of Health and Human Services. *Results from the 2002 National Survey on Drug Use and Health: National Findings.* Washington, D.C.: HHS, 2002a. www.oas.samhsa.gov/nhsda/2k2nsduh/results/2k2Results.htm

United States Department of Health and Human Services. *Substance Abuse Among Older Adults: A Guide for Social Service Providers.* Washington, D.C.: SMA 02–3689, 2000b.

Wasserman, I. "The Effects of War and Alcohol Consumption Patterns on Suicide: United States, 1910–1933." *Social Forces* 68 (1989): 513–30.

Wild, T. "Personal Drinking and Sociocultural Drinking Norms: A Representative Population Study." *Journal of Studies on Alcohol* (July 2002): 469–75.

Chapter 8

Perceptions, Policies, and Social Norms: Transforming Alcohol Cultures over the Next 100 Years

Jeffrey W. Linkenbach, Ed.D.

Contents

The significant problems we face can not be solved at the same level of thinking which created them.

— Albert Einstein

Introduction

At the dawn of a new century, alcohol prevention practitioners, government agencies, and researchers continue the age-old quest to reduce the problems of alcohol in society. Although many strategies have been tried—from increased penalties, to advertising restrictions, to taxes and price controls—the most essential element has been ignored: that of perceptions. People's perceptions closely guide their behaviors and attitudes; thus, the way in which individuals perceive how alcohol is consumed and regulated is key to the success or failure of any alcohol policy or program. Effective long-term solutions require prevention leaders who can implement strategies to steer public perceptions about alcohol, and thereby transform social norms of alcohol use.

The first part of this discussion will address the historical background and context for prevention efforts, and describe the integral relationship between perceptions, policies, and social norms. Part two will address strategies for correcting misperceptions that can set the stage for transforming the culture of alcohol over the next 100 years.

Section 1: Perceptions, Policies, and Social Norms

Background

The history of alcohol control efforts in the United States is many centuries old. From America's earliest colonial days to the present, strategies aimed at impacting alcohol-related norms have encompassed an ever-changing array of philosophies and social policy experiments (Langton 1996). As early as 1327, England had tried and failed to control drunkenness by limiting the number of establishments that could sell alcoholic beverages (Ray and Ksir 1999). Six hundred years later, America enacted the 18th Amendment and launched "the noble experiment" of prohibition, which today is regarded as a failed attempt to legislate morality and social change (Langton 1996, p. 166). Prohibition was seen as a simple solution to a complex social problem, "by which, in relation to more than 100,000,000 people, age-old evils could with one stroke be eliminated" (Fosdick and Scott 1933, p. 5). When the prohibition era officially ended in 1933, so too ended our naiveté and our hope for a magical policy that could mandate the improvement of social behavior.

Since the repeal of prohibition, prevention efforts have been characterized by see-sawing policies and shifting of public sentiments that demonstrate how easily the pendulum swings from one extreme to another, moving the locus of control from the individual to the society and back again, or switching the focus of prevention between education and enforcement (Fosdick and Scott 1933; Engs 1990; Calahan 1991; Goldberg 2004). To keep the public from rejecting or reacting poorly to laws that they perceive as overly liberal or too stringent, it is necessary to balance social behaviors and attitudes with policy (Posner 2000). The key to successfully balancing the relationship between law and social norms is the element of perception. The public's perception of the culture of alcohol and the laws designed to regulate it are as influential as the culture and laws themselves. The challenge for the field of alcohol prevention throughout the next 100 years is to promote interventions that balance the three domains of perceptions, policies, and social norms.

The Three-Tiered System of Alcohol Control

At the end of national prohibition, federal control over alcohol was returned to individual states (Ray and Ksir 1999). Many of the social evils of the pre-Prohibition era resulted from excessive promotion by the suppliers and retailers of alcohol, who were often one and the same (Whitman 2003). The public perception about these "tied-house" arrangements was that they encouraged irresponsible alcohol consumption, allowing purveyors to push to increase sales, no matter what the societal costs (WSWA 1999). The three-tiered system of alcohol control broke this monopoly by dividing the alcohol distribution system into three parts—suppliers, wholesalers, and retailers (Fosdick and Scott 1933; Whitman 2003).

In the forward to *Toward Liquor Control* (Fosdick and Scott 1933), the book that concretized the three-tiered system, John D. Rockefeller, Jr., describes how perceptions determine how the imposition of alcohol law ultimately impacts social behavior. He writes:

> Men cannot be made good by force. In the end, intelligent lawmaking
> rests on the knowledge or estimate of what will be obeyed. Law does

not enforce itself. The Eighteenth Amendment embodied an ideal, but could succeed only with the support of public opinion. (p. xi)

He goes on to note that prohibition failed because of inattention to the social norms of the day: "the majority of people in the country were not willing to support the aim of total abstinence, at least when it was attempted through coercion" (p. vii).

Prohibition sparked a major awakening to the powerful relationship between the legal and social communities, and the realization that "no system of liquor control could be successful which does not command the approval of the community" (Fosdick and Scott 1933, p. 9). Ever since, countless attempts have been made to control alcohol's impacts upon society through strategies that have focused on the individual drinker, the drinking context or the social-ecologic relationship between the two (Stokols 1992; Wallack 1997; Barr 1999). It is only recently, however, that a model has begun to emerge which explicitly captures the interplay between perceptions, alcohol policies, and social norms.

Comprehending a Complex Culture of Alcohol

Although the problems caused by alcohol have been around as long as alcohol itself, there is a constant sense of urgency surrounding them (Hawkins et al., 1992). New, pressing issues appear to sprout overnight. Recent examples include movements to ban alcohol vapor machines, which combine pressurized oxygen with alcohol in the form of a mist (Join Together 2004); controversies associated with underage drinking and youth-preferred products such as "alcopops" (Lee 2002), "hard lemonade" (Anderson 1999), or wine coolers (Goldberg et al., 1994); and numerous disputes over alcohol advertising (Kelly et al., 2002; Saffer and Dave 2002) and online marketing (Carroll and Donovan 2002).

This short list begins to illustrate the complex, ever-changing context in which the prevention of alcohol-related problems resides (Klitzner and Stewart 1991). The following excerpt from a speech attributed to a Midwestern senator around the early 1900s brilliantly depicts the political complexity of issues surrounding alcohol:

> ...You have asked me how I feel about whiskey. Well, here's how I stand on the question. If, when you say whiskey, you mean that devil's brew; the poison spirit; the bloody monster that defiles innocence, dethrones reason, destroys the home, and creates misery and poverty; yes, literally takes the bread from the mouths of little children; if you mean that evil drink that topples the religious man from the pinnacle of righteousness, gracious living, and causes him to descend to the pit of degradation, despair, shame, and helplessness, then I am certainly against it with all my heart.

But if when you say whiskey, you mean the oil of conversation, the philosophic wine, the ale consumed when good fellows get together that puts a song in their hearts and laughter on their lips and the warm glow of contentment in their eyes; if you mean Christmas cheer; if you mean the stimulating drink that puts the spring in an old man's footstep on a frosty morning; if you mean the drink whose sale put untold millions of dollars into our treasury which are used to provide tender care for our little crippled children, our blind, our deaf and dumb, our pitifully aged and infirm, to build highways and hospitals and schools, then certainly I am in favor of it. This is my stand, and I will not compromise. (Svendsen 1986)

One hundred years later, the complexity of alcohol's role in our culture remains essentially the same.

Perceptions, Alcohol Policies, and Social Norms

There are many definitions of social norms; for the purposes of this discussion, social norms are simply the actual majority behaviors or attitudes in any given community or group. For example, if most people in a community do not drink, then not drinking is the social norm. Not drinking is normal, acceptable, perhaps even expected in that population.

Perceptions of social norms are people's *beliefs* about the actual behavioral or attitudinal norms of their peers. If the majority of people in a community perceive that most people drink to excess, then drinking to excess is the perceived social norm. Perceptions of social norms are some of the strongest predictors of future health behavior because people tend to behave in the way they perceive to be most typical or accepted (Berkowitz 1997). When people perceive that there is social support for or against certain activities, they are more likely to either change or continue their behavior to act in accordance with what they believe is normative.

The relationship between perceptions and behavior is complicated by the fact that most people do not accurately perceive the social norms of their peers. Most people make positive decisions about their health and safety. That is almost universally the norm. For example, social norms studies have found that most people drink moderately, wear seatbelts, and are drug and tobacco free (Malenfant et al., 1996; Linkenbach and Perkins 2003a, 2003b; Perkins and Craig 2003). However, social norms studies have also found that people hold remarkably exaggerated views of the risk-taking behavior of their peers (Perkins 2003). These are *misperceptions of social norms.*

Widespread misperceptions have been documented regarding alcohol norms. Studies have found that misperceptions of alcohol use are held by all members of campus communities including undergraduate and graduate students, faculty and staff, students and student leaders (Berkowitz and Perkins 1986b; University of Michigan 1993; Berkowitz 1997). They have been documented in a statewide sample of young adults both in college and not in college (Linkenbach and Perkins 2003b), and among middle and high school students (Beck and Trieman 1996; Botvin et al., 2001; D'Amico et al., 2001; Haines, Barker, and Rice 2003; Perkins and Craig 2003; Rice 2003; Thombs et al., 1997).

Misperceptions of social norms are the "hidden risk factor" that is not addressed in most prevention efforts. There are more than twenty published studies in which misperceptions are positively correlated with drinking behavior or predict how individuals drink (Marks et al., 1992; Perkins 1985, 1987; Prentice and Miller 1993; Beck and Trieman 1996; Perkins and Wechsler 1996; Thombs et al., 1997; Page et al., 1999; Steffian 1999; Thombs 1999; Clapp and McDonnell 2000; Botvin et al., 2001; D'Amico et al., 2001; Sher et al., 2001; Korcuska and Thombs 2003; Kypri and Langley 2003; Trockel et al., 2003; Mattern and Neighbors 2004; Lewis and Neighbors, 2004).

These misperceptions of social norms about alcohol consumption have profound impacts on prevention and enforcement efforts. If people believe that the majority misuses or overuses alcohol, they perceive that the social norm opposes the policies and laws designed to reduce dangerous drinking. This creates a paradigm that falsely dichotomizes social norms and the law, setting them at odds with each other when, in fact, the law supports and enforces the behavior that is already practiced and approved by the large majority. Further, stringent punishments which produce criminal shame can have perverse effects: punishments can actually become badges of status in communities that do not trust the government or enforcing body (Posner 2000).

The process of establishing healthy social environments concerning alcohol is dependent upon equalizing and stabilizing the relationship between perceptions, policies, and social norms (Figure 8.1).

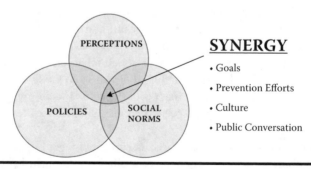

Figure 8.1   MOST of Us® Key Domains.

Cultural Cataracts

The widespread inaccuracies in how we view our communities' alcohol norms are a symptom of cultural cataracts (Linkenbach 2001). Cultural cataracts are a widespread social condition characterized by distorted, negative views of subpopulations, caused by a sensationalized, hyperfocus on rare or extreme behaviors of a small percentage of members that are inaccurately perceived as group norms. This results in the criminalization of health issues and escalating policies of control for political rather than prevention purposes.

The process developing cultural cataracts is fostered by the media, which takes unproven collective beliefs about the risk-taking behaviors of a subpopulation and turns them into cliches that are constantly recycled and supported by "expert opinion" as if they were true. Research demonstrates (Bostrom 2000) that these distorted misperceptions are so powerful that people will omit and overlook positive data and instead focus on the few negative trends by finding ways to reinterpret the facts and numbers in order to reach a negative predetermined conclusion.

Numerous studies and books detail how negatively skewed news reporting affects public perception of specific groups and issues (Males 1999; Dorfman and Schrialdi 2001). We as a nation have for many years had cultural cataracts when it comes to how we view our youth. Widespread misperceptions about our youngest citizens (Males 1996, 1999) have, in the hands of the media, become gross exaggerations of who our young people are (Rothstein 2001). Worse yet, in spite of overwhelming data that our young people are one of the healthiest generations alive today (Howe and Strauss 2000), we are instead "left to perceive distorted shadows of negativity, and pre-defined polarized extremes of a generation at risk" (Astroth 1995; Linkenbach 2001). These entrenched, distorted perceptions have significant impacts on alcohol policy and enforcement. If we believe we have bad, misbehaving youth, then we will support a policy and enforcement environment designed to "catch" and "punish" them, developing ineffective, escalatingly punitive, deterrence-based policies, such as the tough love policies that evolved into three strikes that morphed into zero tolerance—all of which have questionable effectiveness (Skiba 2000).

In short, when public attention is directed at the extreme, atypical behavior of a minority, misperceptions, and associated harm are fostered. Conversely, when the focus and framing of problems and media attention is on health through an accurate portrayal of cultural norms, greater health is encouraged (Linkenbach 2001).

The Tyranny of Health Terrorism

Perception is the key to effective alcohol prevention efforts. "[T]hose who are successful at directing the public's perception of what is normal and acceptable are also those who will largely determine future health and safety trends" (Linkenbach

2001). There appears to be a gap between research findings about the promising effects of positive and perception-based approaches (National Institutes of Health 2004) and the continued application of traditional fear-based strategies by alcohol prevention practitioners.

Fear continues to be used as a major tool in prevention efforts aimed at steering public behavior (Glassner 1999). Many prevention campaigns choose to highlight and publicize the dangerous activity of the minority, ignoring the fact that healthy, protective choices are normative. Prevention specialists typically employ "health terrorist" (Linkenbach 2001) strategies to "scare the health" into people with fear-inspiring sound bites and horrifying media images. Inflating peoples' fears can backlash against the goal of health promotion by supporting and exaggerating misperceptions about social norms (Linkenbach). This distortion of the environment by promoting fear and supporting misperceptions of norms appears to be a coercive tool designed to force healthy norms upon target groups and is having negative effects—especially with regard to youth (Males 1999).

Research panels recently commissioned by leading government agencies to study underage drinking (Bonnie and O'Connell 2004) and other health-risking behaviors in adolescents (The National Institutes of Health 2004) have found that the use of "scare tactics" are not merely neutral and ineffective, but may actually make problems worse. Despite research recommendations that signal the need for alcohol prevention professionals to steer public perceptions and reframe alcohol issues from a positive perspective, the entrenched historical use of negative health messages makes them difficult to eliminate or ameliorate (Olds and Eddy 1986).

Section 2: Perception-Based Prevention

Having established the central role that perceptions play, the following section will outline a strategy for correcting people's misperceptions about the social norms to achieve positive change. It will begin with a detailed discussion of the nature of misperceptions of social norms, and move on to discuss the structure of a perception-based prevention effort.

Causes of Misperceptions

Why do misperceptions of social norms occur? Several factors contribute, ranging from the way we mentally process information to the kinds of cultural stimuli we receive (Perkins 1997, 2002, 2003). Although we are very good observers of the behavior of others, we are typically poor interpreters of the meaning of this information. First, we tend to think that unusual behaviors exhibited by other people are typical of them, whether or not this is the case (an "attribution error," as described by psychologists). We assume that the behavior we observe in others is characteristic—even if it is a once per year or once-in-a-lifetime occurrence—because we do not have enough information about most other people to contextualize such behavior as rare when we hear about or see it happening.

Second, casual conversation tends to focus on the escapades of peers who exhibit extreme or high-risk behaviors. Talk among friends usually emphasizes and exaggerates atypical, risky behaviors (which tend to make funnier or more dramatic stories) rather than the statistically normal behaviors that regularly occur. Amplified talk about risky behavior leads many to think such actions are more prevalent than they actual are. In this way, even people who do not themselves engage in dangerous behaviors may contribute to the problem by acting as "carriers" of the misperception "virus" by spreading it to others through conversation.

The third factor involves the influential role of the media, which is in the business of delivering sensational, memorable material. We are typically attracted to stories—fictional and otherwise—about the most dramatic, arresting, or shocking events. Vivid or emotionally evocative information has increased impact on our perceptions, leading to exaggerated ideas about frequency and prevalence. The result is that people worry about terrorist attacks, whereas some of the most common killers of Americans—obesity, stroke, and heart disease—go practically unnoticed. Thus the way in which the media attends to and disregards information contributes to the misperception of actual norms.

Consequences of Misperceptions

Misperceptions have been shown to fuel a less protective social environment among college students with regard to alcohol abuse (Perkins 2002). These misperceptions have significant consequences. First, people with ambivalent attitudes about a particular high-risk activity—for example, heavy drinking—might nonetheless engage in it if they perceive it as the norm. Meanwhile, those people already at the high-risk end of the drinking continuum wrongly think that their behavior is the acceptable practice of the majority, a misperception that perversely ratifies and reinforces their own choices. Finally, opposition or intervention by others to prevent high-risk drinking (or to ameliorate the problems associated with it) is also inhibited in an environment characterized by widespread misperceptions. People are reluctant to be "the only one" to refrain from a behavior or to intervene in their friends' behavior if, in so doing, they risk social disapproval.

Correcting Misperceptions: The Social Norms Approach to Prevention

The social norms approach to prevention works to shape human behavior by correcting misperceptions of social norms (Perkins and Berkowitz 1986). Identifying and reducing the often great disparity between perceived and actual social norms is the basis of this approach (Perkins 1997, 2003). Social norms interventions have shown that if people's misperceptions of social norms are corrected to reflect the less risky, more protective behaviors or attitudes that are the actual norms in their communities, they are more likely to behave in accordance with those positive standards (Cialdini 2003; Perkins 2003).

Social norms programs focus on the positive majority behavior or attitudes that are almost universally the norm, rather than on the negative behavior and impacts of the minority. By promoting the positive behavior that is the community standard, more good behavior results. Social norms interventions have achieved statistically significant behavioral shifts among a variety of target groups (high school students, college students, young adults) with regard to issues as diverse as alcohol use, seatbelt use, impaired driving, and tobacco use (Berkowitz 2004).

For example, intensive social norms campaigns were implemented at several college campuses to counteract student overexaggerations of the prevalence of heavy episodic drinking. As the students grew informed about the actual majority norms of moderate alcohol use, each campus measured an 18 to 21 percent reduction in high-risk drinking in as little as two years, against a national backdrop that remained virtually unchanged (Haines 1996; Johannessen et al., 1999; Perkins 2002; Perkins and Craig 2002; Jeffrey et al., 2003). A recent media-based social norms intervention on impaired driving achieved statistically positive results across a variety of measures, including message awareness, increased accuracy of perceptions, decreased impaired driving behavior, increased protective behaviors, and increased support for policies to reduce impaired driving (Linkenbach and Perkins 2005).

From Soup to Nuts: How It Works

Social norms campaigns do not seek to change behavioral norms by telling people what they should or should not do. Instead, they work to correct people's misperceptions of social norms by informing them of the healthy behaviors that are actually practiced by the majority. Because people's behavior is determined in large part by their perceptions of what is normal and acceptable, changes in behavior result. In this way, social norms messages do not merely convey what *should* be happening in a given community or population, but rather reflect back what *is* already happening that is positive, protective, and healthy. By reinforcing positive attitudes and behaviors, social norms can enhance the protective factors within the community itself and thus lead to a reduction of the risk-taking behavior of the minority.

Using surveys and other information-gathering techniques, a social norms intervention identifies the positive norms that already exist in a population, and then constructs an intervention that publicizes, reinforces, and strengthens them. Misperceptions of social norms can be corrected using media campaigns, small group interventions, and school curricula, among other strategies, to deliver accurate, data-based messages about actual community norms. These messages correct misperceptions of social norms, giving people a more accurate picture of the behaviors and attitudes of their peers. Through time and message "dosage," this correct normative information translates into corrected perceptions which results in measurable changes in attitudes and behaviors.

The logic model for a social norms campaign looks like this:

Baseline Survey
Identify target's actual and misperceived norms

Intervention
Intensively expose target to accurate norms messages

Correction
Target develops more accurate perceptions of norms

Result
Target practices more safe and healthy behaviors (Perkins 2003)

The Montana Model of Social Norms Marketing

The Montana Model of Social Norms Marketing is a seven-step process that combines social marketing with the social norms approach to prevention. It is a social norms marketing model that can work on regional or statewide levels, for a variety of issues, turning social science into social action by correcting misperceptions and building upon the positive attitudinal and behavioral norms that already exist in a culture. Although the steps are presented in a linear manner, their implementation is a dynamic process that often involves operating within and between each of the steps simultaneously. The Montana Model is the most widely used model for social norms interventions, and has been the foundation for campaigns on issues ranging from impaired driving to tobacco use among teenagers to adult seatbelt use (Figure 8.2).

Step 1: Planning and Environmental Advocacy

Project planning determines the scope and direction of your campaign, and ensures that all of your efforts are aligned with your program goals. Environmental advocacy entails creating a political, economic, and social atmosphere conducive to change.

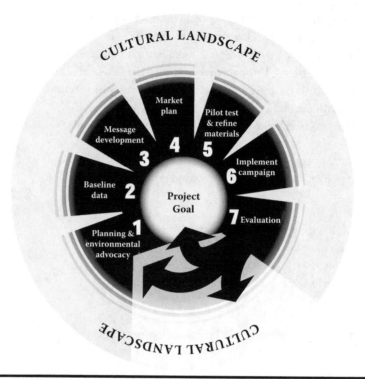

Figure 8.2   The Montana Model of Social Norms Marketing (Linkenbach, 1999).

Step 2: Baseline Data

The disparity between perceived attitudes and behaviors and actual norms is what drives the social norms process. The collection of baseline data is when you measure this disparity in your particular target audience. The survey data you collect will become the actual intervention tool that you will use to create change.

Step 3: Message Development

Message development is a rigorous process that involves deriving stories and statistics from your baseline data. The scope of your message is determined by your target population's readiness for change, their current behavior practices, and their normative perceptions.

Step 4: Market Plan

The creation of a marketing plan begins by seeing things through the eyes of your target population. Traditional and nontraditional media approaches are assessed for their potential to reach the desired audience. The results of these assessments are incorporated into a campaign-specific plan.

Step 5: Pilot Test and Refine Materials

Your normative messages and pilot materials must be tested with your target population for believability and appeal. Focus groups become a key resource for gathering input and information.

Step 6: Implement Campaign

Campaign implementation involves all of the tasks and elements necessary to run and troubleshoot your campaign on a daily basis. It includes placing print and broadcast media messages, running local activities that promote your social norms messages, and managing your campaign's interaction with your target audience and the community at large.

Step 7: Evaluation

The social norms marketing process is driven by continual evaluation of campaign effectiveness. Quantitative and qualitative data are gathered, analyzed, and fed back into the campaign to refine its implementation.

Conclusion: Transforming Culture over the Next 100 Years

Successful prevention research and policy applications over the next 100 years will principally be characterized by their coordinated attention to the three domains of perceptions, policies, and social norms. Although policies and social norms have dominated the focus of prevention efforts, it is perceptions that provide the key to the success of future efforts.

People's misperceptions of social norms (including policy support) surrounding alcohol are "the hidden risk factor" that is the heart of the social norms approach to prevention. The social norms approach has shown that when the focus and framing of alcohol issues are directed at correcting these misperceptions through an accurate portrayal of norms, it encourages greater health. Correcting perceptions, and balancing them with social norms and policy efforts, will transform society's relationship with alcohol by reframing the course of public discussion and improving norms throughout the next century.

Research is needed to better understand the dynamic interplay between the three domains to pave the way for the emergence of a new, three-tiered prevention model.

Research Recommendations

1. Research is needed that will allow better understanding of the three domains of perceptions, policies, and social norms.
2. Develop assessment tools that allow community prevention practitioners to identify where they are in regard to the three domains, and assist them in developing strategic prevention plans based on the balance and interplay between them.
3. Expand social norms research and application to include support for various laws and policies designed to mitigate the harmful effects of alcohol abuse.
4. Frame prevention and research practices that embrace the complexity of alcohol's role in society. Understanding and acknowledging this complex culture will help foster an atmosphere that promotes clear, consistent guidelines and standards concerning alcohol use and misuse.
5. Remove cultural cataracts. It is imperative that we correct our faulty views of subpopulations so that policies and actions do not result in furthering misperceptions and encouraging harm.
6. Avoid possible boomerang effects associated with fear-based campaigns. Create prevention campaigns based on research demonstrating the effectiveness of the positive approach.

References

Anderson, H. "Mike's Hard Lemonade too Easy a Sell to Underage Drinkers." (February 1999). National Consumer's League. Available online from http://www.natlconsumersleague.org/pr2800alco.html. Retrieved Oct. 21, 2004.

Astroth, K. "I'm Okay, You're At Risk: Beyond Ephebiphobia and Toward Research." *Monograph on Youth in the 1990s* 4 (1995).

Austin, G. A. *Perspectives on the History of Psychoactive Substance Use.* Rockville, MD: National Institute of Drug Abuse, 1978.

Balko, R. "Back Door to Prohibition: The New War on Social Drinking." *Policy Analysis* 501 (2003): 1–27.

Bandow, D. *The Politics of Science: the Federal Bureaucracy's War on Social Drinking.* Raleigh, NC: John Locke Foundation, Policy Report No. 13, 1995.

Barr, A. *Drink: A Social History of America.* New York: Carrol & Graf Publishers, Inc., 1999.

Beck, K. H., and K. A. Treiman. "The Relationship of Social Context of Drinking, Perceived Social Norms, and Parental Influence to Various Drinking Patterns of Adolescents." *Addictive Behaviors* 21:5 (1996): 633–44.

Berkowitz, A. D. "From Reactive to Proactive Prevention: Promoting an Ecology of Health on Campus." In *A Handbook on Substance Abuse for College and University Personnel*, edited by P.C. Rivers and E. Shore. Westport, CT: GreenWood Press, 1997.

Berkowitz, A. D. The Social Norms Approach: Theory, Research, and Annotated Bibliography. (August 2004). Retrieved Nov. 19, 2004, http://www.edc.org/hec/socialnorms/theory. Retrieved Nov. 19, 2004.

Berkowitz, A. D., and H. W. Perkins. "Resident Advisors as Role Models: A Comparison of Drinking Patterns of Resident Advisors and Their Peers." *Journal of College Student Personnel* 27:2 (1986): 146–53.

Boccaro. Nova Scotia, Canada: *Youth Research Unity*, Dalhousie University Halifax, 29–37.

Bonnie, R. J. and M. E. O'Connell, editors. "Reducing Underage Drinking: A Collective Responsibility." A publication of the Committee on Developing a Strategy to Reduce and Prevent Underage Drinking. Commissioned by the National Research, 2004.

Bostrom, M. (2000). Teenhood: Understanding Attitudes toward Those Transitioning from Childhood to Adulthood, in S. Bales (Ed.) *Reframing Youth Issues*, Washington, D.C.: Working Papers, Frameworks Institute and Center for Communications and Community, UCLA.

Botvin, G. J., et al. "Preventing Binge Drinking During Early Adolescence: One- and Two-Year Follow-Up of a School-Based Preventive Intervention." *Psychology of Addictive Behaviors* 15 (2001): 360–5.

Cahalan, D. *An Ounce of Prevention: Strategies for Solving Tobacco, Alcohol, and Drug Problems.* San Francisco: Jossey-Bass Publishers, 1991.

Carroll, T. E., and R. Donovan. "Alcohol Marketing on the Internet: New Challenge for Harm Reduction." *Drug and Alcohol Review* 21 (2002): 83–91.

Cialdini, R. B. "Crafting normative messages to protect the environment." *Current Directions in Psychological Science* 12:4 (2003): 105–9.

Clapp, J. D. and A. L. McDonnell. "The Relationship of Perceptions of Alcohol Promotion and Peer Drinking Norms to Alcohol Problems Reported by College Students." *Journal of College Student Development* 41:1 (2000): 20–6.

Council and the Institute of Medicine of the National Academies. The National Academies Press. Washington, D.C.

D'Amico, E. J., et al. "Progression Into and Out of Binge Drinking Among High School Students." *Psychology of Addictive Behaviors* 15 (2001): 341–9.

Dorfman, L., and V. Schiraldi. "Off Balance: Youth, Race & Crime in the News." U.S. Department of Justice Report. Building Blocks for Youth, 2001.

Engs, R. C., editor. *Controversies in the Addiction's Field: Volume One.* A publication of the American Council on Alcoholism. Dubuque, IA: Kendall/Hunt Publishing Company, 1990.

Fosdick, R., A. Scott, and J. D. Rockefeller, Jr. *Toward Liquor Control.* New York: Harper & Brothers Publishers, 1933.

Fox, E. *Power Through Constructive Thinking.* San Francisco: Harper, 1932: 7.

Glassner, B. *The Culture of Fear: Why Americans Are Afraid of the Wrong Things.* New York: Basic Books, 1999.

Goldberg, M. E., G. J. Gorn, and A. M. Lavack. "Product Innovation and Teenage Alcohol Consumption: The Case of Wine Coolers." *Journal of Public Policy & Marketing* 13:2 (1994): 218–27.

Goldberg, R., editor. *Taking Sides: Clashing Views on Controversial Issues in Drugs and Society.* Sixth edition. Guilford, CT: McGraw-Hill/Dushkin, 2004.

Haines, M. P. *A Social Norms Approach to Preventing Binge Drinking at Colleges and Universities.* Newton, MA: Higher Education Center for Alcohol and Other Drug Prevention, 1996.

Haines, M. P., G. P. Barker, and R. Rice. "Using Social Norms to Reduce Alcohol and Tobacco Use in Two Midwestern High Schools." In *The Social Norms Approach to Preventing School and College Age Substance Abuse: A Handbook for Educators, Counselors, Clinicians,* edited by H. W. Perkins. San Francisco: Jossey-Bass, 2003.

Hawkins, D. J., and R.F. Catalano, R.F. Jr. and Associates. *Communities That Care.* San Francisco: Jossey-Bass Publishers, 1992.

Howe, N., and W. Strauss. *Millenials Rising: The Next Generation.* New York: Vintage Books, 2000.

Jeffrey, L. P., P. Negro, D.S. Miller, and J.D. Frisone. *The Rowan University Social Norms project. The Social Norms Approach To Preventing School and College Age Substance Abuse.* San Francisco: Jossey-Bass, 2003.

Johannessen, K., C. Collins, B. Mills-Novoa, and P. Glider. *A Practical Guide to Alcohol Abuse Prevention: A Campus Case Study in Implementing Social Norms and Environmental Management Approaches.* Tucson: Campus Health Service, University of Arizona, 1999.

Join Together Online. County Set to Ban Alcohol Vapor Machines. (2004) Available online at http://www.jointogether.org/sa/news/summaries/reader/0,1854,574757,00.html. Retrieved October 30, 2004.

Kelly, K. J., M .D. Slater, and D. Karan. "Image Advertisements' Influence on Adolescents Perception of the Desirability of Beer and Cigarettes." *Journal of Public Policy & Marketing* 21:2 (2002): 295–304.

Klitzner, M., and K. Stewart. "Factors that Facilitate and Impeded Community Planning to Address Drug and Alcohol Issues." Paper presented at the 50th anniversary meeting of the American Society of Criminology, San Francisco, CA, 1991.

Korcuska, J. S., and D. L. Thombs. "Gender Role Conflicts and Sex-Specific Drinking Norms: Relationships to Alcohol Use in Undergraduate Women and Men." *Journal of College Student Development* 44:2 (2003): 204–15.

Kypri, K., and J. D. Langley. "Perceived Social Norms and Their Relation to University Student Drinking." *Journal of Studies on Alcohol* 64 (2003): 829–34.

Langton, P. A. *The Social World of Drugs.* St. Paul, MN: West Publishing Co., 1996.

Ledermann, S. "Ledermann Hypothesis in Alcohol, Alcoholism, Alcoholization." In *Drink: A Social History of America,* edited by Barr, A. New York: Carrol & Graf Publishers, Inc., 1956.

Lee, T. Alcopops Fuel Underage-Drinking Battle (2002). Available online from *SouthCoast Today*: http://www.s-t.com/daily/03-02/03-10-02/d06bu128.htm. Retrieved October 20, 2004.

Lewis, M. A., and C. Neighbors. "Gender-Specific Misperceptions of College Student Drinking Norms." *Psychology of Addictive Behaviors,* 2004. Vol. 18, NO. 4, 334–339.

Linkenbach, J. W. "Application of Social Norms Marketing to a Variety of Health Issues." *Wellness Management* 15:3 (1999): 7–8.

Linkenbach, J. W. "Cultural Cataracts: Identifying and Correcting Misperceptions in the Media—the Report on Social Norms." (Working Paper #1.) Garfield, NJ: PaperClip Communications, 2001.

Linkenbach, J. W., and H. W. Perkins (2005). "MOST of us Prevent Drinking and Driving: A Successful Social Norms Campaign to Reduce Driving after Drinking among Young Adults in Western Montana." A publication of the U.S. National Highway Traffic Safety Administration—U.S. Department of Transportation. DOT HS 809 69.

Linkenbach, J. W., and H. W. Perkins. "Misperceptions of Peer Alcohol Norms in a State-wide Survey of Young Adults." In *The Social Norms Approach To Preventing School and College Age Substance Abuse,* edited by H. W. Perkins. San Francisco: Jossey-Bass, 2003a, 173–81.

Linkenbach, J. W., and H. W. Perkins. "MOST of Us Are Tobacco Free: An Eight-Month Social Norms Campaign Reducing Youth Initiation of Smoking in Montana." In *The Social Norms Approach To Preventing School and College Age Substance Abuse,* edited by H. W. Perkins. San Francisco: Jossey-Bass, 2003b, 224–34.

Malenfant, L., J. Wells, R. Van Houten, and A. Williams. "The Use of Feedback Signs to Increase Observed Daytime Seat Belt Use in Two Cities in North Carolina." *Accident Analysis and Prevention* 28:6 (1996): 771–7.

Males, M. *The Scapegoat Generation: America's War on Adolescents.* Monroe, ME: Common Courage Press, 1996.

Males, M. *Framing Youth: 10 Myths About the Next Generation.* Monroe, ME: Common Courage Press, 1999.

Marks, G., J. W. Graham, and W. B. Hansen. "Social Projection and Social Conformity in Adolescent Alcohol Use: A Longitudinal Analysis." *Personality and Social Psychology Bulletin* 18:1 (1992): 96–101.

Mattern, J. M. and C. Neighbors. "Social Norms Campaigns: Examining the Relationship Between Changes in Perceived Norms and Changes in Drinking Levels." *Journal of Studies on Alcohol* 64:5 (2004): 489–93.

NIH News—National Institutes of Health. "Panel Finds that Scare Tactics for Prevention are Harmful: Good News Is That Positive Approaches Show Promise." Press release: October 15, 2004, NIH. Available online from http://www.nih.gov/news/pr/oct2004/od-15.htm. Retrieved October 26, 2004.

Olds, R. S., and J. M. Eddy. "Negative Health Messages in Schools." *Journal of School Health* 56:8 (1986): 334–6.

Page, R. M., A. Scanlan, and L. Gilbert. "Relationship of the Estimation of Binge-Drinking Among College Students and Personal Participation in Binge Drinking: Implications for Health Education and Promotion." *Health Education* 30 (1999): 98–103.

Perkins, H. W., ed. *The Social Norms Approach to Preventing School and College Age Substance Abuse.* San Francisco: Jossey-Bass, 2003.

Perkins, H. W. "Parental Religion and Alcohol Use Problems as Intergenerational Predictors of Problem Drinking Among College Youth." *Journal for the Scientific Study of Religion* 26:3 (1987): 340–57.

Perkins, H. W. "Religious Traditions, Parents, and Peers as Determinants of Alcohol and Drug Use Among College Students." *Review of Religious Research* 27:1 (1985): 15–31.

Perkins, H. W. "Social Norms and the Prevention of Alcohol Misuse in Collegiate Contexts." *Journal of Studies on Alcohol,* Supplement 14 (2002): 164–72.

Perkins, H. W., and A. D. Berkowitz. "Perceiving the Community Norms of Alcohol Use Among Students: Some Research Implications for Campus Alcohol Education Programming." *International Journal of the Addictions* 21 (1986): 961–76.

Perkins, H. W., and D. A. Craig. *A Multifaceted Social Norms Approach to Reduce High-Risk Drinking: Lessons from Hobart and William Smith Colleges.* Newton, MA: Higher Education Center for Alcohol and Other Drug Prevention, 2002.

Perkins, H. W., and D. A. Craig. "The Imaginary Lives of Peers: Patterns of Substance Use and Misperceptions of Norms Among Secondary School Students." In *The Social Norms Approach to Preventing School and College Age Substance Abuse: A Handbook for Educators, Counselors, Clinicians,* edited by H. W. Perkins. San Francisco: Jossey-Bass, 2003.

Perkins, H. W., and H. Wechsler. "Variation in Perceived College Drinking Norms and Its Impact on Alcohol Abuse: A Nationwide Study." *Journal of Drug Issues* 26:4 (1996): 961–74.

Prentice, D. A., and D. T. Miller. "Pluralistic Ignorance and Alcohol Use on Campus: Some Consequences of Misperceiving the Social Norm." *Journal of Personality and Social Psychology* 64:2 (1993): 243–56.

Posner, E. A. *Law and Social Norms.* Cambridge, MA: Harvard University Press, 2000.

Rampton, S., and Stauber, J. *Trust Us, We're the Experts.* New York: Jeremy P. Tarcher/Putnam, 2001.

Ray, O., and C. Ksir. *Drugs, Society, and Human Behavior.* Boston: WCB/McGraw-Hill Publishers, 1999.

Rice, R. "An Overview of the 2003 National Conference on the Social Norms Model." The Report on Social Norms: Working Paper # 7, p. 3, Little Falls, NJ: PaperClip Communications, 2003.

Rothstein, R. "Lessons: of Schools, and Crime and Gross Exaggeration." *New York Times* 7 February 2001.

Saffer, H., and D. Dave. "Alcohol Consumption and Alcohol Advertising Bans." *Applied Economics* 34:11 (2002): 1325–35.

Sher, K., E. D. Bartholow, and S. Nanda. "Short- and Long-Term Effects of Fraternity and Sorority Membership on Heavy Drinking: A Social Norms Perspective." *Psychology of Addictive Behaviors* 15 (2001): 42–51.

Skiba, R. "Zero Tolerance, Zero Evidence: An Analysis of School Disciplinary Practice." #SRS2 of Policy Research Report. Indiana Education Policy Center, 2000.

Skrabanek, P. *The Death of Humane Medicine and the Rise of Coercive Healthism.* Bury St. Edmunds, Suffolk, UK: 194 p. 188.

Steffian, G. "Correction of Normative Misperceptions: An Alcohol Abuse Prevention Program." *Journal of Drug Education* 29:2 (1999): 115–38.

Stokols, D. "Establishing and Maintaining Healthy Environments." *American Psychology* 47 1992: 6–22.

Stone, N. (1995). *The Wine Spectator.* August 31, 1995, p. 57.

Svendsen, R. *Chemical Health: A Planning Guide for Congregations in Response to Alcohol and Other Drug Issues.* A publication of the Division for Life and Mission in the Congregation of the American Lutheran Church, 1986: 8.

Thich Nhat Hanh. *Going Home: Jesus and Buddha as Brothers.* New York: Riverhead Books, 1999: 74.

Thombs, D. L. "Alcohol and Motor Vehicle Use: Profiles of Drivers and Passengers." *American Journal of Health and Behavior* 23 (1999): 13–24.

Thombs, D. L., B. J. Wolcott, and L. G. Farkash. "Social Context, Perceived Norms and Drinking Behavior in Young People." *Journal of Substance Abuse* 9 (1997): 257–67.

Trockel, M., S. Williams, and J. Reis. "Considerations for More Effective Social Norms Based Alcohol Education on Campus: An Analysis of Different Theoretical Conceptualizations in Predicting Drinking Among Fraternity Men." *Journal of Studies on Alcohol* 64 (2003): 550–9.

United States Federal Trade Commission. Alcohol and Advertising: A Report to Congress 2003. Available online from www.ftc.gov.

University of Michigan. *University of Michigan Survey Regarding Alcohol and Other Drugs.* UM Initiative on Alcohol and Other Drugs, Ann Arbor, MI, 1993.

Wallack, L. "Media Advocacy: A Strategy for Empowering People and Communities." In *Community Organizing and Community Building for Health,* edited by M. Minkler. New Brunswick, NJ: Rutgers University Press, 1997: 339–52.

Whitman, D. G. *Strange Brew: Alcohol and Government Monopoly.* Oakland, CA: A Publication of the Independent Institute 3 (2003).

Wine and Spirits Wholesalers of America (WSWA). *The History of the Three-Tier System 1999.* Available online from www.wswa.org/whole/history.htm

Chapter 9

Controlling Misuse of Alcohol by College Youth: Paradigms and Paradoxes for Prevention

Elissa R. Weitzman

Contents

Societal paradigms for understanding and labeling youth may affect the type of alcohol-related prevention programming that is supported. Additionally, the degree of understanding about interrelationships between individual- and population-risks for drinking-related harm by levels of alcohol consumption may affect how communities choose specific prevention strategies. These issues are discussed in this chapter in the context of reviewing evidence about risks for heavy and harmful drinking among college youth, prevention models, recent discussions in neurobiology and epidemiology, and evidence from community change initiatives.

Alcohol Use among Young Adults

Alcohol use is the third leading cause of preventable mortality in the United States (McGinnis and Foege 1993). Social costs related to drinking were estimated at $184.6 billion for 1998 (Harwood 2000). In the United States, young adults are among the heaviest drinkers (Naimi et al., 2003). Rates of alcohol abuse and dependence among them appear to have risen sharply over the latter half of the 20th century (Grant 1997).

Drinking poses substantial risk for health problems among young people. Harms include accidents and injuries related to drinking events as well as long-term health and developmental consequences (Hingson and Kenkel 2004). Given the substantial risks for morbidity, mortality, and social costs related to drinking, interest has intensified in identifying effective strategies for delaying the age at which youth begin drinking and for moderating consumption after youth do drink. Achieving objectives of delayed onset and moderated consumption may be important to a comprehensive prevention strategy for reducing immediate and longer term consequences of alcohol consumption among youth and young people (Zucker 1987; Babor et al., 1992).

Multiple Risk Factors

In the United States and abroad, a period of intensive research into causes and correlates of problem drinking by youth began in the mid- to late 1980s. Studies of young people in community, school, and college settings successfully identified a host of individual and environmental risk and protective factors for heavy and problem drinking among youth. Across settings, male gender, positive history for family drinking problems, and very young age of first or regular substance use have been found to be important individual-level risk factors for heavy or problem drinking among young people. Weak enforcement of comprehensive underage drinking laws, poor restrictions on alcohol accessibility, availability and promotions, high alcohol outlet density, low price per drink, low levels of social capital, and school bonding all appear to comprise important environmental-level risk factors (Hawkins et al., 1992; Petraitis et al., 1995; Goldmanet et al., 2002).

Prevention Models

Along with a growing understanding of risk and protective factors for heavy and harmful drinking among young people, the latter 20th century has seen a parallel movement toward applying a developmental perspective toward drinking issues (Schulenberg et al., 2001). The developmental perspective recognizes that patterns of health risk behaviors and influences on their expression may differ across the lifespan. An integrated social development perspective goes further and recognizes both the developmental and multifactorial nature of drinking in which myriad risk and protective can be located at individual, family, peer, neighborhood, and macro-social levels (Weitzman 2004). This perspective acknowledges that issues related to life stage, social role, and setting may be important considerations in understanding young adult health status, health risk behaviors, and outcomes. The developmental perspective may offer a particularly compelling motivation to intervene. Because young adulthood is a time during which young people learn to establish independent social ties and connections, participate in higher education, and begin work and career paths, heavy drinking poses substantial risks for longer term problems. Reflecting on the opportunity costs of heavy drinking in adolescence and young adulthood, Koren Zailckas wrote:

> Nine years after I took my first drink it occurs to me that I haven't grown up. I am missing so much of the equipment that adults should have, like the ability to sustain eye contact without flinching or letting my gaze roll slantwise to the floor. At this point in time, I should be able to hear my own unwavering voice rise in public without feeling my heart flutter like it's trying to take flight. I should be able to locate a point of conversation with the people I deeply long to know as my friends. ...For me abstinence has been nothing but growing pains. It has meant starting from scratch, reliving my awkward phase, and learning all over again what it means to be an adult. (2005: xvii–xx)

A focus on life course patterns for young adults coincides with a trend toward formal conceptualization of "emergent adulthood" as a developmental stage bridging later adolescence and adulthood (Arnett 2000). Emergent adulthood, in fact, appears to encompass three separate but related developmental challenges: *existential* challenges centered on meaning-making as one becomes an adult; *economic* challenges centered on moving toward financial independence from financial dependence on parents and caretakers; and *epidemiologic* challenges centered on moving healthily through a period of peak behavioral and psychological risk.

The net result of this growing awareness about the ways that social developmental issues may affect heavy and harmful drinking among young people may be: 1) growing acceptance of the need for comprehensive prevention programs that target multiple risk and protective factors spanning individual and community levels and

2) a move toward developmentally oriented programs that target risk and protective factors thought to be most salient for young people in a given time, place, and setting. As Schulenberg and Maggs wrote:

> The task now for scientists is to understand more fully how risk and protective factors are linked with substance use within individuals over time and across contexts. (2002: 57)

An excellent case for advancing this more nuanced approached to prevention is made by considering heavy and problem drinking by youth in college in the United States, a group at particular risk for drinking problems who are undergoing dramatic developmental change. In going to college, young people are transitioning from adolescence to young adulthood, often in a new place. As such, they need to repopulate their social networks and supports, assume new roles and responsibilities, and move away from familiar and established supervisory controls and settings. The cumulative effect of these transitions on health behaviors is only beginning to be addressed and may be evident in the very high risks for alcohol misuse and abuse seen among them.

Among young people, college students drink more heavily than their non–college attending peers (O'Malley and Johnston 2002). About two in five students attending college in the United States engage in heavy episodic, or "binge" drinking—defined as consumption of five or more drinks in a row for males and four or more drinks for females on one or more occasion during a two-week period. This rate has been consistent across multiple national surveys employing differing methods and was stable during the 1990s (CDC 1997; Douglas et al., 1997; Presley et al., 1999; SAMHSA 2000; Johnston et al., 2001; O'Malley and Johnston 2002; Wechsler et al., 2002), a period of concentrated research activity on this topic (Dowdall and Wechsler 2002).

In college, about one third of college students and three in five frequent binge drinkers qualify for a diagnosis of alcohol abuse, whereas 1 in 17 (one in five frequent binge drinkers) could be diagnosed as alcohol dependent (Knight et al., 2002) based on clinical criteria (American Psychiatric Association 1994). It is estimated that approximately 1,700 U.S. college students died in unintentional injuries related to alcohol in 2001. During that year, about 2.8 million college youth drove a motor vehicle under the influence of alcohol. Nearly 600,000 college youth were unintentionally injured while under the influence of alcohol and 696,000 were assaulted by another student who was under the influence (Hingson et al., 2005). These problems worsened significantly over the period 1998–2001 (Hingson et al.). Despite their evident problems with alcohol, few college students who drink heavily perceive that they are heavy or problem drinkers and even fewer report that they have sought treatment or counseling for their drinking (Knight et al., 2002; Wechsler et al., 2002).

A growing body of evidence links high risks for misuse and abuse of alcohol in college to environmental exposures. This is significant because environmental exposures can be changed to affect large numbers of youth in a presumably lasting fashion. In contrast, individual characteristics, including patterns of knowledge, attitude, and belief about alcohol must be addressed on an ongoing basis. This is because within the college setting different cohorts of youth enter and cycle through a college annually. Unfortunately for public health, individually oriented preventive interventions have a poor track record of working in college settings (see Larimer and Cronce 2002, for a comprehensive review). In light of the need to repeat them regularly, they may also be deemed inefficient.

The movement toward supporting exploration of environmental prevention programs reflects not only theory and practicality but findings about social patterning of heavy drinking among college youth. For example, researchers found that rates of heavy episodic or "binge" drinking vary dramatically by college (ranging from 1 to 76 percent), by region of the country (lower in the Western states), and by the sets of policies and laws governing alcohol sale and use (Wechsler et al., 1998, 2002a, 2002b, 2003; Presley et al., 2002). The pricing and promotion of alcoholic beverages have been linked to consumption among college students (Chaloupka and Wechsler 1996), for whom low prices and easy access promote underage alcohol use (Wechsler et al., 2000b). Similarly, lower rates of heavy episodic drinking have been observed among students attending colleges where no alcohol outlets exist within a mile of campus (Wechsler et al., 1994). High alcohol outlet density is associated with higher levels of frequent and heavy drinking and drinking-related problems (Weitzman et al., 2003a). Moreover, perceptions about alcohol's accessibility and availability strongly predict the acquisition in college of binge drinking in a national study examining factors that contributed to binge uptake among underage freshmen who reported they did not binge drink in high school (Weitzman et al., 2003b). In fact, the impact of these factors on binge uptake in college far exceeds the impact of other factors related to exposure to educational messages about alcohol, family characteristics, and individual social-demographic characteristics.

Campus policies that target alcohol use are associated with less binge drinking among college students. Substance-free residences, in which students are prohibited from using alcohol and tobacco products, are associated with less alcohol use and fewer secondhand effects of alcohol (Wechsler et al., 2001b). Among underage students who reside on campus, those who live in substance-free housing (i.e., alcohol and tobacco use prohibited) have the lowest rates of binge drinking (Wechsler et al., 2002b). State and local alcohol policies are also associated with drinking behavior among college students. Strong state and local drunk-driving policies targeting youths and young adults are associated with lower levels of drinking (Williams, Chaloupka, and Wechsler 2002). The National Minimum Legal Drinking Age law in the United States appears to be an effective deterrent (Toomey and Wagonaar 2002; Wagonaar and Toomey 2002). Underage students in states with extensive laws restricting underage and high-volume drinking were less likely to drink and to binge drink (Wechlser et al., 2002b). These comprehensive sets of laws were also associated with less drinking and driving among college students (Wechsler et al., 2003).

Clearly, many malleable social, structural, and policy factors influence patterns of heavy and abusive drinking among college youth. Whether society chooses to act to alter these factors hinges on the levels of social and political will available for addressing competing interests, ideologies, and inertia (WHO 2005). Mustering sufficient will also depends on how we understand adolescence versus young adulthood. Arguably, society is reasonably comfortable enacting strong social policies aimed at limiting hazardous exposures for youth insofar as there is a good fit between normative understandings about youth and societal commitment to protecting the vulnerable. By contrast, society tends toward allowing people greater discretion to make their own mistakes by young adulthood, given the fit between normative understandings about adulthood and societal encouragement of independence and autonomy for adults. Finally, willingness to manipulate social, structural, and policy levers to affect behavior change may hinge on society's understanding of individual and population risks for harm as they relate to different levels of alcohol consumption.

Discussions in Neurobiology and Epidemiology

Two recent scientific discussions raise important questions about these issues as they relate to selection and support of prevention strategies for reducing heavy and harmful drinking by college (and other) youth in the United States. The first discussion reflects research into patterns of brain development and the implications of these findings for how we think about health risk behaviors including alcohol and other drug abuse in older adolescence and emergent adulthood. Using nuclear magnetic resonance imaging, National Institutes of Health scientists have documented that development of the frontal lobes—the part of the brain thought to govern risk taking behavior—occurs until at least 25 years of age (Gogtay et al., 2004). This is an age well beyond what many consider "adolescence" with all that term connotes: greater propensity to take risks and seek novel and stimulating experiences, a sense of personal invulnerability, and a lack of fully developed consequential thinking. Findings of an attenuated adolescence call into question the ability of young people to appropriately judge risk and self-regulate to minimize harm, vulnerabilities that may be intensified in the presence of peers. The brain's immature status may increase young peoples' vulnerabilities to alcohol use and misuse. Additionally, it appears that alcohol may differentially affect the adolescent brain, setting up the potential for spiraling risk and harm. Thus new paradigms of risk are emerging that bring together biologic and sociologic insights. They suggest that emergent adulthood is still a period of active development and maturation, even though the social construction of adolescence may deem otherwise.

Understanding of associations between developing neurologic structures and risk-taking is only just beginning. However, this work is sparking debate about the importance for young people's behavior of biologic structures and the implications for policy and prevention of observed associations. In the context of a quickly developing science, it seems that brain structure and development are important considerations with respect to health risk behavior. Moreover it seems that adolescence lasts longer than many people thought—roughly from 13 to 25 years of age. From a policy perspective this age span is notable because it encompasses ages when society permits young people to make decisions with far-reaching implications for their health, including decisions to drive (at 16), vote and enlist in the military (at 18), and purchase and use tobacco and alcohol (at 21). This age span is also when young people may be most likely to live in peer dense settings—as they do in college. It is the time when many young people experience disruption or loss of familiar adult supports and supervisory controls that serve to protect or buffer them including from parents, family primary care providers, teachers, and neighbors. Perhaps not surprisingly, this period of life may be one in which people are most heavily targeted by industries seeking to develop markets, such as the tobacco, alcohol, and food industries.

Findings that young people may be vulnerable to health risk behaviors as a result of their incomplete neurologic development give us pause about the types of influences and opportunities that surround them. Are we overly optimistic about young people's abilities to regulate their own choices and behaviors in the context of powerful influences to drink, smoke, and eat poorly? How do we balance young people's needs and desire for autonomy with societal obligations to practically and frankly consider their vulnerabilities and perhaps need for protection a little later into life than we may have thought? Colleges are one of the institutions most directly confronted with the need to resolve this issue.

A second scientific discussion reflects questions about the magnitude of harm generated by various levels of alcohol consumption and drinking style—and the implication of these patterns for setting prevention priorities and strategies. Epidemiologists have been exploring whether harms from drinking are most likely to reflect patterns of intensive heavy drinking and intoxication—patterns which call for secondary and tertiary prevention approaches (i.e., screening and treatment); or, whether harms disproportionately reflect lower levels of consumption typical of large segments of the general population—patterns not generally considered hazardous and that call for primary prevention approaches (i.e., policy changes targeting supply and availability of alcohol-, media-, and communication-based efforts to change knowledge, attitudes, and beliefs).

Studies suggest that the bulk of all harms may in fact disproportionately arise from patterns of low to moderate consumption in a phenomenon termed the "prevention paradox" (Rose 1992), first investigated with respect to alcohol by Kreitman

(1986). A number of investigators using different methods and approaches have found that the burden of alcohol-related harms experienced by communities disproportionately reflects low to moderate levels of consumption (i.e., two to three drinks per occasion). This pattern exists despite findings that a given individual's risk for experiencing drinking-related harm increases with the amount of alcohol consumed. The paradoxical nature of this finding reflects the distribution of consumption patterns in a community. Because the bulk of drinkers consume at low to moderate levels but experience a non-zero risk for harm from their drinking, the majority of drinking-related harms in a community derive from their drinking behaviors. Studies by Spurling and Vinson (2005) using case control methods and hospital emergency room data, and Weitzman and Nelson (2004) analyzing four panels of a nationally representative survey (approximately 50,000 college youth) both found that the magnitude of drinking harms arising from persons drinking at low to moderate levels outweighed harms arising from persons drinking at heavier and extreme levels. Gruenwald et al. (2003) came to similar conclusions when modeling survey data describing patterns of alcohol consumption and harm among college youth using a dose-response framework. Finally, Stockwell and colleagues (2004) concluded that the prevention paradox applies to measures of alcohol and tobacco but not illicit drug use among adolescents in Victoria, Australia. Examining cross-sectional and longitudinal patterning of substance use by social and developmental risk factors, they found that even across intensities of use, the vast majority of substance use was found among youth with low/average risk.

These findings turn what may feel like common sense on its head and suggest that as a society we focus attention on social and policy factors that incrementally reduce low and moderate consumption among the majority to maximally improve public health. Primary prevention strategies focused on moderating consumption among the majority stand in contrast to tertiary prevention strategies (i.e., treatment). The latter are designed to affect large changes in behavior for the minority of drinkers who consume at extreme levels. Despite the public health logic of targeting prevention resources toward incrementally changing behavior among the majority of drinkers given they account for the largest share of drinking-related morbidity and mortality, considerable challenges exist in affecting these changes. Generating strong support for enacting environmental strategies that foster moderation in consumption requires educating lay people, policy makers, and clinicians about the relationship between consumption and harms and the "prevention paradox." As stated by Weitzman and Nelson (2004, p. 249):

> ...these types of prevention strategies may be both controversial—by seeking to incrementally change the behavior of a majority who may correctly perceive they are at low individual risk of harm—and counterintuitive—by investing prevention resources and attention toward changing the upstream determinants of behaviors that may appear

benign individually while seemingly ignoring the easily identified problems of persons with more acute symptoms or disease.

Despite ample evidence supporting environmental strategies for reducing consumption and harms (SAMHSA 1999; NIAAA 2002; Bonnie and O'Connell 2003), there appears to be resistance globally to making use of these strategies (Room et al., 2003). An example of leadership trying to focus attention on environmental (as opposed to mostly individual) exposures is evident in the World Health Organization's "Declaration on Young People and Alcohol, 2001" (WHO 2001). This call to action intentionally draws attention to societal factors influencing heavy and problem drinking among young people, including the marketing and promotion of alcohol. Additionally, the Declaration highlights links between alcohol, tobacco, and other substances, urging protection of young people within school and university settings.

Moving toward Community Change Initiatives

The evidence base for the effects of environmental prevention programs targeting heavy and harmful alcohol use by college youth is as yet sparse. However, results from comprehensive community prevention efforts targeting noncollege youth show good results (Wagenaar et al., 1999, 2000a,b; Holder et al., 2000), as do findings from a rigorous study of environmental initiatives targeting heavy drinking in college (Weitzman et al., 2004; Nelson et al., 2005). The five-year Community Trials Program in California used multiple complementary environmental strategies to reduce deaths and injuries related to alcohol, including: 1) community-led program-partnered efforts to increase support for public policy interventions through increasing knowledge and concern about alcohol-related deaths/injuries; 2) support for responsible beverage service efforts targeting reductions in alcohol sales to drinkers who are intoxicated and enforcement of local alcohol laws by working with alcohol outlets, Alcohol Beverage Control Commissions, and law enforcement; 3) promotion of efforts to train police and support new police practices around reducing driving while intoxicated behaviors; 4) promotion of efforts to reduce alcohol sales to underage youth by better enforcement of underage sales laws and training of alcohol outlet sales and service staff around underage sales; and 5) better use of local zoning restrictions to limit or reduce alcohol outlet density. In addition, several of these strategies were undertaken with media advocacy and communications components to increase levels of awareness and support about these issues. The Community Trial Program is credited with reducing alcohol sales to minors (Grube 1997), and reducing alcohol-related trauma in participant communities (Holder et al., 2000).

The Communities Mobilizing for Change on Alcohol (Wagenaar et al., 1999, 2000a,b) was a six-year initiative to use community organizing strategies to promote environmental change around multiple availability controls affecting youth access to alcohol in seven Minnesotan and Wisconsin communities. Community organizers led community efforts to enact and enforce local policies affecting supply and sales of alcohol to minor youth. Multiple efforts to address alcohol supply and availability were undertaken including purchase checks to assess patterns of enforcement and compliance with regulations prohibiting sale of alcohol to minors and increase supervision around youth access to alcohol. Over time, the program achieved increases in patterns of supervision and control around alcohol sales to minors by bars and other on-premise consumption settings. Older adolescents were less likely to provide alcohol to their peers. And driving under the influence (DUI) violations, crashes, and arrests declined among youth in intervention sites. The program's significant effects were largely restricted to college-age youth (i.e., 18–20 years old) (Wagenaar et al., 1999, 2000a,b).

In the case of young people in college, new reports give rise to optimism that comprehensive community prevention efforts can moderate consumption and reduce harm. Quasi-experimental evaluation results of the first four years of a program that uses local university–community coalitions in ten high-binge prevalence (i.e., >50 percent) college communities to promote environmental change around alcohol accessibility and availability demonstrated clear patterns of success where fidelity to the environmental change model of the program was high (Weitzman et al., 2004). The evaluation tracked implementation of environmental changes undertaken by ten college communities under the "A Matter of Degree" national prevention demonstration. After four years, five of ten intervention communities had achieved markedly higher levels of environmental change than their peer sites. At the five high-fidelity sites, college youth were less likely to report that alcohol was easily available, less likely to consume heavily, experience harms related to their drinking, and report second hand effects from others drinking. These changes were not evident among youth at low environmental change sites or among youth from 32 comparison communities. Additionally, despite concerns that drinking/driving behaviors would worsen where alcohol was made less readily available, risks for driving after drinking, driving after binge drinking, and riding in a car where the driver was high or drunk also declined among youth at high environmental change sites within the A Matter of Degree program (Nelson et al., 2005). Examples of effective environmentally oriented strategies for moderating consumption include greater enforcement of minimum drinking age laws, training on responsible beverage service, controls on pricing and promotion of alcohol, enactment of parental notification policies to inform parents about illegal or risky drinking behavior of their children, and expansion of substance-free living space capacity.

Synthesis and Implications

So what do we learn about preventing college drinking by considering risks for heavy and harmful drinking among college youth, trends in models for prevention, findings from neurobiology and epidemiology, and results from select comprehensive community prevention programs? First, adolescence through young adulthood appears to be a period of physiologic, psychologic, and sociologic vulnerability—a triple whammy from the perspective of substance use. Given the complexity of this period, the focus on an integrated social developmental model of heavy and harmful drinking for college youth appears to be a good fit to a major health risk behavior. A range of prevention and intervention options reflecting individual and societal or population approaches is available. There is consistently good evidence that altering key environmental factors is effective at moderating alcohol consumption and harms among young people—including those in college. There is poor or mixed evidence that altering individual factors is as effective. It is unlikely that a single "best" strategy for prevention will be identified. Rather, a best approach may be a rational effort that matches primary, secondary, and tertiary prevention strategies to a well-diagnosed problem and clear health objectives that are well supported by a local community. Comprehensive community change approaches do appear to be effective for young adults in community and college settings. Continued attention should be paid to promoting social policy interventions focused on reducing alcohol's supply and availability for college youth. These efforts are challenging to implement however and require a great deal of political will to enact. It may be that our deepened appreciation for the ways in which young people are vulnerable to influences to drink and our reexamined notions of adolescence and adulthood will help generate the political will required to undertake comprehensive community change efforts. This political will may be further supported by an improved understanding of the efficacy of environmental change efforts and the net benefits to society of undertaking them. Undertaking comprehensive community change efforts that include a strong environmental focus is likely to make our environments safer for young people, helping them move through life unencumbered by substance use habits and harms.

References

American Psychiatric Association. *Diagnostic and Statistical Manual of Mental Disorders.* 4th edition. Washington, D.C.: American Psychiatric Association, 1994.

Arnett, J. J. "Emergent adulthood: A theory of development from the late teens through the twenties." *American Psychologist* 55 (2000): 469–80.

Babor, T. F., M. Hofmann, F. K. DelBoca, V. M. Hesselbrock, R. E. Meyer, Z. S. Dolinsky, and B. Rounsaville. "Types of Alcoholics: I. Evidence for an Empirically Derived Typology Based on Indicators of Vulnerability and Severity." *Archive of General Psychiatry* 49 (1992): 599–608.

Bonnie, R. J., and M. E. O'Connell, editors. *Reducing Underage Drinking.* Washington, D.C.: National Academies Press, 2003.

Centers for Disease Prevention and Control (CDC). "Youth risk behavior surveillance: National College Health Risk Behavior Survey—United States, 1995." *MMWR* 46 (1997): 1–54.

Chaloupka, F. J., M. Grossman, and H. Saffer. "The Effects of Price on Alcohol Consumption on Alcohol Related Problems." *Alcohol Research Health* 26:1 (2002): 22–33.

Coate, D., and Grossman, M. 1998. Effects of alcoholic beverage prices and legal drinking ages on youth alcohol use. *Journal of Law and Economics* 31:1 (1998): 145–71.

Douglas, K. A., J. L. Collins, C. Warren, L. Kann, R. Gold, S. Clayton, J. G. Ross, and L. J. Kolbe. "Results from the 1995 National College Health Risk Behavior Survey." *Journal of American Collegiate Health* 46 (1997): 55–66.

Dowdall, G., and H. Wechsler. "Studying College Alcohol Use: Widening the Lens, Sharpening the Focus." *Journal of Studies in Alcohol* 14 (2002): 14–22.

Gogtay. N., J. N. Giedd, L. Lusk, et al. "Dynamic Mapping of Human Cortical Development During Childhood Through Early Adulthood." *PNAS* 101 (2004): 8174–79.

Grant, B. F. "Prevalence and correlates of alcohol use and DSM-IV alcohol independence in the United States: Results of the National Longitudinal Alcohol Epidemiologic Survey." *Journal of Studies in Alcohol* 58 (1997): 464–73.

Grube, J. "Preventing sales of alcohol to minors: Results from a community trial." *Addiction* 92:2 (1997): 251–60.

Gruenewald, P. J., F. W. Johnson, J. M. Light, R. Lipton, and R. F. Saltz. "Understanding College Drinking: Assessing Dose Response from Survey Self-Reports." *J Stud Alcohol* 64 (2003): 500–14.

Harwood, H. *Updating Estimates of the Economic Costs of Alcohol Abuse in the United States: Estimates, Update Methods, and Data.* Report prepared by The Lewin Group for the National Institute on Alcohol Abuse and Alcoholism, 2000. Based on estimates, analyses, and data reported in Harwood, H., D. Fountain, and G. Livermore. *The Economic Costs of Alcohol and Drug Abuse in the United States 1992.* Report prepared for the National Institute on Drug Abuse and the National Institute on Alcohol Abuse and Alcoholism, National Institutes of Health, Department of Health and Human Services. NIH Publication No. 98-4327. Rockville, MD: National Institutes of Health, 1998.

Hawkins, J. D., R. F. Catalano, and J. Y. Miller. "Risk and Protective Factors for Alcohol and Other Drug Problems in Adolescence and Early Adulthood: Implications for Substance Abuse Prevention." *Psychology Bulletin* 12 (1992): 64–105.

Hingson, R., and J. Howland. "Comprehensive Community Interventions to Promote Health: Implications for College-age Drinking Problems." *Journal of Studies in Alcohol* 14 (2002): 226–40.

Hingson, R., and D. Kenkel. "Social, Health, and Economic Consequences of Underage Drinking. In National Research Council and Institute of Medicine." *Reducing Underage Drinking: A Collective Responsibility, Background Papers* [CD-ROM]. Committee on Developing a Strategy to Reduce and Prevent Underage Drinking. Division of Behavioral and Social Sciences and Education. Washington, D.C.: The National Academies Press, 2004.

Holder, H. D., P. J. Gruenewald, W. R. Ponicki, A. J. Treno, J. W. Grube, R. F. Saltz, R. B. Voas, R. Reynolds, J. Davis, L. Sanchez, G. Gaumont, and P. Roeper. "Effect of Community-Based Interventions on High-Risk Drinking and Alcohol-related Injuries." *Journal of the American Medical Association* 284:18 (2000): 2341–7.

Johnston, L. D., P. M. O'Malley, and J. G. Bachman. "National Survey Results on Drug Use, 1975–2000. Volume II: College Students and Young Adults Ages 19–40." NIH Publication No. 01-4925. Bethesda, MD: National Institute on Drug Abuse, 2001.

Knight, J. R., H. Wechsler, M. Kuo, M. Seibring, E. R. Weitzman, and M. A. Schuckit. "Alcohol Abuse and Dependence Among U.S. College Students." *Journal of Studies in Alcohol* 63 (2002): 263–70.

Kreitman, N. "Alcohol Consumption and the Preventive Paradox." *Journal of Addictions* 81 (1986): 353–63.

Larimer M., and J. Cronce. "Identification, Prevention and Treatment: a Review of Individual-Focused Strategies to Reduce Problematic Alcohol Consumption by College Students." *Journal of Studies in Alcohol* 14 (2002): 148–64.

McGinnis, J. M., and W. H. Foege. "Actual Causes of Death in the United States." *Journal of the American Medical Association* 270 (1993): 2207–12.

Naimi, T. S., R. D. Brewer, A. Mokdad, C. Denny, M. K. Serdula, and J. S. Marks. "Binge Drinking Among U.S. Adults." *Journal of the American Medical Association* 289 (2003): 70–5.

National Institute on Alcohol Abuse and Alcoholism (NIAAA) Task Force on College Drinking. "A Call to Action: Changing the Culture of Drinking at U.S. Colleges." *NIH Publication No: 02–5010* National Institute on Alcohol Abuse and Alcoholism, Bethesda, MD, 2002. Available online at http://www.collegedrinkingprevention. gov/Reports/TaskForce/TaskForce_TOC.aspx

Nelson, T. F., Weitzman, E. R., Wechsler, H. The Effect of a Campus-Community Environmental Alcohol Prevention Initiative on Student Drinking and Driving: Results from the "A Matter of Degree" Program Evaluation. *Traffic Injury Prevention.* 6(2005): 323–330.

O'Malley, P. M., and L. D. Johnston. "Epidemiology of Alcohol and Other Drug Use Among American College Students." *Journal of Studies in Alcohol* 14 (2002): 23–39.

Petraitis, J., B. R. Flay, and T. Q. Miller. "Reviewing Theories of Adolescent Substance Use: Organizing Pieces in the Puzzle." *Psychology Bulletin* 117 (1995): 67–86.

Presley, C. A., J. S. Leichliter, and P. W. Meilman. "Alcohol and drugs on American college campuses: Findings from 1995, 1996, and 1997." A Report to College Presidents, Carbondale, IL: Southern Illinois University, 1999.

Room, R., K. Graham, J. Rehm, et al. "Drinking and Its Burden in a Global Perspective: Policy Considerations and Options." *Eur Addict Res* 9 (2003): 165–75.

Rose, G. *The Strategy of Preventive Medicine.* Oxford: Oxford University Press, 1992.

Schulenberg, J. E., and J. L. Maggs. "A Developmental Perspective on Alcohol Use and Heavy Drinking during Adolescence and the Transition to Young Adulthood." *Journal of Studies in Alcohol* Supplement No. 14 (2002): 54–70.

Schulenberg, J., J. L. Maggs, K. Steinman, and R. A. Zucker. "Development Matters: Taking the Long View on Substance Abuse Etiology and Intervention During Adolescence." In: *Adolescents, Alcohol, and Substance Abuse: Reaching Teens through Brief Interventions*, edited by P. M. Monti, S. M. Colby, and T. A. O'Leary. New York: Guilford Press, 2001: 19–57.

Spurling, M. C., and D. C. Vinson. "Alcohol Related Injuries: Evidence for the Prevention Paradox." *Annals of Family Medicine* 3 (2005): 47–52.

Stockwell, T. R., J. Toumbourou, P. Letcher, D. Smart, A. Sanson, and L. Bond. "Risk and Protection Factors for Different Intensities of Adolescent Substance Use: When Does the Prevention Paradox Apply?" *Drug and Alcohol Review* 23:1 (2004): 67–77.

Substance Abuse and Mental Health Services Administration (SAMHSA), Center for Substance Abuse Prevention, Division of State and Community Systems Development. Preventing Problems Related to Alcohol Availability: Environmental Approaches, Reference Guide, Third in the PEPS Series, DHHS Publication No.: (SMA) 99-3298, Rockville, MD: Department of Health and Human Services, 1999. Available online at http://www.health.org/govpubs/PHD822/aar.htm.

Substance Abuse and Mental Health Services Administration (SAMHSA), Office of Applied Studies. 1999 National Household Survey on Drug Abuse summary findings, DHHS Publication No.: SMA 00-3466, NHSDA Series H-12, Rockville, MD: Substance Abuse and Mental Health Services Administration, 2000. Available online at http://www.samhsa.gov/oas/p0000016.htm#special.

Wagenaar, A. C., D. M. Murray, J. P. Gehan, M. Wolfson, J. L. Forster, T. L. Toomey, C. L. Perry, and R. Jones-Webb. "Communities Mobilizing for Change on Alcohol: Outcomes From a Randomized Community Trial." *Journal of Studies on Alcohol* 61:1 (2000a): 85–94.

Wagenaar, A. C., D. M. Murray, and T. L. Toomey. "Communities Mobilizing for Change on Alcohol (CMCA): Effects of a Randomized Trial on Arrests and Traffic Crashes." *Addiction* 95:2 (2000b): 209–17.

Wagenaar, A. C., and T. L. Toomey. "Effects of Minimum Drinking Age Laws: Review and Analyses of the Literature from 1960 to 2000." *Journal of Studies in Alcohol* Supplement 14 (2002): 206–25.

Wechsler, H., J. E. Lee, M. Kuo, M. Seibring, T. F. Nelson, and H. Lee. "Trends in College Binge Drinking During a Period of Increased Prevention Efforts: Findings from 4 Harvard School of Public Health College Alcohol Study Surveys, 1993–2001." *Journal of the American College of Health* 50 (2002): 203–17.

Weitzman, E. R. "Social Developmental Overview of Heavy Episodic or 'Binge' Drinking Among American College Students and Implications for Prevention and Treatment." *Psychiatric Times*, 21:2 (February 2004): Special Report.

Weitzman, E. R., T. F. Nelson, H. Lee, and H. Wechsler. "Reducing Drinking and Related Harms in College: Evaluation of the 'A Matter of Degree' Program." *American Journal of Preventative Medicine* 21 (2004): 187–96.

Weitzman, E. R., and T. F. Nelson. "College Student Binge Drinking and the 'Prevention Paradox': Implications for Prevention and Harms Reduction." *Journal of Drug Education* 34 (2004): 247–66.

World Health Organization. *Declaration on Young People and Alcohol*, 2001. WHO European Ministerial Conference on Young People and Alcohol, Stockholm. (2001) Available online from http://www.euro.who.int/aboutwho/policy/20030204_1. Accessed on May 4, 2005.

World Health Organization. *Seventh Futures Forum—On Unpopular Decisions in Public Health*, WHO Regional Office for Europe, Copenhagen, ISBN 92-890-1069-X, 2005. Available online from http://www.euro.who.int/InformationSources/Publications/Catalogue/20050608_1.

Zailckas, K. Smashed. *Story of a Drunken Girlhood.* New York: Penguin Group, Viking Press, 2005.

Zeigler, D. W., Wang, C. C., Yoast, R. A., et al. "The neurocognitive effects of alcohol on adolescents and college students." *Preventive Medicine* 40 (2005): 23–32.

Zucker, R. A. "The Four Alcoholisms: A Developmental Account of the Etiologic Process." In: *Alcohol and Addictive Behavior,* edited by P. C. Rivers. Nebraska Symposium on Motivation 1986, Vol. 34. Lincoln, NE: University of Nebraska Press, 1987: 27–83.

Chapter 10

How Do Alcohol Screening and Prevention Programs Fare in a Web-Based Environment?

Marc Belanger

M.A., Health Communications

Contents

The year 2005 marked the 10th anniversary of the Internet. As the fastest communication medium in U.S. history, it wasn't long before it became a tool used by health prevention and promotion professionals. Particularly in alcohol abuse prevention, there is an increasing need for more effective message dissemination channels. It is estimated that 18 million Americans abuse alcohol or are alcohol dependent. Annually, this problem takes the lives of 100,000 people and costs the health care system billions of dollars (AlcoholScreening.org 2001). Consequently, many alcohol screening and prevention programs have taken their message online (e.g., AlcoholScreening. org, E-chug.com, MyStudentBody.com, AlcoholEdu.com).

The Internet, however, is a unique means of communication and there are many considerations that must be taken into account before developing an online prevention program. Traditional frameworks of health communication may seem rather anachronistic when placed in a Web environment. This chapter will discuss reasons for this. Starting with some exploration into the growth of the Internet, it will then lead into discussion of current research of Web-based programs, followed by a few words on the convergence of traditional health communication models and the Internet. And last, some contextual caveats, with respect to development and evaluation, will be presented, using AlcoholScreening.org as one example.

The Growth of the Internet

The Internet has been the fastest growing communication medium in U.S. history, taking only seven years to saturate 30 percent of American households. It took 46 years for electricity, 38 years for the telephone, and 17 years for television to do the same. In 1997, 19 million Americans were accessing the Internet. One year later, that number tripled, and, in 1999, it surpassed 100 million users (Lebo 2000). In 2004, the 10th anniversary of the Internet's availability to the general public, 75 percent of Americans were going online (Lebo 2004).

As Internet access grows, so does the amount of content. In 2000, research estimated that the Internet was increasing by more than 3.2 million Web pages and 715,000 images every 24 hours (Lebo 2000). By February 2005, the Google search engine reported that it was indexing 4.28 billion Web pages and 880 million images (Caslon Analytics 2005). Fifty-five percent of Internet users consider this information to be "a very important or extremely important source of information for them." Seventy-four percent of people consider most or all of the information on government sites to be accurate and reliable when compared with established media sites and sites posted by individuals (Lebo 2004, p. 50).

More people every day are using the Internet to access health information. According to a 2005 study by the Pew Internet & American Life Project, 116 million Americans are going online. Eighty percent have searched at one time for information about one or more major health topics. (Interestingly, on a typical day, 6 percent of Internet users are seeking health or medical information, whereas only 5 percent are buying products.) Of those people searching for health information, 8 percent have searched at least once for information specifically about alcohol and drug problems (Fox 2003).

American news media quickly recognized this as a growing trend and began tracking it. The word "Internet" first started to appear in American media and thus they began reporting on in 1990. That year, there were 346 mentions. By 1995, that number increased to 70,944 and continued to grow; 219,866 in 1997, 529,343 by 1999, and surpassed 700,000 during the first three quarters of 2000 (Lebo 2000, p. 4). More recently, research on the opinions of Internet users has allowed news programs to create stories around it. Below is one example from a 2002 story called "Health Online" aired by a New England television news program:

> More than half of all Americans with Internet access have used the web for medical advice and information. Some do it because it's easy. Others do it because they say it's too difficult to see a doctor…52 million Americans have used the web to learn about diseases and treatments. Plus other health related matters, like diet and exercise. 92 percent of those surveyed found their internet search helpful. 81 percent learned something new (Kim 2002).

Eventually, the government began to respond. In 1996, the Science Panel on Interactive Communication and Health was created by the Office of Disease Prevention and Health Promotion of the U.S. Department of Health and Human Services. The panel consisted of fourteen experts from various disciplines, including interactive technology, public health, health promotion, and communication studies. The goal of the panel was "to examine interactive health communication technology and its potential impact on the health of the public." In addition to the Internet, they also evaluated other media forms such as DVD and dial-in services. The end result was a final report, *Wired for Health and Well-Being: The Emergence of Interactive Health Communication,* published in 1999. This report explores quality and evaluation of "interactive health communication" and provides recommendations for future development and use of this means of communication (Science Panel 1999).

The same government office later created a Health Communication Focus Area within its Healthy People 2010 initiative. The goal was simply "to use communication strategically to improve health." In 2003, Healthy People 2010 released its report, *Communicating Health: Priorities and Strategies for Progress,* and, for the first time, included objectives proposed by the Health Communication Focus Area.

Several of those objectives focused on Internet health communication (e.g., Internet Access in the Home, Disclosure of Information To Assess the Quality of Health Web Sites) (U.S. Dept. of Health, 2003).

Current Research of Web-Based Programs

Although limited, the research so far on Web-based screening has had some encouraging findings. Some studies have shown distinctive benefits of Web-based programs. One study comparing Web-based screening programs with paper-and-pencil screening programs reported a decrease in data collection and entry errors, presumably from the removal of human error (Miller, 2002). Online screening programs that require disclosure of high-risk or stigmatized behaviors, including alcohol, have shown significantly lower reporting bias (Turner, 1988; Flicker, 2004). In other words, the responses were more honest and closer in accuracy to the actual behavior. One can assume this is a result of an increased sense of anonymity and confidentiality.

Web-based screening programs targeting youth seem to have higher response rates (Flicker, 2004). Generation Y, as they are called, is the first generation to grow up with the Internet and are oftentimes very familiar with and not intimidated by the Internet. Also, when presented with a choice, screening participants find online surveys very convenient, and prefer them over paper and pencil, oftentimes leading to increased response rates (Cunningham et al., 2000; Matano et al., 2000; Miller 2002).

Fortunately, many studies have also begun examining the efficacy of Web-based screening programs (Kypri, Gallagher, and Cashell-Smith, 2004; Linkel et al., 2004). One university-based study reported that its Web-based program was nearly as equal as its in-person program (Kypri, Saunders et al., 2004). One workplace study reported an 8 percent change in drinking behavior (Westrup et al., 2003). Another study, based in a university setting, reported lower consumption rates during a six-week follow-up, and lower personal problems and academic problems at a six-month follow-up (Kypri, Saunders et al., 2004).

AlcoholScreening.org

The information used as a foundation during the development of AlcoholScreening. org will be presented in this section as a way of illustrating the development process of Web-based alcohol screening and brief intervention programs. This Web site was chosen as an example because the author of this chapter was the former Program Manager for AlcoholScreening.org and was privy to the development process.

AlcoholScreening.org is a free public Web site created by Join Together, a project of the Boston University School of Public Health, in collaboration with Richard

Saitz, MD, Boston University School of Medicine, Clinical Addiction Research and Education Unit. Funded primarily by the Robert Wood Johnson Foundation, Join Together's mission is to advance effective alcohol and drug policy, prevention, and treatment. Its Web site, www.JoinTogether.org, is a leading source of information for professionals working in the substance abuse field.

Join Together developed AlcoholScreening.org as a response to the increasing interest in searching for health information online. As a resource to help visitors understand how their drinking behavior may likely be affecting their health, now or in the future, AlcoholScreening.org is meant to be widely accessible and nononsense in its presentation. Since its launch during National Alcohol Awareness Month (April) 2001, AlcoholScreening.org has been visited by more than 600,000 people who have completed nearly 350,000 screens.*

AlcoholScreening.org has received extensive recognition. It's been featured on the television programs CNN Presents and Dateline NBC, and in online reports on CNN, MSNBC, and several other media Web sites. It was featured as the Web site of the Week by the British Medical Journal, and hundreds of Web sites have linked to it, including WebMD.com, the Massachusetts State Health Department, Delta Airlines, and the New York State Office of Alcoholism and Substance Abuse Services.

AlcoholScreening.org has three sections; Screening, Learn More, and Find Help. The Learn More section provides information about a wide range of alcohol-related health topics including alcohol consumption guidelines, how to cut down on drinking, tips for teens, what to do if someone you know has a problem, as well as several other topics. All information provided in the Learn More section was provided by the U.S. Department of Agriculture, U.S. Department of Health and Human Services. Government information is used because most users feel that government information is the most credible (Lebo 2004).

The Find Help section contains links to support resources such as face-to-face support groups, online support groups, support for family and friends, and resources for other addictions. Much of the information is provided by credible sources such as Alcoholics Anonymous and the U.S. Government. Find Help also incorporates the Substance Abuse and Mental Health Association's treatment provider database which is a searchable database of 11,000 local treatment programs throughout the United States.

The Screening section of AlcoholScreening.org is comprised of three demographic questions, twelve screening questions, and one final question. All questions require an answer. The three demographic questions ask the user's age, gender, and zip code. Age and gender are needed to provide personalized feedback, which is discussed later in this chapter. Age is also collected to know whether that person fits within the valid age range (i.e., 14–99) for the screening questions. Zip code

---

*AlcoholScreening.org data provided in this article was collected from January 1, 2001, through February 28, 2004.

information is collected for research and data analysis. The final question is a choice between:

- I am completing this test based upon my own alcohol-use experience.
  or
- I am just curious about the test and the related feedback, or answered the questions with someone else in mind.

As with a zip code, this last question is asked solely for the purpose of research and data analysis. The data collected from users who are completing the test based on their own alcohol-use experience is considered valid and only this data is included in any analyses. The next page lists the twelve screening questions as they are listed on AlcoholScreening.org. The answer choices online, however, are drop-down menus.

AlcoholScreening.org Screening Questions

1. How often do you have a drink containing alcohol?
   Never
   Monthly or less
   2–4 times a month
   2–3 times a week
   4 or more times a week

2. How many drinks containing alcohol do you have on a typical day when you are drinking?
   1 or 2
   3 or 4
   5 or 6
   7, 8, or 9
   10 or more

3. Thinking about a typical week, on how many *days* do you have at least one alcoholic drink? (If you don't drink every week, answer for a typical week in which you do.)
   1
   2
   3
   4
   5
   6
   7

4. How often do you have six or more drinks on one occasion?
   Never
   Less than monthly

Monthly
Weekly
Daily or almost daily

5. Thinking about the past year, what is the greatest number of drinks you've had on any one occasion?

1
2
3
4
5
6
7
8
9 or more

6. How often during the last year have you found that you were not able to stop drinking once you had started?

Never
Less than monthly
Monthly
Weekly
Daily or almost daily

7. How often during the last year have you failed to do what was normally expected from you because of drinking?

Never
Less than monthly
Monthly
Weekly
Daily or almost daily

8. How often during the last year have you needed a first drink in the morning to get yourself going after a heavy drinking session?

Never
Less than monthly
Monthly
Weekly
Daily or almost daily

9. How often during the last year have you had a feeling of guilt or remorse after drinking?

Never
Less than monthly
Monthly

Weekly
Daily or almost daily

10. How often during the last year have you been unable to remember what happened the night before because you had been drinking?
   Never
   Less than monthly
   Monthly
   Weekly
   Daily or almost daily

11. Have you or someone else been injured as a result of your drinking?
   No
   Yes, but not in the last year
   Yes, during the last year

12. Has a relative or friend or a doctor or another health worker been concerned about your drinking or suggested you cut down?
   No
   Yes, but not in the last year
   Yes, during the last year

All questions, except #3 and #5, make up the Alcohol Use Identification Test (AUDIT). The AUDIT is an alcohol screening instrument created by the World Health Organization (WHO). In 1982, WHO convened an international committee with the goal of creating a screening instrument that had not yet existed—a screening instrument "for the early identification of harmful drinking rather than alcoholism" (Babor 1992, p. 5). This was a significant step in the field of substance abuse prevention and treatment because harmful drinkers (i.e., low risk and at-risk, rather than dependent drinkers) make up the majority of the population (Institute of Medicine, 1990). The Drinker's Pyramid shown below illustrates the stratification of the general population according to their reported drinking behavior (Figure 10.1).

AlcoholScreening.org uses the AUDIT instrument for several reasons. For one, it has been validated across various populations, in many different countries, and

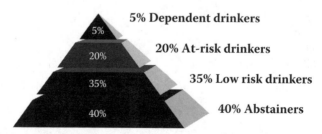

Figure 10.1   Drinker's pyramid.

in many languages. Although AlcoholScreening.org is in English and uses U.S. drinking guidelines, it was important to use a screening instrument that has been so widely validated. It was also shown to be successful as a self-screener. The third reason for choosing the AUDIT was because it "...emphasizes identification of hazardous drinking rather than long-term dependence and adverse drinking consequences, and focuses primarily on symptoms occurring during the recent past rather than "ever" (Babor 1992, p. 11). This is the same goal of AlcoholScreening. org. To screen harmful/hazardous drinkers early allows for the possibility of shifting their behavior before it becomes a dependency problem.

Originally, the AUDIT was not valid for anyone younger than 18 years old. However, a study by John R. Knight published in January 2003 has shown that, with some changes to the scoring algorithm, the AUDIT is also valid for youth 14 through 17 years old (Knight et al., 2003). AlcoholScreening.org incorporated Knight's recommendations in August 2004 and began allowing this age group to take part in the screening process. Data is also being collected, but it is too recent to be included in the examples provided in this chapter.

To take into account current drinking trends, two additional questions were added to the screening tool. Questions #3 and #5 were added to assess binge drinking:

> *Question #3:* Thinking about a typical week, on how many *days* do you have at least one alcoholic drink? (If you don't drink every week, answer for a typical week in which you do.)
> *Question #5:* Thinking about the past year, what is the greatest number of drinks you've had on any one occasion?

Binge drinking did not gain much public attention until thoroughly evaluated in a 1993 study, "Health and Behavioral Consequences of Binge Drinking in College," published in the *Journal of the American Medical Association* (Wechsler et al., 1995). This study defined binge drinking in the context of college students; however, the application of its definition was generalized to the greater public soon after. Since then, binge drinking has been recognized as a national problem and has been the subject of many scientific studies.

Even though binge drinking was placed on the research platform only within the past decade, binge drinking was briefly used as a categorical term a decade earlier. In a 1984 article in the *American Journal of Public Health*, P. M. O'Malley (1984) defined five or more drinks in a sitting as binge drinking. O'Malley was reporting on data from the University of Michigan's Monitoring the Future project, which studies the health behavior of high school seniors. Monitoring the Future adopted this five-drink measure after it was described in a 1969 report as a valid measurement of drinking with reasonable potential for harmful consequences (Cahalan et al., 1969).

Although the definition of binge drinking has changed slightly over time, the official definition today remains similar to the original "5 or more drinks in a sitting." Today's definition is:

For men, 5 or more drinks on one occasion (in a row or within a short span of time, usually 2 hours).
For women, 4 or more drinks on one occasion (in a row or within a short span of time, usually 2 hours).

The male/female differentiation was established later by Henry Wechsler. It takes into account the biologic difference between genders in how alcohol is metabolized.

AlcoholScreening.org Personalized Feedback

Contrary to how health communication programs should be established, AlcoholScreening.org does not focus on any specific audience. After all, this is nearly impossible for any public Web site that can be accessed by anyone with Internet access, at anytime, anywhere in the world. Contrary to one main health communications rule, the response to the proverbial question, "Who is your audience?", in this case is "everyone."

This makes it difficult for AlcoholScreening.org to work under the paradigm of traditional health promotion teachings, which say that a program's audience must be focused and the message to that audience must take into account the specific needs, barriers, and self-efficacy of that audience. It would be nearly impossible to provide different and truly personalized feedback for every visitor; however, it does use several tools for successful personalization.

After answers have been submitted to all twelve questions, AlcoholScreening.org uses the data to create a personalized feedback page. The feedback is meant to provide some insight as to whether the user's reported alcohol consumption is within safe limits or may likely be harmful to their health, either now or in the future. It is meant to be supportive, while encouraging change in behavior, if necessary. It does not label anyone as an alcoholic; instead, it focuses on health risks, both immediate and long term.

The feedback pages were created using the Brief Intervention Model and the Health Belief Model as conceptual frameworks. Brief interventions (BI) are counseling sessions (typically conducted in person) that can be as short as five minutes. In face-to-face situations, they have been shown to be highly effective reducing alcohol use as well as reducing health care utilization thus reducing health care costs (World Health Organization 1996; Gentilello et al., 1999). Most often, BIs incorporate the six elements of FRAMES: feedback, responsibility, advice, menu of strategies, empathy, and self-efficacy. The goal of BIs is to activate the person to take the next step in positive behavior change.

Obviously, there are inherent differences between face-to-face BIs and feedback provided online. This is even acknowledged in the "About This Site" section of AlcoholScreening.org:

> Research to date on Internet-based [screenings and brief interventions], while preliminary, points to significant potential to effectively reach many more individuals than can be physically screened in health-care and other offline encounters. While no online health screening and information tool can take the place of individual advice from a quali-fied health professional, Join Together believes that online screening will play an increasingly important role in increasing public and per-sonal awareness about alcohol consumption and health.

The second health communication model that was used as a framework while developing the feedback pages is the Health Belief Model (HBM). In the 1950s, public health professionals were baffled by the lack of participation in free screen-ing programs (e.g., tuberculosis, flu). As part of an effort to explain this, social psychologists in the U.S. Public Health Service developed the HBM (University of Florida 1999). The National Cancer Institute (2003, p. 3) describes the HBM as "one of the most widely recognized conceptual frameworks of health behavior." Freudenberg (1995, p. 293) describes this model as such:

> The health belief model…predicts that individuals will act to protect their health if they regard themselves as susceptible to a condition, if they believe the condition has serious consequences, if they believe that an available course of action will reduce their susceptibility or the sever-ity of the condition, and if they believe the benefits of action outweigh its costs or disadvantages.

The HBM attempts to explain and predict future health behaviors by focusing on attitudes and beliefs. Table 10.1 highlights the six key concepts, the definition of each concept, and the application of the each concept in health promotion pro-grams (The Communications Initiative 2003).

Below are the six HBM concepts with examples of AlcoholScreening.org feed-back provided in each. The feedback examples help illustrate which concepts Alco-holScreening.org has successfully or unsuccessfully incorporated into the feedback text.

Table 10.1 Health Belief Model Key Concepts		
Concept	*Definition*	*Application*
Perceived susceptibility	One's opinion of chances of getting a (harmful) condition	Define populations at risk, risk levels. Personalize risk based on a person's features or behavior. Heighten perceived susceptibility if too low
Perceived severity	One's opinion of how serious a condition and its sequelae are	Specify consequences of the risk and the condition
Perceived benefits	One's opinion of the efficacy of the advised action to reduce risk or seriousness of impact	Define action to take: how, where, when; clarify the positive effects to be expected
Perceived barriers	One's opinion of the tangible and psychological costs of the advised action	Identify and reduce barriers through reassurance, incentives, assistance
Cues to action	Strategies to activate "readiness"	Provide how-to information, promote awareness, reminders
Self-efficacy	Confidence in one's ability to take action	Provide training, guidance in performing action

Perceived Susceptibility

Using the data provided by the user, the feedback pages describe susceptibility in various ways, dependent on the severity of the reported behavior. For example, someone with a low AUDIT score (low-risk drinker overall), but seems to binge every so often, would receive this feedback (italics have been added to highlight examples):

Your results on the AUDIT (Alcohol Use Disorders Identification Test) are below the range usually associated with harmful drinking or alcoholism.

However, *you may be at increased risk for health problems due to the number of alcoholic drinks you reported consuming per week,* and from how much you have consumed on at least one occasion. For men aged 65 and under, consuming more than 14 drinks a week increases their risk.

In addition, *consuming too much alcohol on one occasion increases your risk for injury and other immediate consequences.* This risk is associated with having more than 4 drinks per occasion if you are a man aged 65 or under.

Finally, if you experience any of the following:

■ you are not able to stop drinking once you have started;
■ you fail to do what is normally expected from you because of drinking;
■ you need a first drink in the morning to get yourself going after a heavy drinking session;
■ you feel guilt or remorse after drinking;
■ you're unable to remember what happened the night before because you had been drinking;
■ you are injured as a result of your drinking;
■ a relative, friend, or doctor expresses concern about your drinking or suggests you cut down;
■ this may indicate an early alcohol problem or one that the AUDIT did not detect.

All users receive feedback illustrating normative data that compare their reported alcohol consumption with that of others of the same age and gender as a way to illustrate if the person drinks more or less than his or her peers. For example, *"More than 80.5 percent of the general adult American population and 71 percent of men consume fewer drinks per week than you reported consuming."* This normative data are provided by the Alcohol Research Group in Berkeley, California. Using normative data, AlcoholScreening.org is an extremely telling way of "making it real" for the users and heightening their perceived susceptibility and perceived severity.

Perceived Severity

The appropriate application of this concept would be to "specify consequences of the risk and the condition." AlcoholScreening.org could do a better job at listing specific consequences of risky drinking. It touches on risks, but only in the most general way. For example, this is the feedback provided to a user with more severe drinking behaviors:

> *It is likely that your current drinking patterns are hazardous or harmful to your health and well being.* Your responses to the AUDIT (Alcohol Use Disorders Identification Test) are in a range believed to be consistent with problems related to drinking.

And this is the feedback provided to the user with less severe drinking behavior overall, but possible binge occurrences:

> Your results do not suggest that a pattern of excess drinking is harming your health. However, the amount you reported consuming on at least one occasion *may increase your risk for injury or other immediate consequences.* This risk is associated with having more than 3 drinks per occasion if you are a woman or someone over 65, or 4 drinks per occasion if you are a man age 65 or younger.

Perceived Benefits

This is the concept where AlcoholScreening.org lacks the most. The benefits to lowering the number of drinks per week or the numbers of times a person binges are significant, and they can easily be listed (e.g., greater concentration, lower risk of cardiovascular disease, lower risk of accidents). However, the feedback pages fail to include such information. The concepts are key to convincing the person of why they should change their behavior, and providing encouragement to do so.

The final three concepts (Perceived Barriers, Cues to Action, and Self-Efficacy) are each implemented into the last paragraph of every feedback page, which starts with "Recommended Action." The same paragraph will be used for each section following; however, the key concept is in italics.

Perceived Barriers

> Because your results indicate that your drinking patterns may be hazardous or harmful, consider seeking further evaluation from *your doctor or other qualified health professional, who can help you determine if your alcohol consumption* is adversely affecting your health or interfering with your work and relationships. You may also want to learn more about health problems related to drinking and ways to reduce your risk. The links below will assist you in locating a local health professional for further assistance, and in making well informed health decisions about alcohol.

■ Learn more about alcohol and health
■ Find help and support

Or for those who reported less severe behavior:

> Because your results indicate that your alcohol consumption may be increasing your risk for health problems, consider cutting back the

amount of alcohol you drink to safer levels. For some people, especially those with an early or undetected alcohol problem, quitting may be the best choice. And, in some situations no amount of alcohol is safe.

- Learn more about alcohol and health
- Find help and support

The two bulleted items presented are hypertext links to the respective section on the Web site—Learn More or Find Help. They appear at the bottom of all feedback pages.

Cues to Action

Because your results indicate that your drinking patterns may be hazardous or harmful, consider seeking further evaluation from your doctor or other qualified health professional, who can help you determine if your alcohol consumption is adversely affecting your health or interfering with your work and relationships. *You may also want to learn more about health problems related to drinking and ways to reduce your risk.* The links below will assist you in locating a local health professional for further assistance, and in making well informed health decisions about alcohol.

- Learn more about alcohol and health
- Find help and support

Self-Efficacy

Because your results indicate that your drinking patterns may be hazardous or harmful, consider seeking further evaluation from your doctor or other qualified health professional, who can help you determine if your alcohol consumption is adversely affecting your health or interfering with your work and relationships. You may also want to learn more about health problems related to drinking and ways to reduce your risk. *The links below will assist you in locating a local health professional for further assistance, and in making well informed health decisions about alcohol.*

- Learn more about alcohol and health
- Find help and support

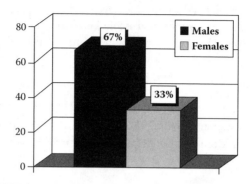

Figure 10.2   Gender breakdown of AlcoholScreening.org users.

User Behavior Immediately after Receiving Personalized Feedback

The big question now is, "Do users heed the advice given in the feedback?" After all, isn't that the goal of this site? And, if users did heed the advice, then it would illustrate some validity to Web-based alcohol screening and prevention programs. The data provided in this section were collected at AlcoholScreening.org between January 1, 2001, and February 28, 2005 (Figure 10.2). A piece of these data was used in the study *Web-based Screenings and Brief Intervention for the Spectrum of Alcohol Problems* (Saitz et al., 2004).

Some Demographic Information

All Visitors

Of all AlcoholScreening.org users between 18 and 99 years old (valid age range for the AUDIT), 67 percent were men, 33 percent women. The average age was 32. Of those 18 years old and older, 89 percent reported binge (per occasion) drinking, and 55 percent reported typically exceeding weekly risky drinking limits. Most (73 percent males vs. 62 percent females) had alcohol screening test results (AUDIT score) consistent with alcohol abuse or dependence (AUDIT score ≥ 8).

Visitors Younger than Twenty-One Years Old

Seventy-seven percent were between 18 and 20 years old. The average age for all visitors younger than 21 was 18 years old, and 56 percent were men, 44 percent women. Seventy-six percent of males and 69 percent of females had alcohol screening test results consistent with alcohol abuse or dependence (AUDIT ≥ 8).

Ninety-two percent of male visitors between 18 and 20 years old reported binge drinking at some point over the past year; 91 percent of the females reported the same. Within this same age cohort, 78 percent of the males had alcohol screening test results (AUDIT ≥ 8) consistent with alcohol abuse or dependence; 72 percent of the females scored the same.

Behavior after Receiving Feedback

There are several behaviors encouraged in the "Recommended Action" section (e.g., "consider cutting back," "consider seeking further evaluation from your doctor," "quitting may be the best choice"). The recommended action depends on the user's reported behavior. Knowing whether or not the user followed the recommended action seems nearly impossible to measure, because AlcoholScreening.org does not ask for follow-up information.

However, everyone is encouraged to 1) learn more about the issue, and, if appropriate 2) seek help for a possible alcohol use problem. Each one is further encouraged by the placement of a hypertext link to each of the respective sections at AlcoholScreening.org; Learn More and Find Help. These sections were both discussed earlier in this chapter. To measure whether or not the feedback is, in fact, influencing the user to take the recommended action, his or her immediate next click of the mouse, after being presented with feedback, is logged by Web traffic software. There are three possible options for the immediate next click of their mouse: 1) leave the site entirely, 2) click-through to the Learn More section, or 3) click-through to the Find Help section. While maintaining anonymity, these data are saved to a database and connected to the user's AUDIT score and binge drinking information.

Using these data, the study *Web-based Screening and Brief Intervention for the Spectrum of Alcohol Problems* set out to examine the influence of AlcoholScreening. org feedback on behavior. Below is the results summary as printed in the study abstract (Saitz et al., 2004):

> …One-fifth of visitors visited portions of the Web site that provided additional information about alcohol use and referrals. Visitors with possible alcohol abuse or dependence were more likely than those without these disorders to visit a part of the Web site designed for those seeking additional help (33 percent vs. 8 percent, $P < 0.0001$).

This says that there is some connection with the recommended action and the immediate next step. The study does report on more specific data, further demonstrating this connection. For example, Figure 10.3 shows the percentage of users who immediately visited the Learn More or Find Help section, broken down according to their reported drinking behavior.

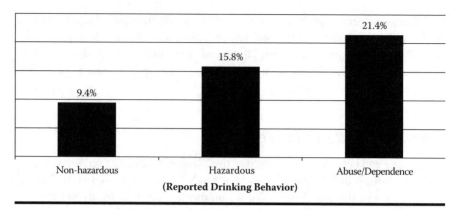

Figure 10.3   Percent of users who immediately clicked-through to learn more or get help.

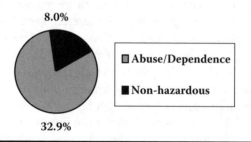

Figure 10.4   Which users immediately visited the Find Help section?

In other words, users with greater drinking severity level are more likely to visit one of those two sections of AlcoholScreening.org (rather than leave the site altogether).

Now, looking specifically at those users who clicked-through to Find Help after receiving feedback, 32.9 percent reported alcohol abuse or dependence, while those who reported nonhazardous drinking behaviors only made up 8 percent of this group (Figure 10.4).

Conclusion

Even though the Internet has infiltrated many aspects of our daily lives and become the fastest growing communications medium this country has ever seen, it's still a communications medium in its infancy. The Internet lives in an environment all its own, and special considerations should be thoroughly examined before using it as a channel for disseminating health messages and encouraging behavior change. There is so much to learn about its abilities, drawbacks, consequences, and effectiveness.

For instance, alcohol screening programs for some special populations (e.g., elderly) should not be considered as a Web-based program. The digital divide—that which separates Internet users from nonusers—still exists and has remained stable since late 2001. According to the Pew Internet & American Life Project, 42 percent of the American population reported themselves to be non-Internet users, although many of them reported some indirect access (e.g., through friend's/family's use). Twenty-four percent reported being "truly disconnected," having no direct or indirect experiences with the Internet (Lenhard 2003). The elderly make up a large part of the nonusers and would be missed completely if a screening and prevention program tried to reach them via the Internet.

AlcoholScreening.org is only one example of many using traditional health communication frameworks to build itself online. It won't be surprising if, in time, there are additional models and theories of health communication created that speak directly to programs being developed on the Internet.

Research on current Web-based programs has finally begun to increase and provide much information, and, as of yet, the research findings are nothing short of encouraging. Many studies show positive results equal to that of offline programs. They are also reporting a greater acceptance by the public of Web-based programs over more traditional modalities. There is, however, so much more to be done. Creating Web-based screening programs may be easy and cost-effective, but more research must be pursued into examining whether or not these great benefits are helping or hindering an ever-growing public health problem.

References

AlcoholScreening.org. About this Site (April 2001). Available online from http://www. AlcoholScreening.org. Retrieved August 1, 2005.

Babor, T. F., de la Fuente, J. R., Saunders, J., and Grant, M. "The Alcohol Use Identification Test (AUDIT): Guidelines for Use in Primary Health Care." World Health Organization, 1992.

Cahalan, D., I. H. Cisin, and H. M. Crossley. "American Drinking Practices: A National Study of Drinking Behavior and Attitudes." Monograph No. 6, New Brunswick, NJ: Rutgers Center of Alcohol Studies, 1969.

Caslon Analytics. Caslon Analytics: net metrics and statistics guide (February 2005). Available online from Caslon Analytics website: http://www.caslon.com.au/metricsguide2.htm#pages. Retrieved August 2, 2005.

Cunningham, J. A., K. Humphreys, and A. Koski-Jannes. "Providing Personalized Assessment Feedback for Problem Drinking on the Internet: A Pilot Project." *Journal of Alcohol Studies* 61:6 (November 2000): 794–8.

Flicker, S., E. Goldberg, S. Read, T. Beinot, A. McClelland, P. Saulnier, et al. "HIV-Positive Youth's Perspectives on the Internet and eHealth." *Journal of Medical Internet Research* 6:3 (2004): article e32.

Fox, Susannah. Health Information Online. Washington, D.C.: Pew Internet and American Life Project (July 2003).

Freudenberg, N., E. Eng, B. Flay, G. Parcel, T. Rogers, and N. Wallerstein. "Strengthening Individual and Community Capacity to Prevent Disease and Promote Health: In Search of Relevant Theories and Principles." *Health Education Quarterly* 22:3 (1995): 290–306.

Gentilello, L. M., F. P. Rivara, D. M. Donovan, G. J. Kovich, E. Daranciang, C. W. Dunn, et al. "Alcohol Interventions in a Trauma Center as a Means of Reducing the Risk of Injury Recurrence." *Annals of Surgery* 230:4 (1999): 437–80.

Institute of Medicine. Broadening the Base of Treatment for Alcohol Problems. Washington, D.C.: National Academy Press, 1990.

Kim, Kristy. Health Online (May 1, 2002). Available online from Channel 7 News (WHDH) at http://www2.whdh.com:80/features/articles/healthcast/H521/. Retrieved August 1, 2005.

Knight, John R., L. Sherritt, S. K. Harris, E. C. Gates, and G. Chang. "Validity of Brief Alcohol Screening Tests Among Adolescents: A Comparison of the AUDIT, POSIT, CAGE, and CRAFFT." *Alcoholism: Clinical and Experimental Research* 27:1 (2003): 67–72.

Kypri, K., S. Gallagher, and M. Cashell-Smith. "An internet-based survey method for college student drinking research." *Drug and Alcohol Dependence* 76 (2004): 45–53.

Kypri, K., J. B. Saunders, S. Williams, R. O. McGee, J. D. Langlely, M. Cashell-Smith, et al. "Web-based Screening and Brief Interventions for Hazardous Drinking: A Double-Blind Randomized Controlled Trial. *Addiction* 99(11) (2004): 1410–7.

Lebo, Harlan. *Surveying the Digital Future: Year Four.* University of Southern California: Center for the Digital Future, November 2000.

Lebo, Harlan. *The UCLA Internet Report: Surveying the Digital Future.* University of California Los Angeles: Center for the Digital Future, November 2004.

Lenhard, Amanda. *The Ever-Shifting Internet Population: A New Look at Internet Access and the Digital Divide.* Washington, D.C.: Pew Internet and American Life Project, April 16, 2003.

Linkel, S., A. Brown, and P. Wallace. "Down Your Drink: A Web-Based Intervention for People With Excessive Alcohol Consumption." *Alcohol & Alcoholism* 39:1 (2004): 29–32.

Matano, R. A., K. T. Futa, S. F. Wanat, L. M. Mussman, and C. W. Leung. "The Employee Stress and Alcohol Project: The Development of a Computer-based Alcohol Abuse Prevention Program for Employees." *Journal of Behavior Health Services Research* 27:2 (May 2000): 152–65.

Miller, E. T., D. J. Neal, L. J. Roberts, J. S. Baer, S. O. Cressler, J. Metrik, et al. "Test-Retest Reliability of Alcohol Measures: Is There a Difference Between Internet-Based Assessment and Traditional Methods?" *Psychology of Addictive Behaviors* 16:1 (2002): 56–63.

National Cancer Institute. *Theory at a Glance: A Guide for Health Promotion Practice* (February 27, 2003). Available online from http://www.cancer.gov/aboutnci/oc/ theory-at-a-glance/page3. Retrieved August 10, 2005.

O'Malley, P. M., J. G. Bachman, and L. D. Johnston. "Period, Age, and Cohort Effects on Substance use Among American Youth, 1976–82." *American Journal of Public Health* 74 (1984): 682–8.

Saitz R., E. D. Helmuth, S. E. Aromaa, A. Guard, M. Belanger, and D. L. Rosenbloom. "Web-based Screening and Brief Intervention for the Spectrum of Alcohol Problems." *Preventive Medicine* 39:5 (2004): 969.

Science Panel on Interactive Communication and Health. Wired for Health and Well-Being: The Emergence of Interactive Health Communication. Washington, D.C.: U.S. Department of Health and Human Services, U.S. Government Printing Office, April 1999.

The Communications Initiative. *Change Theories: Health Belief Model* (detailed) (July 29, 2003). Available online from http://www.comminit.com/changetheories/ctheories/changetheories-31.html. Retrieved August 8, 2005.

Turner, C. F., L. Ku, S. M. Rogers, L. D. Lindberg, J. H. Pleck, and F. Sonenstein. "Adolescent Sexual Behavior, Drug Use, and Violence: Increased Reporting with Computer Survey Technology." *Science* 280 (May 1988): 867–73.

University of Florida, Community and Family Health (January 11, 1999). Available online from http://www.med.usf.edu/~kmbrown/Health_Belief_Model_Overview.htm. Retrieved August 8, 2005.

U.S. Department of Health and Human Services, Office of Disease Prevention and Health Promotion. (July 2003). Communicating Health: Priorities and Strategies for Progress. [Electronic Version]. Available online from http://odphp.osophs.dhhs.gov/projects/HealthComm/background.htm. Retrieved August 9, 2005.

Wechsler, H., B. Moeykens, A. Davenport, S. Castillo, and J. Hansen. "The adverse impact of heavy episodic drinkers on other college students." *Journal of Studies on Alcohol*, 56 (1995): 628–634.

Westrup, D., K. T. Futa, S. D. Whitsell, L. Mussman, S. F. Wanat, C. Koopman, A. Winzelberg, and R. Matano. "Employees' Reactions to an Interactive Website Assessing Alcohol Use and Risk for Alcohol Dependence, Stress Level and Coping." *Journal of Substance Use* 8:2 (June 2003): 104–11.

World Health Organization Brief Intervention Study Group. "A cross-national trial of brief interventions with heavy drinkers." *American Journal of Public Health* 86:7 (1996): 948–55.

Chapter 11

Instituting Innovation: A Model of Administrative Change in a State-Level Liquor Control Board

Raymond W. Cox III
Kelley A. Cronin

Contents

Introduction

The policing of alcoholic consumption in the United States has had a checkered history. The Volstead Act of 1919 implementing a constitutionally mandated prohibition on the sale and consumption of most alcoholic beverages proved a short-lived disaster. The repeal of prohibition returned the control of the production, distribution, and sale of alcohol to state and local jurisdictions (Peters 2004, p. 48). Thus, since the early 1930s, the enforcement of the regulations controlling the sale and distribution of alcoholic beverages has been, primarily, a joint effort involving state and local officials.[1]

Such arrangements are common in the United States, yet also they are replete with the same hazards and conflicts that typify intergovernmental relationships (O'Toole 1993, p. 16–17). The law enforcement agencies of the State of Ohio, no less than those in the other forty-nine states, have found the complex set of political and social relationships that are part of the state-level intergovernmental system (Sharp 1989; Keller 1989) make the task of intergovernmental law enforcement cumbersome and often ineffective. Conflicts of goals and administrative approach make intergovernmental management *arguably* the most difficult of all management environments.

The State of Ohio's CODE 2000 Program

In 1999, a major reorganization of the Ohio Department of Public Safety led to the combining of food stamp and liquor control under one unit renamed the Ohio Investigative Unit (OIU). The reorganization per se is less important than the conscious attempt to reorient and redirect the relationship between those in the unit and local law enforcement. Before the reorganization, the perception within the agency and the consensus among local law enforcement was that there was essentially no coordination between the Ohio Department of Public Safety, Investigative Unit, and local law enforcement (Duvall 2004). The Investigative Unit was not a well-liked organization and had the image, much like the FBI, of coming into a community, making a lot of noise, taking all the glory, and then leaving without really helping local law enforcement. As part of this change, a new direction was established and built into a program called *CODE 2000* (Community Oriented Directed Enforcement). The mandate for this program was to bring the services of this liquor control agency back to the people they were supposed to serve, local law enforcement and their respective communities. *CODE 2000* was to be both a philosophy and a standard by which to judge how the OIU does its job. This was essentially an experiment in "reinventing" government.

A basic theme of the reinventing government movement is the need to create "customer-driven governments." Central to this theme is the idea of treating citizens as customers to improve service performance (Osborne and Gaebler 1992; Garvey and Kettl 1993; Kettl and DiIulio 1995; Osborne and Plastrik 1997; Milakovich 2003). Although this reform movement has had exceptional staying power throughout the 1990s and beyond, few empirical studies have been conducted testing its implementation. Brudney, Wright, and Hebert (1999) surveyed state government agencies and concluded reinvention is happening on a state wide level. Kearney, Feldman, and Scavo (2000) surveyed city managers across the nation and found that a large majority support key principles of reinvention and a smaller portion have actually taken actions to implement reinvention programs. Yet neither of these studies addresses in depth the principle of customer service. Despite the complexities of the issue, there is an overriding reality that citizens expect to be treated with responsiveness and consideration (DiIulio, Garvey, and Kettl 1993). The problem is that citizens have become more vocal over the type and quality of service they receive. This is especially true in the area of public safety. Police agencies are being forced to reassess their relationships with their customers. As a result, many law enforcement agencies are looking for ways to get closer to the citizens of their jurisdictions and develop positive relationships with the people they serve (Cole 1993).

The *CODE 2000* program of the OIU was created to specifically and consciously reflect this orientation. Here a newly reorganized state agency is actively seeking "customer" approval and making its services known to those who may be potential recipients, or "customers" of it. The OIU has put forth a "problem-solving attitude" to meet the needs of local law enforcement and their communities. Although a strict adherence to customer service may not be plausible, nor advisable (Osborne and Plastrik 1997), compliance agencies can use customer standards and customer voice to improve their services.

The OIU's *CODE 2000* program presents a unique opportunity to examine how a program can be implemented under the guise of a "customer-driven government" philosophy. Information was collected from a variety of sources including public documents such as unit annual reports and interviews with key personnel in the various field offices of the OIU. This research seeks to present an example of how a state police agency can use the concept of a customer-driven government to implement a program.

Enforcement of underage drinking laws has a strong deterrent effect on youth consumption of alcohol and binge drinking. Strong enforcement helps to reduce underage drinking by limiting access to alcohol, reducing the opportunities for youths to drink excessively, binge drinking, and curbing impaired driving. But strong enforcement requires not only a consistent, vigorous program, but the coop-eration of the community at large. As a customer service program, *CODE 2000* is aimed at eliciting the effective cooperation of state of Ohio law enforcement agen-cies to solve many problems, particularly those associated with youth consumption of alcohol and binge drinking. Using a customer service perspective, OIU agents are teaming with local law enforcement and liquor permit premise holders to crack down on underage drinking throughout Ohio. The agents have criminal jurisdic-tion and serve as the sole law enforcement agency in the state of Ohio with the power to administratively cite a liquor permit premise before the Liquor Control Commission.

Reinventing Public Organizations

Several bodies of literature offer explanations of how a customer-driven government can be used to improve the performance in a police agency.

Before the onset of the flurry of rhetoric surrounding reinvention and before Osborne and Gaebler published their now-famous book, an article appeared in *Public Administration Review* foretelling the importance of "customer" service (Wagenheim and Reurink 1991). Wagenheim and Reurink make a compelling case for customer service in public administration. They state that customer service is a management strategy that focuses on meeting customer expectations. It is based on the concept that the organization will reach its goals effectively and efficiently through satisfaction of the customer (p. 3).

John Alford (2002) of the University of Melbourne attempted to take the cus-tomer-perspective debate further by defining the client in the public sector from a social exchange perspective. Alford contends that one of the crucial features of the customer model is the notion of exchange. Government organizations need things from service recipients such as cooperation and compliance which are crucial for effective organizational performance. Eliciting those things necessitates meeting not only people's material needs but also their symbolic and normative ones. Engag-ing in these different forms of exchange with clients is not necessarily inconsistent with an active citizenship model.

Others have viewed citizens not only as customers, but as owners and inves-tors. Smith and Huntsman (1997) espouse a customer-centered public administra-tion where there is a value-centered perspective in which citizens are viewed not as shop-walking proprietors who supervise government employees or as consumers who choose to buy this or that brand of government. Instead citizens are intelligent investors and co-invest their resources in the community and government, from which they expect to receive value (p. 310). In a value-centered model, citizens are shareholders of the community enterprise, and government is a trustee, steward, and manager of the assets, programs, and services that deliver value to its citizen investors. A value model suggests that citizens interact with government because they are fundamentally motivated to create value for themselves and for the community. Citizens may not buy shares of a community or government, but they do invest by choosing to live in a community, by buying property there, and by giving community service. They expect a reasonable return for their efforts. Government employees are similar. They not only deliver city services to their constituents, but they create value for them as well. Smith and Huntsman argue that viewed from this lens, public servants and citizens may begin to view the citizen-government relationship differently, not as one party overseeing the other but as mutual stakeholders who have common interests in increasing the worth of the community (p. 317).

Based on the concept that the organization will reach its goals effectively and efficiently through satisfaction of the customer presents a unique opportunity for keeping underage drinking enforcement a priority. *CODE 2000* is supported by strong Ohio liquor laws and an aggressive education effort by OIU agents.

International Perspective

In contrast to past reforms, reinvention is notable for its apparent relationship to similar administrative reforms beyond the borders of the United States. New public management has spread from the Westminster countries of the United Kingdom, New Zealand, and Australia to the United States. Light (1997) speculates that its adoption abroad has occurred because of an extensive decline of trust in government in these countries and a search for ways to strengthen government by borrowing from the private sector. Others have examined management reforms internationally and concluded that, although the reforms have many similarities, they also vary substantially across countries (Pollit and Bouckaert 2000). Some reforms emphasize privatization, others decentralization, and still others governmental deregulation (Peters 1996; Peters and Pierre 1998).

There have been two ways in which the basic idea has been played out. In some countries such as Australia and Sweden, government reformers argued for the need to let managers manage. The belief by reformers there is that managers knew the right things to do, but that existing rules, procedures, and structures created barriers to doing it. The consensus is that by focusing managers on the problems that have to be solved and then by giving them the flexibility to solve them promotes organizations that can adapt and governments that work better (Senge 1990; Barzelay 1992; Howard 1994; Kettl 1994). Underage drinking is frequently viewed as a low priority for enforcement, in part, perhaps, because American society has often viewed it as a rite of passage and an adolescent problem. Developing support within a law enforcement agency for an underage drinking program begins with the officer in charge making enforcement of underage drinking laws a priority (www.nhtsa.dot.gov). The OIU made this commitment in 1999 with the reorganization of the Investigative Unit and a renewed focus to stop underage drinking.

Alcoholic beverage control in Canada reflects this shift toward more "privatized" approaches to the problem of alcohol consumption by youth and "overconsumption" and binge drinking. In 1994 the Province of Saskatchewan privatized its liquor wholesaling and distribution operations (Thomas 2004). In 2001, the Province of Nova Scotia replaced its Liquor Control Commission with the quasipublic Nova Scotia Liquor Corporation, a royal corporation with responsibility for controlling liquor wholesaling, distribution, and "package" sales in that province (www.nslcweb.thenslc.com). This new corporation has the legal mandate to promote "intelligent consumption," yet it also has a mandate to be "profitable" in its operations. As the Canadian Centre on Substance Abuse reports:

> This trend is fairly universal in Canada and has caused some critics to suggest that even though most package alcohol is sold through public monopoly arrangements, "back door" privatization is occurring under the guise of business development and consumer convenience. … For example, one of the main "corporate objectives" set out in the 2004–2005 Performance Plan for the Saskatchewan Liquor and gaming Authority is to "support fair access to liquor and gaming products and services" (Government of Saskatchewan 2004, p. 8). … From a public health perspective, there are likely to be some legitimate concerns about a provincial liquor and gaming authority promoting "fair access to alcohol and gambling" as a major corporate objective when their mandate also includes controlling the harms associated with these activities (Thomas 2004, p. 28n).

Thus management reforms that have emerged in Canada have not always yielded reduction in the consumption of alcohol. For example, the "privatization" of liquor stores in 1993 in Alberta has resulted in a doubling of the number of liquor establishments in that province in the years from 1994 to 2004 (Thomas 2004, p. 25n). Also, the Centre has noted that alcoholic consumption, which had held steady through the 1980s and early 1990s, has grown by approximately 3% per year since 1994 (Thomas 2004, p. 1). On the other hand, the number of alcohol related highway fatalities continues to decline even as consumption grows (Thomas 2004, p. 16). The privatization and quasiprivatization of liquor control in Canada has meant that agencies, which are expected to "show a profit," are simultaneously expected to address the harmful effects of that consumption.

Typology of a Customer-Driven Government

To better understand the reform initiatives in Ohio, this section presents several frameworks and issues associated with the notion of customer service. Because of the vastness of this subject matter, it is useful to organize the literature around the question, "how do you define a customer-driven government?" For this task, a typology was developed around three theoretical frameworks of public administration: reinvention, new public administration, and new public management (Appendix 1). Lists were made for each framework describing how the concept of a customer-driven government is viewed through that particular framework. These frameworks are important to understanding the customer service perspective each agent-in-charge uses in the enforcement of underage drinking laws in Ohio.

After these lists were made, similar patterns were discovered. For instance, innovation is a concept embraced by all three frameworks. However, the difference lies in how that innovation is approached. Reinvention *directs* innovation, traditional public administration *facilitates*, and new public management *supports* innovation. Differences for each framework were listed and were broken down into seven distinct areas. Each framework was given a "catch phrase" for easy identification: "reinventor type" for reinvention, "citizen type" for public administration, and "consumer type" for new public management. After these three columns were made, a fourth column was added with a descriptor name for each of the practices: agency-client relationship, innovation/change, service strategy, problem solving, power direction, accountability, and performance measurement focus. Each of these practices describes one aspect of performing customer-service activities. The following discussion will break these practices down.

Customer service activities aimed at effective enforcement of underage drinking may take a myriad of forms. Compliance checks are probably the most identifiable. Vigorous use of compliance checks can reduce the illegal sale of alcohol to underage youth. These compliance checks, sometimes referred to as covert underage buyer or decoy programs, are designed to encourage compliance by alcohol vendors. Compliance checks encourage licensees to be diligent in complying with the law and therefore help to reduce the availability of alcohol to minors. In 2003 and 2004, the OIU was nationally recognized by the Pacific Institute of Research and Evaluation as one of the top four state agencies in the country enforcing alcohol compliance checks. The success of this program has become a model for other state law enforcement liquor enforcement agencies.

Another customer service activity directly related to the enforcement of underage drinking is the *Cops in Shops* program. Originally developed in Delaware, the program places undercover law enforcement officers or alcohol beverage control agents in off-premise stores that sell alcohol. Officers issue citations or make arrests for underage purchase, attempts to purchase, and related violations, including adults who purchase alcohol for underage youth, according to the current law of the jurisdiction where the program is in operation. Key to this program is the training that is provided to both enforcement officers and retailers. From a customer service perspective, the offered training to liquor permit premises is a way to conduct customer service activity while tackling the enforcement of underage drinking. Alcohol Server and H.E.L.P. (Hire Education for Liquor Permits) are two programs within the OIU Merchant Education Program Division. These programs are tailored to meet the needs of alcohol retailers. These partnerships in training are effective means by which the OIU has taken its customer perspective to improve their performance in addressing underage drinking issues in Ohio.

Ohio and Enforcement of Underage Drinking Laws

Binge drinking among youth and subsequent fatalities have contributed to a strong enforcement of underage drinking laws in Ohio. Recently, a Jackson County court sentenced a beverage store clerk to 90 days in jail, 250 hours of community service, three years' probation, and a $400 fine for the sale of beer to a minor that resulted in his death. Executive Director Dwight Holcomb stated, "Our commitment to enforcing Ohio's liquor laws and prosecuting those who violate them stem from our desire to prevent tragic accidents and deaths like this" (OIU Press Release, October 13, 2005).

Ohio has an aggressive strategy for enforcement of underage drinking laws that begins with the OIU. Agents are actively involved in working with local law enforcement agencies and sheriff's offices in Ohio's 88 counties. Exceptional educational programs round out this aggressive strategy. Sober Truth, Promotional Programs, H.E.L.P, Alcohol Server, and the 1-877-4MINORS tip line are all community-based programs designed to educate Ohio youth and adults on Ohio liquor laws. Aiding these educational programs is *CODE 2000*, which guides how the programs will reach out to local law enforcement, liquor permit premises, and the community at large.

Adding to the Ohio success has been yearly liquor enforcement grants from the Governor's Highway Safety Office. This yearly grant totals $100,000. The purpose of the grant is to monitor and investigate events and permit premises that cater to intoxicated and underage individuals. Money obtained from this grant has been used to offset labor costs associated with running such labor intensive projects. In 2001, the Investigative Unit shifted its concentration efforts to underage person's sources of alcohol. As a result, the number of permit premises cited before the Liquor Control Commission for selling alcohol has increased 310% (OIU Annual Report 2002). This streamlined effort to go after the source, those persons, or establishments selling alcohol to minors, and using a customer service perspective are what has made the OIU example so noteworthy.

Finding the Customer

DiIulio, Garvey, and Kettl (1993) cite four competing approaches that drive government in four different directions in seeking to serve the customer. This can be directly related to the enforcement of underage drinking laws as serving the customer as the catalyst for successful enforcement of these laws. These consist of 1) the citizen as service recipient, 2) partners in service provision, 3) overseers of performance, and 4) citizens as taxpayers. DiIulio et al. conclude that the approaches they outlined and the perspectives they represent—responsiveness, effectiveness, accountability, and efficiency—cannot all be balanced evenly, simultaneously or permanently. The effort to improve government performance is important but understanding it requires working through a series of complications.

- Any government program or agency has multiple customers with multiple levels of interest. These interests change over time. Charting the process helps to identify who is likely to appear as a customer.
- Different customers are likely to have different ideas about how they ought to be served, and these are likely to be different from the ideas of service providers. What is important is to create an ongoing relationship of trust, not necessarily in the vein to satisfy every customer.
- Customers will have a hard time finding their way to the service. Those who might be disenfranchised by power and politics must be identified and their needs must be represented.
- There are many intermediate customers. Because of the complexity of government programs and the multiple steps required to go from program design to execution, many customers have other customers. That means they rely heavily on the integrity of the process, from top to bottom. How well citizens are treated depends on how well the process works along the way.
- The job of serving the customer means not only making the individual programs more responsive but also integrating programs so that junctures appear seamless. Bottom line, citizens don't care who solves the problem, they just want it solved.

DiIulio et al. (1993) conclude that these complications require that all government workers must strive to make customer service, not their own needs, the focus of their activity. If we follow this line of logic and rely more on making customer service the focus of activity rather than the end result in a customer-driven government, we can begin to accept the customer service initiative as a good thing. In Ohio, customer service as a focus of activity is clearly present in the OIU's *CODE 2000* program. The goal of the program is activity driven, meaning the building of joint partnerships and relationships between local law enforcement agencies, liquor permit premises, and the OIU are continuous. These cooperative activities (i.e., an IU agent working with a local cop in an undercover effort to bust underage drinkers in a college bar) generate underage drinking prevention coalitions.

Customer Service at the OIU

Can a "customer strategy" be applied to the Ohio Department of Public Safety Investigative Unit? Although a strict adherence to customer service may not be plausible or advisable (Osborne and Plastrik 1997), compliance agencies can use customer standards and customer voice to improve their services to compliers, as a means to improve their voluntary compliance—which helps the community at large. They are different from other public agencies in that they offer a service which really in essence results in no choice. However, they can learn to focus more on problem solving and continuous improvement (Osborne and Plastrik 1997). This analysis suggests that the success of any customer service initiative within a liquor control agency must address the four aspects of customer service noted previously.

- "Finding" the customer
- Empowering the customer
- Defining accountability, and
- Balancing the competing values

These are the standards by which to judge the OIU (or any other state-level law enforcement agency).

Finding the Customer

CODE 2000 placed heavy emphasis on reaching out to local law enforcement to let them know of the services available to them. Many small police agencies throughout the state were unaware of services the OIU provided and, if they were aware, they were not certain such services would be of much use to them based on past performance and poor image of state policing agencies (Duvall 2004). Furthermore, the outreach was needed to build back trust from local law enforcement that had been diminished under the old liquor control agency.

Empowering Customers

Local law enforcement, as a customer of the state of OIU, will have a multitude of their own customers to include citizens, the courts, witnesses, victims, and prosecutors. Their ability to serve their customers effectively and efficiently, in situations wherein the OIU is needed, will depend largely on the type of service they received in collaboration with the OIU.

The agency actively sought "customer" approval and advocated a "problem-solving attitude" to meet the needs of local law enforcement and their communities.

Accountability

Customer-focused accountability as described by Milakovich (2003) is a good test of the *CODE 2000* program. The ability of district agents to develop positive, one-to-one relationships with chiefs of police and sheriffs should improve customer service and accountability. The OIU specifically states in its mission statement that it exists to

> Provide quality enforcement of state, federal, and local laws with emphasis on liquor, food stamp, and tobacco offenses, further offering educational guidance and professional assistance to law enforcement agencies and the general public. (OIU annual report 2000)

Hence local law enforcement, police and sheriff, are both stakeholders and customers.

Achieving Balance

Although most law enforcement agencies rigidly hold members accountable for adherence to rules and procedures, little else is measured or demanded in many cases. Because the rules are seemingly the only standard of *accountability*, members may develop the attitude that what they accomplish is unimportant as long as they don't violate directives. Rules, policies, and procedures are necessary in any organization, especially in a police organization where power and authority is given to them. But police departments need to move beyond rule adherence. First they must identify what performance standards are important and how they contribute to the mission of their organization. Next they need to demand accountability for those standards. Serving citizens, solving their safety-related problems, effectively employing enforcement and investigative resources, adhering to agency values, and providing effective stewardship of public resources are at least as important as complying with procedures. Individuals must work together as a team and truly commit themselves to the agency's mission. This is in effect combining performance with satisfaction (Shafer 1997).

Customer Service as a Model for Liquor Control

The key question is to what extent do the employees of the OIU use the theoretical framework of reinvention to implement *CODE 2000* in their districts? Stated another way, to what extent has a reinventing culture become the norm within the OIU district enforcement offices?

The results of this study yield decided mixed results with regard to these questions. The decision to make the reinvention-mandated concern for customer service the centerpiece of the reorganization of the former Liquor Control Board is a worthwhile endeavor. On the other hand, the program as implemented was more of a public relations initiative than an attempt to change the organizational culture. The program never really progressed beyond the "get out the word" stage of customer interaction. Most tellingly, the record keeping that is critical to performance measurement was never initiated. The impression left with many local law enforcement agencies (and even some inside the OIU) was that the program made for good "conversation," but changed relatively few actions in the districts. *CODE 2000* lacks a performance measurement strategy. Although the Ohio Department of Public Safety has put forth such a plan in a business proposal, there is no current system in place. Second, many of those in the field were "doing *CODE 2000*" type initiatives long before the program was mandated. They just were not calling it *CODE 2000*. These prior activities were born out of necessity for some and clearly thought out for others. Third, there was a mix of responses in the reinventor and citizen perspectives, which is not so surprising because the reinvention and new public administration literature are very much intertwined.

The agency-client characteristic is approached by most of the agents-in-charge from the customer perspective. A dual relationship with local law enforcement is also practiced: first as customers and second as consumers. Most agents-in-charge use a collaborative approach to innovation and present an environment for change within the organization. Responsibility for *CODE 2000* is given to all OIU agents with an emphasis on a customer service strategy. Problem solving is also approached as a collaborative effort and is practiced on two levels: with local law enforcement agencies and district enforcement offices. In general, district agents-in-charge seek to empower both customers and citizens through implementation of the *CODE 2000* program. Accountability is expected and practiced by all agents, though it is understood that the agent-in-charge has ultimate accountability. Finally, the program lacks a performance measurement strategy.

Other findings show the more seniority with the organization, the more often the agent-in-charge exhibited reinventor characteristics. Additionally, other issues emerged implying problems with the reorganization from the Ohio Department of Liquor Control Enforcement Division to the Ohio Department of Public Safety Investigative Unit. These issues include: the name change, dispelling myths of the old liquor control agency, using *CODE 2000* as a marketing tool, and the suggestion that budget cuts are responsible for a larger problem of reduced manpower.

It was found that a reinvention culture does exist with many of the district agents-in-charge preferring the reinvention framework in their administrative approaches and practices. However, this preference seems to be more in idea or philosophy than in consistent practice. Meaning, customer service sounds like a good idea but really when we interact with local law enforcement we do so on a different level. In practice, many of the approaches to administrative practices by the district agents-in-charge resemble a combination of the reinvention and public administration frameworks. For example, the agents-in-charge view the relationship they have with local law enforcement easily as customer and sometimes consumer but practice innovation and change, problem solving, and accountability from the new public administration framework. Collaboration and facilitation of joint efforts by the OIU agents and the law enforcement agencies they serve are key to their operations. One of the OIU's major concerns is to stop underage drinking and illegal sales of alcoholic beverages. This is a huge problem and requires much collaboration. It is concluded that some strategy of performance measurement would enhance these efforts. Further, it is recommended that the OIU refocus their program *CODE 2000* and decide on the managerial purposes to which a performance measurement may contribute.

Major Findings

This research examines "reinventing government" at a state agency level and develops a typology of a "customer-driven government" to explain ways the agents-in-charge implement the OIU's *CODE 2000* program. The typology frames an explanation of the approaches taken by the agents-in-charge as they conduct this program. The results of the interviews show that the district agents-in-charge advocate many of the reinvention characteristics. Therefore, they are operating the program *CODE 2000* using the theoretical framework of reinvention. The results from the open-ended discussions show the agents-in-charge doing *CODE 2000* activities long before they were required. The results also say that the OIU has not taken the program to the next level: a performance measurement system. For the field of public administration, this research affirms the view that we still do not know how to turn philosophy into management practices. It also suggests that the citizen versus customer debate is a hindrance to turning these philosophies into management tools.

For the field of public administration these findings have strong implications. As scholars, we still are not connecting philosophy with management practices. In short, we are not giving the practitioners the tools they need to do their jobs. On the issue of reinvention, we keep returning to the citizen versus customer question and spend way too much time arguing over which "term" is right (Frederickson 1992, 1997; Moe 1994; Schachter 1997; King and Stivers 1998; deLeon and Denhardt 2000; Alford 2002). Academics need to get past this argument. It is counterproductive and it will never be fully answered.

The situation with the OIU illustrates a common problem in the field of public administration. We take a new philosophy to the point of support and it fades. For example, the OIU Annual Report of 2000 report was dedicated to the program and all the wonderful goals and objectives that were anticipated. By 2003, there is barely a mention of the program. Still, superiors of the OIU firmly believe that this is a program entrenched in its organizational structure. It even has a prominent place on the official OIU Web site. Yet the OIU seems hard pressed to define *CODE 2000* beyond the initial "let's get our name out there." It has barely skimmed the surface of a philosophy put into practice. Why is it that public administration continues to have the inability to connect philosophy with management practices, especially since we are an "applied field"? Several reasons come to mind.

First is the old argument of theory versus practice. Some in the field have suggested that this theory practice gap is constructed and not a naturally occurring phenomenon (King 1997; King and Stivers 1998). The findings from this study show a different result. One of the keys for a customer-driven government is the use of measurement for results (Osborne and Gaebler 1992). The OIU is not doing this. There is a gap between what they claim to be doing and what they are actually doing. This is not a socially constructed phenomenon, but rather failure of police management to require that performance measures program be instituted.

There is another problem, more specific to police professionals. The finding that many were doing *CODE 2000* before the program illustrates lack of the necessary knowledge to properly implement this program. Some of these agents have prior experiences which influenced their decision to conduct these activities. However, the finding of no performance measurement shows that they do not have the right tools. Although this is not a new argument, the lack of connecting the theory with the practice, it is a strong reminder to academics that we need to start focusing on the tools. We tell practitioners what is wrong, but we don't tell them how to fix it. In the field of policing, many police administrators are hungry for ways to streamline their departments and make them more customer-oriented.

Reinvention efforts also fall short because it is hard to tell the difference between a client and a customer. The behaviors associated with a citizen versus those exemplified by a customer are not easily identified. Furthermore, most people do not care if our government refers to them as a citizen or a customer. They just want a law enforcement officer there when they need one. Looking at reinvention as a set of practices rather than trying to fit them into the theory mold is much more beneficial for the field of public administration. Looking at reinvention as a set of management practices has value for the field. Central to the set of practices are the key issues of measurement and quality (Osborne and Gaebler 1992; Milakovich 2003). There is real value in performance measurement and pushing for quality in government services. But tasks associated with performance measurement and total quality management (TQM) never get done. As a result, reinvention ends up focusing on a difference in semantics (customer versus citizen) rather than practices, which can effect real organizational change. We never seem to get past this argument (Milakovich 1995; Kettl 1997; Kelly 1998; Terry 1998, 1993, 1990; deLeon and Denhardt 2000) and as a result we have programs that end up going nowhere. Practitioners do not see a difference. The district agents-in-charge all answered the agency-client relationship question with both a citizen and customer perspective in mind. Service recipients do not see a difference either. It has become an introspective argument with no chance of a winner.

We need to concentrate on strategies for implementation rather than questions of semantics. We need to offer solutions to practitioners and identify steps by which they can achieve them. Gianakis and Davis (1998) said it best, "if the sound bites of the reinventing government are ever to attain the status of sound scripture, they must first be operationalized in terms of specific services" (p. 485). It is not enough to simply change the organizational culture, as the OIU has shown. An organization needs to have a performance measurement in place so that the organization has a real opportunity to reinvent itself.

Implications for the OIU and Liquor Control

The OIU set out to change its organization by imposing the concept of a customer-driven government onto its seven agents-in-charge. The *CODE 2000* program was well-received and basically accomplished what it set out to do. The notion of a customer-driven government is embedded within this organization and to that extent reinvention has worked quite well. The results of the survey confirm this finding with many of the agents-in-charge responding that they follow reinvention characteristics. Many have their own version of *CODE 2000* and were "doing" these customer service type activities within their districts before the program came about. The key finding from the interviews was that none of them is doing any sort of performance measurement. So, although some notions of a customer-driven government are found in the threads of the organization, the program never got past "opening night." This finding supports similar studies in which programs never got past the advocacy stage (Gianakis and Davis 1998; Brudney, Hebert, and Wright 1999; Kearney, Feldman, and Scavo 2000). For the OIU, this means that the program is currently dead. Although it accomplished what it set out to do, educating the state of Ohio law enforcement community on the name change and the services they offer, there is no real change for this organization. The next step for the OIU would be to first decide if in fact they wish to go further with the *CODE 2000* program. If they wish to continue, they will need to take the program to the next step. This would involve setting up a performance measurement system as well as strategies for education and training.

Beyond the OIU

Overall, this study can be generalized to other enforcement agencies, as many have in place programs of a customer service nature. However, the results would render the same outcome unless the program has a built in system of performance measurement. This would hold true if we tried to recreate the study in other types of public agencies as well. Because this study looks at common practices of management, it could be replicated in many other instances. The state or local level, police or other type agency, would all be appropriate landscapes for this study. Further, the typology of a customer-driven government is a unique concept that could be retooled to fit a certain agency. The framework and characteristics could be changed to fit the descriptions of the agency. This matrix is a workable tool whereby an organization can learn about its services and the philosophies by which they are implemented.

Through *CODE 2000*, combining law enforcements' resources to target underage drinking has been an innovative and highly effective method of prosecuting offenders who place alcohol in the hands of teens. The Ohio experience can be a model for other states wanting to incorporate successful underage drinking enforcement strategies. What is unique about the OIU compared to other states is the customer perspective of the *CODE 2000* program. Many states have alcohol server programs and enact such underage drinking enforcement strategies as compliance checks, Cops in Shops, and party buster hotlines. California's TRACE (Target Responsibility for Alcohol Connected Emergencies) program identifies a protocol whereby officers will immediately try to determine where youths obtained or consumed alcohol before an event and alert the appropriate enforcement agency immediately. Similarly, Texas has a program called Operation Fake Out. This program is a cooperative venture involving alcoholic beverage retailers and the Texas Department of Public Safety, and, when possible, local law enforcement (Texas Alcoholic Beverage Commission: www.tabc.stat.tx.us/enforce). Although both of these programs exemplify enforcement strategies, neither uses the unique OIU perspective of a customer-driven government. The reason the OIU has had such success in their efforts to stomp out underage drinking and upholding the law is the acknowledgment that they cannot do it alone. By understanding the customer and developing a customer service program, *CODE 2000*, the OIU has had a significant impact on changing the nature of underage drinking in Ohio.

References

Alford, John. "Defining the Client in the Public Sector: A Social-Exchange Perspective." *Public Administration Review* 62:3 (2002): 337–46.

Ammons, David N. "Overcoming the Inadequacies of Performance Measurement in Local Government: The Case of Libraries and Leisure Services." *Public Administration Review* 55:1 (1995): 37–47.

Ammons, David N. "A Proper Mentality for Benchmarking (Mini-symposium on Intergovernmental Comparative Performance Data)." *Public Administration Review* 59:2 (1999): 105–9.

Arnold, Peri E. "Reform's Changing Role." *Public Administration Review* 55:1 (1995): 407–17.

Aucion, Peter. *The New Public Management: Canada in Comparative Perspective.* Montreal, Quebec, Canada: Institute for Research on Public Policy, 1996.

Barzelay, Michael, and Aramajani Babak. *Breaking Through Bureaucracy: A New Vision for Managing Government.* Berkeley, CA: University of California Press, 1992.

Bouchaert, Geert. "Measurement and Meaningful Management." *Public Productivity & Management Review* 17:1 (1993): 31–44.

Box, Richard C., Gary S. Marshall, B. J. Reed, and Christine M. Reed. "New Public Management and Substantive Democracy." *Public Administration Review* 61:5 (2001): 608–17.

Brudney, Jeffrey L., F. Ted Hebert, and Deil S. Wright. "Reinventing Government in the American States: Measuring and Explaining Administrative Reform." *Public Administration Review* 59:1 (1999): 19–30.

Carroll, James D. The Rhetoric of Reform and Political Reality in the National Performance Review. *Public Administration Review* 55:3 (1995).

Conlan, Timothy J. "Federalism and Competing Values in the Reagan Administration." In *American Intergovernmental Relations,* 2nd edition, edited by L. O'Toole. Washington DC: CQ Press, 1993: 359–377.

DeLeon, Linda and Robert B. Denhardt. "The Political Theory of Reinvention." *Public Administration Review* 60:2 (2000): 89–97.

Denhardt, Robert B., and Janet Vinzant Denhardt. "The New Public Service: Serving Rather than Steering." *Public Administration Review* 60:6 (2000): 549–59.

DiIulio, John J., Jr., Gerald Garvey, and Donald F. Kettl. *Improving Government Performance: An Owner's Manual.* Washington, DC: Brookings Institution, 1993.

Duvall, Ed, Jr., Deputy Director Ohio Investigative Unit. Interview October 2004.

Ferlie, E., L. Ashburner, L. Fitzgerald, and A. Pettigrew. *The New Public Management in Action.* Oxford: Oxford University Press, 1996.

Frederickson, George H. "Comparing the Reinventing Government with Public Administration." *Public Administration Review* 56:3 (1996): 263–70.

Frederickson, George H. *Ideal and Practice in Council-Manager Government.* Washington, DC: ICMA, 1989.

Guide 5, Enforcement—Community How To Guide on Underage Drinking Prevention. Available online at the National Highway Transportation www.nhtsa.dot.gov.com

Heinrich, Carolyn J. "Outcomes-Based Performance Management in the Public Sector: Implications for Government Accountability and Effectiveness." *Public Administration Review* 62:6 (2002): 712–25.

Kamensky, John M. "Role of Reinventing Government Movement in Federal Management Reform." *Public Administration Review* 56:3 (1996): 247–55.

Kearney, Richard C., Barry M. Feldman, and Carmine P. F. Scavo. "Reinventing Government: City Manager Attitudes and Actions." *Public Administration Review* 60:6 (2000): 535–48.

Keller, Lawrence F. "City Managers and federalism: Intergovernmental relations" in *Ideal and Practice in Council-Manager Government,* edited by H. G. Frederickson. Washington, DC: ICMA, 1989: 33–44.

Kettl, Donald F. *The Transformation of Governance: Public Administration for a 21st Century America.* Baltimore: Johns Hopkins, 2002.

Kettl, Donald F. *Inside the Reinvention Machine.* Washington, DC: The Brookings Institution, 2002.

Kettl, Donald F. "Building Lasting Reform: Enduring Questions, Missing Answers." In *Inside the Reinvention Machine: Appraising Governmental Reform*, edited by Kettl, Donald F., and John J. DiIulio, Jr. Washington, DC: Brookings Institution, 1995.

Kettl, Donald F. *Reinventing Government? Appraising the National Performance Review* (CPM Report 94-2). Washington, DC: The Brookings Institution, 1994.

Kettl, Donald F. *Sharing Power: Public Governance and Private Markets*. Washington, DC: The Brookings Institution, 1993.

King, Cheryl, and Camilla Stivers. *Government is Us: Public Administration in an Anti-government Era*. Thousand Oaks, CA: Sage Publications, 1998.

Kravchuck, Robert S., and Ronald W. Schack. "Designing Effective Performance-Measurement Systems under the Government Peformance and Results Act of 1993." *Public Administration Review* 56:4 (1996): 348–58.

Light, Paul C. *The Tides of Reform: Making Government Work 1945–1995*. New Haven, CT: Yale University Press, 1997.

Milakovich, Michael E. (2003). "Balancing Customer Service, Empowerment and Performance with Citizenship, Responsiveness and Political Accountability." *International Public Management Review* 4:1 (2003): 61–83.

Moe, Ronald C. "The 'Reinventing Government' Exercise: Misinterpreting the Problem, Misjudging the Consequences." *Public Administration Review* 54:2 (1994): 111–22.

National Performance Review. *Report: Creating A Government That Works Better and Costs Less*. Washington, DC: U.S. Government Printing Office, 1993.

Nova Scotia Liquor Corporation Web site. Available at http://www.nslcweb.thenslc.com

Osborne, David, and Peter Plastrik. *Banishing Bureaucracy*. Reading, MA: Addison-Wesley, 1997.

Osborne, David, and Ted Gaebler. *Reinventing Government*. Reading, MA: Addison-Wesley, 1992.

O'Toole, Laurence, J., Jr. *American Intergovernmental Relations,* 2nd ed. Washington, DC: CQ Press, 1993.

Peters, B. Guy. *American Public Policy: Promise and Performance,* 6th ed. Washington, DC: CQ Press, 2004.

Poister, Theodore H., and Greg Streib. "Performance Measurement in Municipal Government: Assessing the State of Practice." *Public Administration Review* 59:4 (1999): 325–35.

Pollit, Christopher, and Geert Bouckaert. *Public Management Reform*. Oxford: Oxford University Press, 2000.

Sharp, Elaine B. "City Management in an Era of Blurred Boundaries." In *Ideal and Practice in Council-Manager Government*, edited by H. G. Frederickson. Washington, DC: ICMA, 1989: 3–15.

Thomas, Gerald. "Alcohol-Related Harms and Control Policy in Canada," Canadian Centre on Substance Abuse, 2004.

Wagenheim, George D., and John H. Reurink. "Customer Service in Public Administration." *Public Administration Review* 51:3 (1991): 263–70.

Appendix I
Customer Driven Government

Characteristic	Reinventor Type (Osborne and Gaebler/National Performance Review)	Citizen Type (Public Administration Literature)	Consumer Type (New Public Management Literature)
Agency-client relationship	Easily as customer	Client as citizen	Client as consumer
Innovation/change	Directs innovation and an environment for change	Facilitates innovation and an environment for change	Supports innovation and an environment for change
Service strategy	Emphasizes service to customers	Service strategy not clearly defined because of citizen vs customer debate	Emphasizes service to consumers
Problem solving	Advocates a collegial/but top down problem-solving work environment	Advocates a collaborative problem-solving work environment	Gives managers the flexibility to solve problems: "letting the managers manage"
Power direction	Empowers customers	Seeks to empower citizens	Empowers front-line employees
Accountability	Managers accountable to customers	All accountable to politics and citizens	Manager accountable for result
Performance measurement focus	Results	Program purposes	Outputs and/or outcomes

Despite actions such as the Reagan administration-initiated mandate approved in Congress in 1984 to create a uniform, national legal age for the purchase of alcoholic beverages, in general, the production, distribution, and sale of alcohol has remained primarily a state-level concern. (See Conlan, Timothy J. "Federalism and Competing Values in the Reagan Administration" in *American Intergovernmental Relations*, edited by O'Toole. Washington D.C.: CQ Press, 1993: 359–77).

Chapter 12

Toward Liquor Control: A Retrospective

Mark R. Daniels

Contents

Introduction

More than seventy years have passed since Raymond B. Fosdick and Albert L. Scott published *Toward Liquor Control*. The book was published because of the authors' anticipation of the repeal of the 18th Amendment that prohibited the manufacture, sale, transportation, importation, or exportation of intoxicating liquors. The authors interviewed a wide array of experts, including but not limited to judges, lawyers, clergymen, social workers, newspaper editors, representatives of the Foreign Language Information Service, distillers, brewers, members of the Federal Bureau of Industrial Alcohol and the Prohibition Bureau, law enforcement officers, police officials, college presidents, and members of the state boards of control already established. Their research was assisted by a staff of at least thirteen researchers who traveled across the United States and Canada collecting information, in addition to traveling to England, France, Germany, Italy, Russia, Poland, Finland, Sweden, Norway, and Denmark. The goal of the study was to establish what measure and plan of liquor control was feasible once prohibition ended.

The report reviewed the problems with alcohol that led to prohibition, examined the legacy of prohibition, and then made a substantial set of recommendations for liquor control after repeal of prohibition would occur. These recommendations included policies for beer and wine that would be different from policies for spirits, licensing, regulations for advertising, state monopolies for distribution, and sale of heavier alcoholic beverages, issues involving taxation and education policies aimed at temperance. The publication of the report in 1933 was a precedent setting event, intended to frame the policy agenda for states that would face enacting alcohol control legislation immediately after prohibition would be repealed. The report provides an answer to the question: "What defenses shall the law set up to guard society against the abuses of alcohol?" (Fosdick and Scott 1933, p. 131). This chapter will review *Toward Liquor Control* with the objective of summarizing the comprehensive recommendations of the report offered on the eve of the repeal of prohibition. After a summary of the recommendations, this chapter will then assess to what extent the recommendations have been adopted by the federal and state governments.

Part 1: Recommendations from *Toward Liquor Control*

The Legacy of Prohibition

Fosdick and Scott accepted the conclusion that with the passage of the 20th Amendment, the American people "attempted to impose on law a burden which law itself is not equipped to carry" (p. 5). Another way of expressing this sentiment is that a society cannot legislate morality. "Permanent advance in human society," they continue, "cannot be brought about by night-sticks and patrol wagons. Men cannot be made good by force" (p. 7).

Prohibition occurred, however, before the passage of the 18th Amendment. Thirteen states adopted prohibition legislation between 1846 and 1855, but by 1904 only three retained their prohibition policies (p. 2–3). During 1907 to 1913, twenty-three states enacted prohibition legislation and on the eve of American entry into World War I, a total of twenty-five states were dry (Moore and Gerstein 1980, pp. 156–7).

The authors do not discuss why prohibition occurred in the first place, if it did not have the support of the American people. Prohibition came about primarily through the efforts of the Anti-Saloon League to influence close local elections by offering support to one of the candidates if the candidate supported prohibition. The Anti-Saloon League in the early 20th Century has been compared with the current tactics of the National Rifle Association (Meier 1994, p. 136). Saloons of this early time were often owned by large breweries and offered discounts, free food, and credit to market beer. The saloon was a poor man's social club, attracting working class customers in the industrial cities, and offering an escape from tenements and harsh working conditions. The Anti-Saloon League was aligned with Protestant churches and clergy who believed that alcohol was the primary cause of poverty, domestic violence, serious illness, and early death. Eventually, leading businessmen who thought that alcohol posed a threat to increasingly automated, assembly line industrial plants joined with the Anti-Saloon League. Prohibition was a result of the efforts of a small but disciplined cadre of voters, backed by big business, who could throw their support behind a candidate in a close race, or have a strong turn out in a referendum election. Ratification of the 18th Amendment by the respective states once again involved the pressure tactics of the Anti-Saloon League. A minority of voters in each state were able to influence alcohol policy that was to be enforced on the vast plurality of Americans.

The passage of the 17th Amendment, giving the U.S. Congress the power to collect income taxes, ended the federal government's dependence on alcohol taxes. The loss of federal revenue from the passage of prohibition was eliminated as a potential obstacle after the Federal Income Tax became law.

The authors conclude that illegal alcohol trafficking has been greased by payoffs to courts, police, and politicians, and has corrupted society. The result was widespread civil disobedience, and the rise of organized crime in America. One shortcoming of prohibition, they argue, is that prohibition had exceptions. For example, manufacturing beer, wine, and cider in the home was legal. By 1919, grocery stores quickly stocked their shelves with home brew equipment and supplies. The authors correctly observe that the combination of illegal liquor and home brew prevented the country from ever going completely dry.

The authors also do not mention the positive effects of prohibition. By 1919, the first year that national prohibition was in effect, 170,000 saloons were closed (Moore and Gerstein 1981, p. 159). Between 1911 and 1929, death from cirrhosis of the liver dropped from 29.5 to 10.7 per 100,000, admissions to hospitals for alcoholic psychosis dropped from 10.1 to 4.7 per 100,000 between 1919 and 1928, and arrests for drunk and disorderly behavior were cut in half from between 1916 and 1922 (p. 165). From 1919 through 1933 the consumption of ethanol (the alcoholic chemical common to wine, beer, and spirits) dropped from 1.96 to .97 gallons per year per person (Nephew et al., 2003).

By 1932, the plurality of Americans opposed to prohibition expressed their preferences by electing Franklin D. Roosevelt as President, and a lame duck Congress passed the 20th Amendment with the stipulation that it be ratified by conventions in the respective states instead of being ratified by state legislatures. Most states opted to organize conventions composed of elected citizen delegates, the result of which minimized the pressure the Anti-Saloon League could exert on career legislators.

What Does the Community Want?

Fosdick and Scott conclude that any system of alcohol control must have the approval of the community. After conducting extensive interviews, they conclude that Americans of 1933 want six essential things from alcohol control policies (p. 15–18). First, bootlegging and racketeering must be eliminated from alcohol production and transportation. Second, temperance education should be adopted as a public policy by all governments. Third, brewery controlled saloons must not be allowed to return. Fourth, Americans do not want breweries and distilleries to violate social standards through their pursuit of profit. Fifth, Americans support the return of beer, but are apprehensive about the return of spirits. The authors embrace the accepted opinion of the time, however erroneous, that because the alcohol content of beer is less than other ethanol drinks, it is therefore less dangerous. And, sixth, the authors conclude that Americans want control over alcohol, but something that is an alternative to prohibition: they want to strike out on a fresh trail.

Light Wines and Beers vs. Spirits

The authors discuss the intoxicating effects of different kinds of intoxicating drinks, and conclude that beer containing 3.2 percent of alcohol, and wines containing 10 to 12 percent of alcohol should be regulated differently than spirits that contain 30 percent or more of alcohol (p. 28–34). They conclude that state governments should offer permits for the sale of 3.2 percent beer and up to 12 percent wine for off premise consumption, for the sale of 3.2 percent beer on premises, and for the sale of 3.2 percent beer and wine up to 12 percent for on premise consumption at hotels, clubs, and restaurants with meals.

Regulation by License or by Authority

Two methods of liquor control are discussed by Fosdick and Scott: control by license and control by government authority. The authors criticize the way the licensing systems in the American states worked before Prohibition. The primary problem with licensing before Prohibition was that the alcohol manufacturers had control of both the politicians who issued the licenses, and the saloons that sold their particular brands. They believe that the breakdown of the licensing system actually led to the Prohibition movement (p. 39). The authors advocate a new licensing system with ten essential characteristics.

First, there should be a single state licensing board, appointed on a merit basis, with statewide authority. This statewide board would be less likely to come under the control of local politicians. Second, board members should be given long terms of office, be eligible for reappointment, and well paid. This would ensure a bipartisan board. Third, licenses should not be awarded to any "tied house" retailer (p. 43). Tied houses were those saloons, before Prohibition, which sold only one manufacturer's product. Fourth, the board should establish a limit on the number of licenses awarded, and also establish prohibited locations such as next to schools or churches. Fifth, licenses should be classified consistent with what the authors viewed as differences between beer, wine, and spirits. Sixth, the hours of retail shops and saloons should be regulated in a way similar to England, where pubs are required to close down for two hours in the afternoon. Seventh, licenses should be awarded not only to the person who is selling the alcohol, but also to the premises where the alcohol is sold. This would assist in identifying problem locations where there have been police reports of disorderly conduct or fighting. Eighth, advertising should be strictly controlled. Newspaper and magazine ads should only contain the name of the establishment or the name of the product, with a simple description of the saloon or product. All other advertising must be approved by the board. No advertising prohibitions or restrictions, however, would apply to 3.2 percent beer. Ninth, the board should control prices to limit the profiteering from alcohol sales. A minimum and maximum price could be set so as not to discourage competition among manufacturers and retailers. Finally, they also encouraged the adoption of a local option to allow local governments to decide whether or not to allow any sales of alcohol. Local option would allow local governments to continue to practice prohibition, if that is what the voters preferred.

The authors think that any license system is flawed. First, there will still be a profit motive behind selling alcohol, and that is inconsistent with temperance education. If the motivation is to stimulate sales of alcohol, then attempts to educate the public about the virtues of temperance would be undermined. Second, even making the licensing board part of civil service does not remove it completely from politics, and where there is politics, there is room for corruption and graft. Finally, licensing manufacturers and retailers allow for the development of proprietary interest. A saloon owner, for example, would invest in the building, the land, fixtures, and inventories and would certainly have vested interest in retaining the license and promoting the business of the saloon. No doubt, the authors believe that such vested interest would result in aggressive tactics to expand the business base and increase the margin of profits. Fosdick and Scott find the licensing system falls short of achieving liquor control and temperance, and for that reason advocate the establishment of government authorities.

Modeled after monopolies in Quebec, Sweden, Norway, Finland, and England, Fosdick and Scott recommend an American state liquor authority plan (referred to as the "Authority") by which the state government takes over, as a monopoly, the retail trade and sale of heavier alcoholic beverages (p. 63–93). Sale of heavier spirits is through state owned and operated liquor stores, for off-premises consumption. The responsibilities of the Authority include: fixing prices on all alcohol products; regulating the sale of all alcoholic beverages in saloons, hotels, restaurants, dining cars, and passenger boats, with or without meals; auditing the records of all private businesses that manufacture alcohol in the state; holding hearings about complaints involving the manufacture or purchase of alcohol. The authors rightly identify this Authority as a public corporation, similar in structure to the London Passenger Transport Authority, the British Broadcasting Corporation, the Port Authority of New York, and the Tennessee Valley Authority. Part of the revenue collected by the Authority would be spent on temperance public policies. Compared with the licensing plan, Fosdick and Scott are of the opinion that the Authority plan is superior.

Although both the licensing and Authority plans have the same objective of placing the sale of alcohol under a series of restrictions devised to curtail excessive consumption, the authors think that the Authority plan is preferable. First, licensing systems impose negative rules and regulations from without, on private businesses that are motivated to make a profit (p. 79). In contrast, the Authority system imposes controls through positive management within a public corporation that is motivated to benefit society. Second, the Authority plan would restrict the advertising of alcoholic beverages more so than the licensing plan. The authors worry that private retailers will always be trying to get around the advertising regulations of the licensing board. Under the Authority plan, the authority board members would decide how their monopoly would advertise their alcoholic beverages. Third, the Authority would be better able to control prices. The objective is to set a price high enough to discourage high consumption, but low enough so as to not encourage bootlegging. The Authority's ability to fix prices on liquor it owns and sells is a more straightforward method than the regulation over the range of prices set by the licensing board. Fourth, the physical appearance of the stores operated by the Authority would be easier to control than under the licensing board. The liquor stores would be owned and operated by the Authority, but under the licensing plan the board would rely on rules and regulations to control the physical appearance of liquor stores. Fifth, the authors argue that the Authority would be able to sell alcohol products to customers in dry areas of the state for home consumption, thereby discouraging the trade of bootlegging to dry areas.

Finally, Fosdick and Scott make the argument that only under the Authority plan can the profit motive be taken out of alcohol sales. It is the profit of motive, they believe, that has destroyed past licensing systems, corrupted politicians, and exploited citizens all in the quest for breweries and distilleries to expand and increase their profits. It is in the public interest, they argue, to have public corporations, the Authorities, to control the production of all alcoholic beverages, and to own and sell the stronger alcoholic beverages.

Taxation

Fosdick and Scott argue that the objective of taxing alcoholic beverages should not be to collect revenue, but should instead be to maintain social control over the consumption of alcohol. They warn that high sales taxes may make it difficult for consumers to purchase alcohol from retail stores, and give rise to the illegal liquor trade of bootleggers. The authors also point out that alcohol sales taxes in the past have not been paid by the manufacturers or retailers but have instead been passed on to the consumer in higher prices. In this sense, the alcohol sales taxes regressive and are a burden on those consumers who can least afford the tax.

A reasonable rate structure is recommended that would be built on a number of different bases (p. 199–120). One base could be the variations in the content of alcohol for different alcoholic products, for example, if whiskey has twelve times the content of beer, taxes could be twelve times as high for whiskey than for beer. Another base could be variations in the value of the product, for example, if whiskey costs three times as much to manufacture than beer, its tax should be three times as high as beer. Another base could be structured on the notion of social control, for example, the authors think that beer and wine are more desirable alcoholic beverages because of their lower alcohol content compared with heavier spirits, and therefore taxes on beer and wine should be less than the heavier spirits. They also argue that all revenue from alcohol taxes should go into the general fund instead of being earmarked for certain public services, such as education. Basing public programs on the revenue generated by liquor taxes would potentially result in the dependency of these programs on the consumption of alcohol, and consumption is something the authors want to have controlled and limited.

Education

Fosdick and Scott observe that "alcoholic indulgence is too deeply rooted in human nature to be dug out by summary process" (p. 131), and turn to education as a way of teaching temperance. They feel that the family is most instrumental in creating values and that the family must somehow be involved in any temperance education policy. In addition to having temperance education programs in the schools for children and young adults, there should also be adult education programs available through school districts, Chambers of Commerce, Parent Teacher Associations, civic agencies, churches, and other organizations created specifically for this purpose. The method of instruction they prefer is teaching from facts and illustrations, and curriculum should include the advantages resulting from sobriety, correction of fallacies about alcohol consumption, scientific knowledge of the subject, and a practical application of knowledge about alcohol consumption that can solve individual and community problems created by alcohol consumption. The authors call for greater scientific research on the subject of alcohol consumption that could become part of the curriculum on temperance education.

Part 2: Assessment of Recommendations Adoption and Implementation

Prohibition

After the ratification of the Twenty-first Amendment, eight states decided to remain dry, and became prohibition states through state legislation (Meier, 162). These states were Alabama, Georgia, Kansas, Mississippi, North Carolina, North Dakota, Oklahoma, and Tennessee. Most of these were conservative, Southern states with large protestant populations. North Dakota shared a border with Canada, a prohibition country. However, these states permitted the sale of at least 3.2 beer, with the exception of Alabama and Kansas. All of these states eventually became wet; the last of the eight to become wet were Kansas (1948), Oklahoma (1957), and Mississippi (1966). Currently, Oklahoma is the only state that allows sales of only 3.2 beer, with sales of beer over 3.2 prohibited. The national repeal of prohibition resulted in the eventual repeal of prohibition at the state level.

Consumption

The consumption of alcohol after the repeal of Prohibition steadily increased but did not reach the levels of the pre-Prohibition years until the 1970s. In 1860, for example, the consumption per capita was 2.53 gallons per year, in the period 1906–1910, it was 2.60 gallons, and in the period 1911–1915 it was 2.56 (Nephew et al., 2003). As states began passing state level prohibition laws, consumption started to drop and was only 1.96 gallons per capita between 1916 and 1919, the eve of Prohibition. Since the repeal of Prohibition, consumption increased from 0.97 gallons per capita in 1934 until it reached a high of 2.76 gallons per capita in 1980. The trend since 1980 has been a slight decrease each year, to 2.18 gallons per capita in 2000. Figure 12.1 contains a line chart that shows the variation in per capita consumption of alcohol from 1850 until 2000, and the reduction in consumption

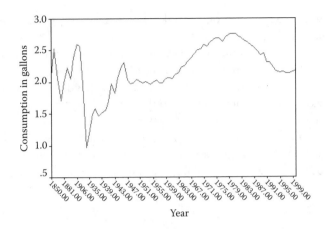

Figure 12.1 Source: National Institute for Alcohol and Alcoholism, online databases, various years.

resulting from Prohibition by 1934, and the steady reduction of consumption after 1980, is displayed.

The decrease in alcohol consumption since 1980 has been attributed to what some researchers call "the new temperance movement" (Miller 1984). Prevention specialists abandoned the old paradigm of individual responsibility and early school based informational approaches to alcohol prevention and replaced it with environmental, policy, and legislative methods of prevention (Room 1992). There is a lack of agreement, however, about what type of approach is best in reducing consumption. The first approach argues that there should be public policies and legislation that will reduce alcohol consumption by all drinkers, regardless of where they are on the light to heavy drinker scale, with a special emphasis on reducing the consumption by heavy drinkers (Moore and Gerstein 1981, p. 67). The second approach targets heavy drinkers only because of the higher social and health costs of their high intake (Rehm, Ashley, and Room 1996). These two approaches are not so much opposing as they are complimentary.

Immediately after the end of Prohibition, there was a sizeable gender gap regarding consumption of alcohol. In an annual Gallup Poll, surveyors found that 70 percent of men and 45 percent of women responded that they drink alcohol. By 1994, 70 percent of men and 61 percent of women surveyed responded that they drink alcohol.

Hazardous consumption of alcoholic beverages is defined as five or more drinks in a day, which is approximately 60–70 grams of ethanol. The top 2.5 percent of Americans who drink on an average of eight drinks per day accounts for a quarter of all alcohol consumed (Greenfield and Rogers 1999). Sixty-three percent of this group is in the 18–29 age group and is mostly male. A majority of beer (59 percent) is drunk in hazardous amounts compared with 37 percent for spirits and 14 percent for wine. Twenty-four percent of all drinking occurs in a bar; however, 37 percent of hazardous drinking occurs in a bar.

Fosdick and Scott recommended fewer restrictions on beer and wine consumption, because the alcohol content of these beverages is less than spirits. However, hazardous drinking involves how many drinks a person has drank, how many hours the person has been drinking, and how old the person is, and how much the person weighs. A person's blood alcohol content, then, is more dependent on how much and how long the person has been drinking than on what the alcohol content is of the beverage. Consumption patterns show that beer drinking is the source of most hazardous drinking, and beer drinking is in no way a lesser temperance problem than heavier spirits.

Costs of Alcohol Consumption

Costs to the United States from alcohol consumption are estimated to be somewhere between $100 and $130 billion each year (NIAAA 1997; Heien 2004). These costs are derived from medical expenditures, morbidity (health problems) and mortality (early death), crime, victims of crime, incarceration, motor vehicle crashes, fire destruction, social welfare administration, and fetal alcohol syndrome. Morbidity accounts for 37 percent of all alcohol costs, and mortality 34 percent.

Revenue from Alcohol

Fosdick and Scott recommended that alcohol taxes be used as a form of social control over alcohol and were fearful that government would become dependent on the consumption of alcohol because of the revenue generated. Since the end of prohibition, state governments have steadily increased their revenue from alcohol, including both taxes and revenue from state store sales. Revenue is of course tied to consumption, but even with the new temperance movement and the decrease of alcohol consumption starting in 1980, revenue continues to climb. Figure 12.2 shows the increase in revenue since the end of Prohibition. Even though consumption has decreased since 1980, state revenue has increased from $5,243 million in 1980 to $8,257 in 2001. Figure 12.3 shows federal revenue from alcohol, and a steady increase, similar to that of the state revenue, is displayed.

State Monopolies and Licensing

By the end of 1933, five states had already passed monopoly legislation. These five states were Pennsylvania, Montana, Oregon, Michigan, and Ohio (StateWays, 1988, p. 66). Another ten states adopted monopolies by 1935: Washington, Iowa, Virginia, Vermont, New Hampshire, Maine, Wyoming, West Virginia, Idaho, and

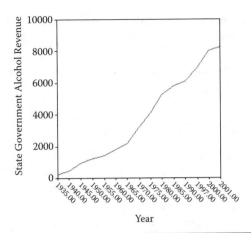

Figure 12.2   Source: U.S. Bureau of the Census, online databases, various years.

Utah (*Ibid*). Much later, an additional three states set up monopolies: Alabama, North Carolina, and Mississippi (*Ibid*).

Although much variation exists among the monopolies, some similarities do exist. For example, none of the monopolies involve manufacturing, and manufacturing and importation are conducted under license by private enterprises involving licensing by both state and federal governments. No state has set up monopoly drinking establishments or state-owned taverns or restaurants. All monopoly states also license the private sale of alcohol. Some monopoly states have opted to privatize wine sales, responding to the lobbying of the Wine Institute, a lobbying arm of the California wine growers. In Ohio, for example, wine sales were privatized and

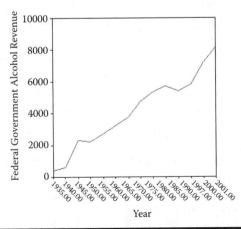

Figure 12.3   Source: Office of Management and the Budget, *Budget of the United States,* online databases, various years.

as a result the consumption of wine increased even though overall consumption of alcohol declined, following the national trend. All monopoly states except Wyoming, Iowa, and Michigan sell alcohol in state-owned retail liquor stores. North Carolina differs from its monopoly neighbors in that it allows for state level, county level, and city level government-owned stores.

Even the nonmonopoly license states have provisions for locally run monopolies (StateWays, 68). For example, Maryland, South Dakota, Wisconsin, and Minnesota allow local governments to operate retail liquor stores. Of course, the federal government also operates monopolies on its military bases, including on-base and off-base retail liquor stores, and on-base "open messes" that offer liquor and beer to go. Native Americans also operate monopolies, with ten tribes on fifteen reservations providing for tribal liquor stores. In 1981, American Inuits (Alaskan Native Americans) were allowed by state law to operate monopolies on reservation land.

These monopolies allow states, the federal government, and Native American tribes to band together as purchasers and receive deep discounts in wholesale transactions from alcohol manufacturers. This is turn allows the monopolies to add a greater proportion of taxes to each bottle of alcohol sold, compared to license-only states, and the overall cost per bottle of alcohol for consumers is less in wholesale states compared to license-only states.

Recommendations for monopolies and licensing made by the Fosdick and Scott have been implemented for the most part by state governments, and states have adopted a strict policy of legal control over the sale of alcoholic beverages. All states, regardless of whether or not they operate monopolies, use licensing as a method of regulating the purchase of alcohol.

Underage Drinking

Underage drinking is a national problem. It is estimated that of the nation's 113 million drinkers, 10 million are underage (Nation's Health, 2000). The total cost of underage drinking is $58 billion annually, including costs from traffic accidents, violent crime, suicide attempts, and medical treatment. One-third of high school students reported binge drinking in the past month, but only three percent of parents believe their teens use alcohol. Efforts have been made by colleges to reduce underage drinking. Fraternity or sorority parties are the primary source of underage drinking on campus, and strict restrictions have been demonstrated to reduce alcohol consumption (Wechler, Lee, Nelson and Kuo, 2002). Elimination of freshman-only dorms, and diversifying residence halls with higher percentages of women and older students are associated with lower levels of underage alcohol consumption (Wechsler and Kuo, 2003).

Both state and local governments fund alcohol education programs for youth, and all school districts include alcohol education as part of the curriculum. The recommendations advanced by Fosdick and Scott regarding alcohol education have been enacted. However, there are only mixed results concerning the effectiveness of these programs. The most successful education programs rely on the concept of social norms. Most studies agree that peer pressure is the major factor behind underage drinking: Students want to be accepted by their peers and therefore engage in underage drinking to be consistent with "what everyone else is doing." However, students report higher perceived drinking among their peers than does actually occur. Social norms education programs emphasize ending the misperceptions of peer drinking behavior and educating students to the real incidence of underage drinking. For example, researchers at Hobart and William Smith Colleges conducted a controlled experiment using the social norms concept and found that students achieved a significant increase in their awareness of actual drinking patterns and as a response significantly reduced their own drinking consumption (Perkins and Craig, 2002).

The New Temperance Movement

The decrease in alcohol consumption since 1980 has been attributed to what some researchers call "the new temperance movement" (Miller, 1984). Prevention specialists abandoned the old paradigm of individual responsibility and early, school-based informational approaches to alcohol prevention and replaced it with environmental, policy and legislative methods of prevention (Room, 1992). There is a lack of agreement, however, about what type of approach is best in reducing consumption. The first approach argues that there should be public policies and legislation that will reduce alcohol consumption by all drinkers, regardless of where they are on the light to heavy drinker scale, with a special emphasis on reducing the consumption by heavy drinkers (Moore and Gerstein, 1981, p. 67). The second approach targets heavy drinkers only because of the higher social and health costs of their high intake (Rehm, Ashley and Room 1996). These two approaches are not so much opposing as complimentary.

Mothers Against Drunk Driving (MADD) set the agenda for the a new temperance movement. From 1975 to 1980 there was a 182 percent increase in arrests for Driving Under the Influence (DUI), a 124 percent increase from 1980 to 1985, and a 118 percent increase from 1985 to 1990 (Meier, 165). MADD is an interest group with no opposition: no one wants to argue for drunk driving, and even major breweries are included in MADD's list of contributors. MADD has given rise to additional temperance interest groups, for example, Students Against Drunk Driving (SADD). Most high schools across the nation have a SADD chapter.

MADD was also instrumental in lobbying for a national drinking age law set at 21 years of age. Starting in the early 1970's, states began to enact legislation that reduced the drinking age to 18 or 19 years of age. By 1979, twenty-three states had set their minimum drinking age at 18 or 19 years of age. However, by the early 1980's there were numerous, highly-publicized studies that claimed teenage alcohol use was out of control and was turning into a devastating problem of epidemic proportion. MADD seized on this issue and flooded the offices of U.S. congressmen with letters from members supporting a national drinking age. With overwhelming support from the U.S. Congress, the National Minimum Drinking Age Act of 1984 was passed. The actual bill required state governments to raise their minimum drinking age to 21 within two years or lose a portion of their Federal-aid highway funds. It also and encouraged states, through incentive grants programs, to pass mandatory sentencing laws to combat drunk driving.

Advertising Retrictions

The U.S. Congress, in 1988, adopted a labeling policy that required alcohol manufacturers to include health warning labels on alcohol containers, similar to the health warnings on cigarette packages. Public opinion overwhelmingly supports the labeling policy (170).

State governments have adopted a variety of policies regarding alcohol advertising (Center for Alcohol Marketing and Youth, 2003). These regulations include prohibitions: on misleading alcohol advertising; against advertising that targets minors or uses images of children in advertisements; against images or statements that associate alcohol with athletic achievement or that encourage intoxication. Additional regulations restrict outdoor advertising in locations where children are likely to be present, or advertising near colleges, schools, playgrounds and churches. Other regulations restrict alcohol contest giveaways, such as contests and raffles.

Conclusion

It is perhaps ironic that in writing about the failure of prohibition and recommending government policies in the face of its repeal, authors Fosdick and Scott overlooked the positive accomplishments of prohibition. Because of prohibition, hundreds of thousands of saloons were closed, consumption of alcohol dropped to the lowest level in American history, drunk and disorderly arrests dropped, and the nation's overall health improved. Of course, prohibition continues to be perceived as a failure due to the rise of organized crime and substantial civil disobedience connected with it.

Many of Fosdick and Scott's recommendations for prohibition's repeal have been enacted by state and local governments. Brewery saloons do not exist, and bootlegging and racketeering have been widely eliminated. Eighteen states have adopted monopolies to control the pricing and retail sale of alcohol, and all states engage in the licensing of retail stores and by-the-drink establishments.

Many states adopted Fosdick and Scott's recommendation about regulating beer and wine differently than the stronger alcoholic spirits. However, research has shown that the alcohol content of a person's blood is a more precise measure of alcohol abuse than the alcohol content of the drink.

With prohibition's repeal, alcohol consumption began an upward trend which peaked in 1980. Along with increased alcohol consumption came the narrowing of the alcohol consumption gender gap: the percentage of women drinkers also steadily increased after prohibition's repeal. As alcohol consumption increased, the nation's health declined. For example, cirrhosis rates increased steadily until 1970, and much of the annual $100–130 billion cost of alcohol consumption is spent on health-related illnesses.

Despite the National Minimal Drinking Age Act of 1984, underage drinking is a national problem. The educational programs aimed at temperance among youth have not been effective in reducing the incidence of underage drinking. One educational approach, the social norms concept, has been proven effective on college campuses.

Most certainly, Fosdick and Scott would be pleased about the emergence of the New Temperance Movement. This movement pursues a reduction in alcohol consumption by all drinkers and advocates moderation. The movement also targets heavy drinkers and underage consumption. MADD has been an instrumental part of this movement, and has advocated increased apprehension and prosecution of drunk drivers. The MADD organization has paved the way for other temperance organizations to form, most notably SADD. The federal government has adopted advertising policies for alcohol, and state and local governments have adopted laws and regulations regarding the advertisement of alcohol products.

The federal and state governments have become dependent upon alcohol-related revenue. Taxes on alcohol have steadily increased since the repeal of prohibition, and governments are fiscally dependent upon the drinking patterns of their citizens. Fosdick and Scott warned against the pernicious relationship between taxation and alcohol consumption: They recommended that taxation should be a way of regulating the consumption of alcohol, not as a way of financing government services.

Overall, Fosdick and Scott would be pleased at the adoption of so many of their recommendations from 1933. They would, no doubt, express disappointment at some post-prohibition trends, such as underage drinking and the reliance of governments on alcohol revenue. Both supporters of the temperance movement a century ago, Fosdick and Scott would feel vindicated by the New Temperance Movement, a movement that has proven, so far, to dull the sharper edges of prohibition's repeal. For the most part, the repeal of prohibition has followed a course consistent with their recommendations.

References

Center on Alcohol Marketing and Youth. 2003. *State Alcohol Advertising Laws: Current Status and Model Policies.* Washington, D.C.: Center on Alcohol Marketing and Youth.

Fosdick, Raymond B., and L. Scott Albert. *Toward Liquor Control.* New York: Harper and Brothers Publishers, 1933.

Gallup Poll. 2004. "Percent Who Drink Beverage Alcohol, by Gender, 1939-2000." http://www.niaaa.nih.gov/databases/dkpat1.htm

Greenfield, T. K., and J. D. Rogers. "Who Drinks Most of the Alcohol in the U.S.? The Policy Implications." *Journal of Studies on Alcohol* 60:1 (1999): 78–89.

Heien, Dale M. 2004. "Are Higher Alcohol Taxes Justified?" Available online at www.cato.org/pubs/journal/cj152-3-7.html

Meier, Kenneth J. *The Politics of Sin: Drugs, Alcohol, and Public Policy.* Armonk, NY: M. E. Sharpe, 1994.

Miller, N. *Prohibitive Tendencies? The New Temperance Movement.* Boston, MA: Phoenix, 1984.

Moore, M., and D. Gerstein. *Alcohol and Prohibition: Beyond the Shadow of Prohibition.* Washington, D.C.: National Academy Press, 1981.

National Institute on Alcohol and Alcoholism. *Alcohol and Health: Special Report to the U.S. Congress.* Washington, D.C.: Department of Transportation, 1997.

Nation's Health. 2000. "Underage Drinking Takes its Toll on the Nation." *The Nation's Health* (February).

Nephew, T. M., G. D. Williams, H. Yi, A. D. Hoy, F. S. Stinson, and M. C. Dufour. *Alcohol Epidemiologic Data System,* Surveillance Report #62, Apparent Per Capita Alcohol Consumption: National, State, and Regional Trends, 1970–2000. Rockville, MD: National Institute on Alcohol Abuse and Alcoholism, Division of Biometry and Epidemiology, August 2003.

Perkins, W., and D. Craig. 2002. A Mulitfaceted Social Norms Approach to Reduce High Risk Drinking: Lessons from Hobart and William Smith Colleges. Newton, MA: Higher Education Center for Alcohol and Other Drug Prevention.

Rehm, J., M. J. Ashley, and R. Room. "On the Emerging Paradigm of Drinking Patterns and Their Social and Health Consequences. *Addiction* 9:1 (1996): 1615–22.

Rogers, J.D. and T.K. Greenfield. 1999. "Beer Drinking Accounts for Most of the Hazardous Alcohol Consumption Reported in the U.S." *Journal of Studies on Alcohol* 60: 732–739.

Room, R. "The Impossible Dream? Routes to Reducing Alcohol Problems in a Temperance Culture." *Journal of Substance Abuse* 4 (1992): 91–106.

StateWays, 1988. "Control: How and Why, A History of 'Monopolies' in the U.S." *StateWays* May/June: 64–68.

Wechsler, H., Lee, J., Nelson, T., and M. Kuo. 2002. "Underage College Students' Drinking Behavior, Access to Alcohol, and the Influence of Deterrence Policies." *Journal of American College Health* 50 (5): 223–236.

Wechsler, H., and M. Kuo. 2003. "Watering Down the Drinks: The Moderating Effect of College Demographics on Alcohol use of High-Risk Groups." *American Journal of Public Health* 93 (11): 1929–1933.

Index